IRS Whistleblower

IRS Whistleblower

MY 33 YEARS AS AN IRS INSIDER WILL SHOW YOU THE SECRETS OF HOW TO ENGAGE THE IRS AND WIN.

Richard M. Schickel

ISBN: 0692514937
ISBN 13: 9780692514931

Notice from Author and Publisher

THE AUTHOR AND THE PUBLISHER disclaim all liability for any damages resulting from the application of the information presented in this book. This book is a memoir of the author's experiences in the IRS. All names, dates, and case circumstances are compilations and have been sanitized to prevent disclosure of confidential tax information. This book is designed to share the author's findings and opinions based on life experiences, research, analysis and experience with the subject matter covered. This information is not provided for purposes of rendering tax, legal, accounting, or other professional advice. If tax, legal or accounting advice is required, the services of a qualified attorney, CPA or Enrolled Agent should be sought.

Dedication

THIS BOOK IS DEDICATED TO all the employees of the Internal Revenue Service past and present.

This book is dedicated to all the taxpayers who have had the Internal Revenue Service in their lives, like it or not.

This book is dedicated to all people who suffer stress, worry and fear because of the actions of government, courts and institutions including those veterans who suffer from lack of care from the Veterans Administration.

For people who are the victims of neglect and abuse from the mental health care system. See www.NAMI.ORG.

For the disabled and elderly who lack resources to provide for their wellbeing or who suffer abuse from elder care abuse, guardianship fraud. See www.KillingSeniors.org

Acknowledgments

THANKS TO RACHEL THERON OF Lekka Media Design and Marketing for the cover design and internet design.

I thank all the editors, proofreaders and technical editors who worked on this project with me. None wish to be identified due to fear of repercussions from the IRS.

Thanks to my friends and family who acted as editors, technical editors, and proofreaders because many professionals I approached and hired were afraid of any project involving the IRS.

Thanks to my friends and family who have encouraged and guided me, including Frank and JoAnne, Kathleen, Kay and Deane, William, Reina, Billie, Jean, Becky, Juanita, Larry, Lupe, Kay, Christy, Alice, Robert Milne, Jessica Schickel, Marge Schickel, Colleen Schickel, Rachel, and many others who provided wise counsel, emotional support and financial investment in this project. Thanks to Valerie Porter for her edits and suggestions.

Acronyms Used in this Book

ACS	Automated Collection System
ACTC	Additional Child Tax Credit
ADP	Automated Data Processing System/Computer Master File
BASIC	Beginners All Purpose Symbolic Instructional Code
BIR	Bureau of Internal Revenue
CAU	Caution on Contact
CI	Criminal Investigation
CIC	Coordinated Industry Case Program
DEA	Drug Enforcement Agency
DIF	Discriminant Index Function
EIC	Earned Income Tax Credit
EIN	Employer Identification Number
EITC	Earned Income Tax Credit
EPA	Environmental Protection Agency
FBI	Federal Bureau of Investigation
ITIN	Individual Taxpayer Identification Number
HIRTI	High Income Fast Track Initiative
HNWI	High Net Worth Individuals
HRAA	High Risk Assault Area
ICE	Immigration and Customs Enforcement
ICS	Integrated Collection System
IDRS	Integrated Data Retrieval Service

IRC	Internal Revenue Code
IRM	Internal Revenue Manual
ISP	Industry Specialization Program
LUG	Large, Unusual or Questionable items on tax returns
MSSP	Market Segment Specialization Program
NTEU	National Treasury Employees Union
NRP	National Research Project
OIC	Offer in Compromise
PII	Personal Identifiable Information
PDT	Potentially Dangerous Taxpayer
RCA	Reasonable Cause Assistant
R/A	Revenue Agent
R/O	Revenue Officer
RPAP	Return Preparer Audit Project
RRA	IRS Restructuring and Reform Act of 1998
SAR	Suspicious Activity Report
SFR	Substitute for Return Program
SBU	Sensitive But Unclassified
SSN	Social Security Number
TAO	Taxpayer Assistance Order
TAS	Taxpayer Advocate Service
TCMP	Taxpayer Compliance Measurement Program
TFF	Treasury Forfeiture Fund
TIGTA	Treasury Inspector General for Tax Administration
UIDIF	Unfiled Income Discriminate Income Function
UNAX	Willful Unauthorized Access to taxpayer records.

Table of Contents

Acknowledgments · · · · · ix
Preface: I'm a Hero. · · · · · xxi

1 Introduction · · · · · 1
My Life in the Internal Revenue Service · · · · · 1
Why I Joined the IRS · · · · · 4

2 Welcome to the World of the IRS · · · · · 7
The History of the IRS · · · · · 7
Income Tax Rates over the Years · · · · · 13
Inside an IRS Office · · · · · 14
Take Care of Yourself First, Best and Always · · · · · 19
My First Day at the IRS · · · · · 23
IRS Training Bad Revenue Officer Training School · · · · · 24
The Start of My IRS Journey · · · · · 27
Why I Stayed · · · · · 29
Happy Times? · · · · · 30
Who Does the IRS like to hire to be Revenue Officers? · · · · · 32
What Does a Revenue Officer Really Do? · · · · · 34
How Did I Feel About the Work? · · · · · 38
The Toll it Took · · · · · 40
Time for Change · · · · · 40
Who is a Typical Taxpayer? · · · · · 42

3 **The IRS Computer System** **45**

4 **The Mission of the IRS** **53**
How I Felt Doing This Job 57
It Flows Down Hill 57
The Queue is a Wonderful Place to Be 62
The IRS, the President and Congress 64
The IRS Congressional Hearings in 1997 67
The IRS Organization 68
The IRS Demographics 69

5 **What Do You Really Pay in Taxes?** **71**

6 **The IRS Culture** **75**
Lead Us Not into Temptation 75
What the IRS Does Well 79
IRS Management Stories 80
Past History of IRS Management 82
Anti-Semitism and More 85
Manager Madness 88
Al Capone Lives On Forever at the IRS 91
Sexual Harassment and Discrimination 93

7 **The Big Seizure** **95**
Never Ignore the IRS 101

8 **Field Calls** **105**
Bribe Attempts 108
I Got a Feeling 110

9 **Greed, Abuse and Loss** **113**
ATAT Group 114
The IRS Does Not Follow the Law 115

It's Nothing Personal 118

10 IRS Employees Doing Bad Things 121
IRS Employees Caught and Jailed 121
The IRS Got Caught 123
Attempting to Corrupt Tax Administration
Is Big Business for those Outside the IRS 124
The IRS System Business Results-Abuses and Benefits 125
The IRS Rewards Employees Who Do
Not Pay Income Taxes 125
IRS Employees Who Are Now Convicted Criminals 126
Temptations in Tax Administration 126
Chasing the Bad Guys 127
Temptations within the IRS 127
The Snoop 128
Credit Card Abuse 129
More IRS Employees Arrested 129
It's Nothing Personal 134

11 Seizures 135
Never Seize This... 135
Pay Me and Then you Can See the Doctor 136
A Smelly Seizure 136
I Make Full and Final Demand for Payment 137
Revenue Officer Schickel and the FBI,
IRS Criminal, ATF, and DEA 138

12 IRS Abuse of Taxpayers 141
Collection Abuse 141
IRS Fear 142
Special Classes of Taxpayers 144
Wealthy People Suffer Too 145
Make an Offer that the IRS Can't Refuse 146

IRS Scares Contractors · · · 148
Chasing the Bad Guys · · · 148
Closing a Case as in Business - Currently Not Collectible · · · 155
Exigent Circumstances Seizure · · · 156
Tax Professionals Abused · · · 156
What Happens in the Field? · · · 157
A Sound and Legal Way to Close Cases · · · 157
Employment Tax Abuse · · · 158
Collection Statute Waiver Abuse · · · 159
Penalty Assessment and Abatement Abuse · · · 159
Two Secrets the IRS Does Not Advertise · · · 159
Jeopardy and Termination Assessments · · · 161
IRS Seizure and Sale Abuse Cases · · · 162
Seizure Harassment · · · 163
IRS Abuse Nearly Destroyed This Woman's Life · · · 163

13 Audit Abuse · · · 171
How the IRS Picks Who They Will Audit · · · 171
The IRS Can't Tell You How to Do Business · · · 175
Big Corporations - Big Tax Assessments · · · 175
Knock, Knock – I'm from the IRS · · · 176
Audit and RRA 98 · · · 177
We Liked Your Old Address Better · · · 177

14 IRS Service Center Abuse · · · 181
IRS Correspondence · · · 181
The CP2000 Program · · · 181
The Excess Collections Fund and Unidentified Remittance Fund · · · 182
Where the IRS Gets Free Money · · · 183
The Statute of Collections and Assessment · · · 183

15 Criminal Investigation Abuse · · · · · · 185
Who is Criminal Investigation Interested In? · · · · · · 185
What Happens If CI Doesn't Get Who They Want · · · · · · 187
Undercover Criminal Agents · · · · · · 187
Civil Forfeiture · · · · · · 188
Suspicious Activity Report · · · · · · 189
Informants and Whistleblowers · · · · · · 191

16 Treasury Inspector General Abuse · · · · · · 193

17 Abuse from Taxpayers · · · · · · 197
The Social Security Loophole · · · · · · 197
Abuse in Action · · · · · · 201
Man Arrested for Petty Theft · · · · · · 201
This is Not a How to Cheat the IRS Book · · · · · · 203
File First and Claim the Kids · · · · · · 203
Your Kids are Worth Money to Other People · · · · · · 204
Additional Child Tax Credit Fraud · · · · · · 204
Alimony Fraud · · · · · · 204
Earned Income Tax Credit Fraud · · · · · · 205
Net Operating Loss Fraud · · · · · · 205
Slavery Reparations Tax Credit Fraud · · · · · · 205
Federal Excise Tax Refund for Highway Use Tax Fraud · · · 206
Illegal Immigrants and Un-Documented Workers · · · · · · 206
Receiving Form 1099 is Used to Hide Income · · · · · · 207
Taxpayers Lying to Each Other · · · · · · 208
Underreporting Income Fraud · · · · · · 208
Cost of Goods Sold Fraud · · · · · · 209
Retirement Contributions Fraud · · · · · · 210
Made-to-Fail Businesses · · · · · · 210
Businesses that Hide Behind the Shield of the Law · · · · · · 211
Money Laundering · · · · · · 212

Catch Me if You Can · · · 212
Nuns, Priests, Rabbis and Ministers
Abusing the System · · · 213
First Time Homebuyers Credit Fraud · · · 215
Like-Kind Exchanges Fraud · · · 216
Higher Education Tax Credit Fraud · · · 216
Unethical Tax Professionals · · · 217
Chronic Delinquent Taxpayers and Serial Non-Payers · · · 217
Loans to Shareholder · · · 218
Lost Treasures Found · · · 218
Prisoners Winning the IRS Lottery · · · 219
Tax Exempt Organizations Fraud · · · 220
Government Contractors as Delinquent Taxpayers · · · 221

18 IRS Seizures and Sales · · · 223
He Could Have Been Really Rich · · · 223
They Hide - I Seek · · · 224
Anything to Save a Few Bucks · · · 224
Tax Protester Advice · · · 226
The Mills of God Grind Slowly But
they Grind Exceedingly Fine · · · 226

19 Physical and Verbal Threats to IRS Employees · · · 229
Security in the Field and the Office · · · 231
Please Don't Shoot · · · 232
Dangerous Tax Professionals · · · 237
Dangerous Taxpayers · · · 237
IRS Employees in Danger · · · 240

20 Identity Theft · · · 241
Identity Theft and Refund Fraud · · · 243
What is the Source of the Social
Security Number Leaks? · · · 244

Refund Fraud · · · 246
Business Identity Fraud · · · 247
Individual Identity Fraud · · · 248
Identity Fraud/Ghosting · · · 248
What is the Underground Economy? · · · 249
Where Did the Money Go? · · · 252

21 Who Manages Your Money? · · · 255
The Trusted Rip-off Artists · · · 257
It's a Ponzi Scheme · · · 257
Conmen I Have Known · · · 259
Embezzlement · · · 260

22 IRS Survival Strategies · · · 263

23 Solutions to the IRS Situation · · · 285
Goals: · · · 285
Employees: · · · 286
Collection · · · 288
Offer in Compromise · · · 289
Audit · · · 290
Tax Professionals · · · 291

24 A New Direction For The IRS · · · 293

Endnotes and Sources · · · 297

Preface

I'M A HERO.

IRS work suited me perfectly. It was as if I was my own boss. I was a tax collector - a Revenue Officer looking for people who owed money or were negligent in sending tax returns to the Government.

My job required me to be out in the field much of the time driving around making cold calls on delinquent taxpayers. Sometimes I would be looking for people who did not want to be found. IRS Revenue Officers do not announce that they are coming; they simply knock on your door whenever they are in the neighborhood. That way they can observe your actual lifestyle and it is safer, since no harmful situations can be planned in advance.

One freezing day right before Christmas in 1982, I was looking for a taxpayer and was very lost. I found myself on an isolated street with only six houses and surrounded by cornfields. I was lost and alone. There was no one around to ask where I was. But I was about to learn being lost was a minor problem in comparison to what was ahead.

As I was staring at my map book, I looked up and saw a woman drive past me. She went to the house on the far side of the street behind me. I watched her in my rearview mirror. I saw her unload some groceries and then open the front door of the two-story house. When she opened the front door, thick black smoke came pouring out. The smoke was coming from the ceiling, reaching her at waist level. She started screaming.

Strangely, my first instinct when I saw what was happening was "I should get the hell out of there." Before I could finish processing that thought, I was out of my car running to help.

The woman was hysterical, but was able to tell me that she had gone out to the store and left her eight-year-old daughter Bridgett alone in the house asleep. Bridgett was trapped in the second floor bedroom. I could see the terrified little girl behind the window and storm window and saw smoke starting to fill her room. I yelled to her "close the bedroom door and stuff clothes at the bottom of the door." She was afraid but did as I told her.

Bridgett was a scared little girl in her pajamas. I could see that she had "bed hair" and had apparently been asleep a short time ago. Mucus was flowing out of her nose from the smoke inhalation, kind of like someone had squeezed a tube of toothpaste from both nostrils. She was trapped behind two windows that were locked up tight for winter. She could not unlock the window or push it open. I had no idea how to get access to her on the second floor. Running into the house was out of the question, so I thought of getting help. This was before we had cell phones. I ran to the six houses on the street and banged on every door screaming, "Fire!" and "Help!" No one was home. It was early winter and no ladders or lawn furniture had been left outdoors - nothing that could help me reach the little girl.

The mother was hysterical and sobbing, and of no help at all. Then two German shepherds came from the back yard and started attacking me, biting my legs, ankles and pants. I yelled at them in what I hoped was a scary, commanding voice that I had never heard myself use before or since. "BACK OFF! I am trying to save the little girl." Miraculously they backed off as if they understood what I was there for, but they looked at me like they would attack again if I messed up.

I ran into the backyard and finally found a metal garden table and chair. I stacked the chair on the table and climbed until only my fingertips could reach the bottom of the windowsill. I am six feet tall but the bottom of the windowsill was still about six feet higher above my head. I was too low to get the window open. I saw some landscape rocks that must have weighed about 10-15 lbs. each, located around the house. They were partially frozen into the ground. I broke some from the frost and put them on the table. I told the girl's mother to get more stones, and then I stood on the rickety chair on the rickety table throwing these heavy stones over my head to break the windows.

I was amazed that I could throw these rocks. It was like I was throwing shot putts over my head. Of course, the first few rocks fell short of their mark and bounced off the screen, hit the table and almost knocked me down. Quickly I figured out how to throw harder and kept throwing the small rocks up over my head. I was able to break the screen and then broke the storm window next. When I broke the storm window, shards of glass started to fall on me, cutting me.

Now the little girl was beyond terrified and actually afraid of me. Finally, I broke the inside window. I could smell the smoke from the fire. The girl looked relieved as she gasped for the fresh, freezing air outside the window. I ordered her to jump into my arms. She was beyond processing my directions because she was scared of me and terrified of the fire. She was slowly dying in that room - we both knew that from the look in each other's eyes.

I told her to climb up onto the windowsill so she could jump down into my arms. She said, "No!" wisely pointing out the large pieces of sharp glass sticking out. She was coughing worse now as more smoke was starting to come through her room seeking the outside air to feed the fire. I told her to use one of the rocks and start smashing the broken glass so there were smaller pieces of broken glass sticking up. She did. Then I told her to get up onto the windowsill and jump into my arms.

She was coughing, bleeding, sobbing. It is surreal to even remember this scene now. I was standing on a lightweight chair on a rickety metal table and I was trying to gain her confidence so she would jump into my waiting arms. When she climbed onto the windowsill her feet and her hands were on the broken glass shards. She started bleeding from more cuts. The smoke inhalation had caused more fluid to pour from her mouth and nose and she was coughing, trying to gasp for more air.

I screamed at her, "Jump now!" I was in an unstable situation and was at first asking, then yelling, at this girl, and finally commanding her to jump. She was too afraid. I told her, "You are going to die in that room if you don't jump!" She and her mother were both hysterical and sobbing. She kept looking behind and beyond me thinking that surely someone would see the thick black smoke and come and help. I told her, "No one is coming. Jump!" She was determined not to jump and then in a move that surprised us both, she jumped safely into my arms. I believe that an angel pushed her out of the window.

When she finally jumped into my arms, the table held. I carried her down from the table and ran with her and her mother to my car. I dropped her in the middle of the front seat on to my tax collector files. I threw a box of the tax papers into the back seat. She had gotten blood on many of them getting into the car. She was going into shock from the combination of freezing weather, the thin pajamas she was wearing, and the considerable bleeding. Secretions were still pouring out of her nose and mouth. I had picked up my dry cleaning that morning and ripped apart one of my dress shirts, and tied it on each hand and foot to stop the bleeding. I also had a grey suit jacket from the cleaners and I wrapped her up in it for warmth. I was thinking at that moment, "I hope I don't get in trouble with my manager for getting the case files bloody." In fact, I continued to use the bloody case files and closed them over the next year. That is just how it is at the IRS - use it up - wear it out - never waste anything. Funny what runs through your mind in a crisis.

I started to drive, but the mother was so hysterical, terrified and sobbing, that I could not concentrate enough to be able to drive. I reached over and slapped her face just like in some gangster movie with Jimmy Cagney. She stopped crying and I was able to drive on. The slap brought her back to reality, but I regretted that I had to do that in the moment.

Although I was lost, my sixth sense directed me to the roads I needed to take to get to the hospital. Bridgett told me that the house was her grandparents' house and they were visiting.

At the hospital I called the Fire Department. The emergency room doctor said that Bridgett had had a close call with death and that another 15 minutes of smoke inhalation would have caused her to die. He said she would be okay. Her mother said nothing the whole time. It was strange, to me, that her daughter was clutching me the whole time when she was on the examining table. I guess her mother was in shock. The father arrived shortly thereafter. That was also a strange interaction, because he addressed me as if I had caused the problem.

I never heard a thank you from Bridgett, her mother or father and I never saw or heard from any of them again. Maybe they did not like the IRS, I don't know. I later learned from the Fire Chief that she had fully recovered and he said that I was a "hero". The story was on the TV news and in the newspapers.

I stopped by the house on the way home and the only things left were smoldering timbers in the flooded basement. The cause of the fire had been a faulty chimney. Ashes from the fireplace fire the night before had smoldered in the wall and ignited the next day.

I received a Silver Medal from the Treasury Department, an Award for Heroic Action and Meritorious Service from the Secretary of the Treasury and a letter from President Reagan. I never really felt like a hero. God had put me in that place at that time for a reason. My destiny that day was to save this eight- year - old girl.

I was pretty shaken up after the rescue. Why was I at that exact place at that exact time when that mother and child needed help? Why me? Was this the Universe at work? Was there a God and a plan? Before that day they had all just been words in a book. Was it destiny, fate, accident or coincidence that brought me there? I now believe that God put me in that exact place to save Bridgett's life.

It was humbling when it first occurred to me that God knew who I was and had used me to help another person.

Little did I know how many more times God would use me to help other people. My life really began on that day. I felt good and happy that I had finally figured out what I was supposed to do in my life. Just show up, be available and God would use me to help people.

THE WHITE HOUSE

WASHINGTON

May 26, 1983

Dear Mr. Schickel:

Through the kindness of your parents, I was pleased to receive word of your heroic life-saving efforts. By assisting Bridget Caparelli in a time of urgent need, you proved yourself to be courageous and quick-thinking and you saved her life. I am proud to commend your fine deed.

Nancy joins me in sending our best wishes for the future. God bless you.

Sincerely,

Ronald Reagan

Mr. Richard M. Schickel
Apartment 2-C
1140 Lorraine Road
Wheaton, Illinois 60187

UNITED STATES

DEPARTMENT OF THE TREASURY

MERITORIOUS SERVICE AWARD

TO *Richard M. Schickel*

In recognition of meritorious service in the Treasury Department

Donald T. Regan

Secretary of the Treasury

CITATION

MERITORIOUS SERVICE AWARD

RICHARD M. SCHICKEL

The Treasury Department bestows the Meritorious Service Award on Richard M. Schickel for his courageous efforts in saving the life of an eight year old, Bridget Caparelli.

In December 1982, Revenue Representative Schickel responded to cries for help by the child's mother who, upon attempting to enter a nearby house at #9 Eagle Nest Court, found it completely enveloped with smoke. Neither Mr. Schickel nor the child's mother could enter the house to rescue Bridget, who was trapped inside near an upstairs window. Mr. Schickel broke the window and convinced the child to jump to him. Mr. Schickel then drove the child and her mother to the hospital where the child was released after treatment for cuts and smoke inhalation.

Thanks to the timely actions and good judgment demonstrated by Revenue Representative Schickel, the child survived. This award recognizes Mr. Schickel's concern and presence of mind which led to his successful effort in saving a life.

2 Daily Courier-News, Tuesday, December 28, 1982

Passerby credited with saving girl, 8, from burning home

Fire destroyed a house in rural Elgin Monday afternoon, but an 8-year old girl sleeping inside when the fire started escaped with minor injuries.

South Elgin Fire Chief Louis Oine credited a Wheaton man with saving the girl's life.

The tri-level house at 9 Eagles Nest Court, off MacDonald Road southwest of Elgin, was gutted by the fire which apparently started in the lower level. A cause has not yet been determined, but Oine ruled out arson.

When firefighters arrived, the house was engulfed in flames, Oine said.

The fire apparently started while the girl, Bridget Caparelli of Lombard, was sleeping in an upstairs bedroom, Oine said.

The house is owned by Salvatore Titone, but neither he nor his wife were home at the time of the blaze.

Shortly after the fire started, Caparelli's mother came to the house, discovered the fire, and called for help.

A PASSING motorist, Richard Schickel, 25, of Wheaton, came to assist her, Oine said.

"He is a real hero," Oine said. "As far as I'm concerned, he saved the girl's life."

Oine said Schickel broke some windows at the front of the house with large rocks and eventually persuaded the girl to jump into his arms. The girl was awakened by a smoke alarm and the barking of a family dog, Oine said. The dog perished in the fire.

The girl's mother took her to St. Joseph Hospital in Elgin, where she was treated for cuts on her hands and feet and for smoke inhalation. She was later released.

The state fire marshal was expected to inspect the scene today, Oine said.

Pingree Grove and Countryside firefighters assisted South Elgin in fighting the blaze.

1

Introduction

My Life in the Internal Revenue Service

This book contains my memories of 33 years as a Senior Revenue Officer (Tax Collector) in the Internal Revenue Service (IRS) and about situations in which I was involved, heard about or witnessed. Some of them point out the strengths and the failings of the IRS. The names and case facts have been changed to protect the privacy of people I have worked with.

The intent of this book is to show that the IRS is an agency broken by years of budget cuts, an antique computer, an aged workforce 40% of which can retire by 2019, inexperienced employees and a failed approach to its Mission. The IRS budget has been cut over one billion dollars over the past five years and new laws from Congress placed more responsibilities on the IRS and are quickly destroying the old tax administration system. IRS management is responsible for mismanagement, inefficiency, waste and confusion of their mission and purpose. I desire to expose what is not working at the IRS, to draw attention to limitations of the existing system, so that a new tax administration system can be developed for the next fifty years.

The IRS of today is not what it was when I signed up for service in 1981. The people of the United States seemed to be more cohesive and wanted to contribute to the good of all society and their fellow citizens in need. Today I have witnessed a more - "I am going to take what I can get attitude". This book is about numbers. It has to be.

I have tried to spread them out. But the IRS is about numbers and money and statistics. The numbers tell the story.

I trust in the system - the budget system, the Congress and the Whistleblower System. Tax assessment and collection are one of the fundamental jobs of the government and should not be contracted out to private collectors. I have faith a little information will go a long way to correct the wrongs that are prevalent at the IRS; the wrongs that I have not only witnessed but objected to and then been made to suffer from.

Having faith and trust in the system is not enough. I also have hope. I believe in the Constitution of the United States that proclaims that we the people are all created equal and deserve equal protection under the law. I believe in the right of due process. I hate favoritism, inequality, racism and discrimination against any person or class of people. I want this book to expose to the light of day the crimes and abuses that are being committed by the Internal Revenue Service against the taxpaying public, but also the crimes and abuses against the IRS from the public. Most importantly, I offer solutions.

The IRS is an amazingly efficient tax collector with many employees who want to help and serve the taxpayers of the United States. But it can be arbitrary, capricious and mean spirited, and that is just for starters. When challenged, the IRS can turn into a cruel, bitter, vindictive enemy that will do whatever it can, using whatever federal government resources available to it, to not only win its case but also to teach a lesson to those who have challenged it. I have been at the end of that whip for years.

People have asked me if writing a book about the IRS is a wise thing to do. I have asked myself the same question, many times. One friend said "I think your book and your tax consulting business is cool, it's a great way to help people. The IRS is this thing that people are afraid of and you are in the position to help them understand how the system works and that they don't need to lose hope anymore." A quote from a philanthropist named Harris Rosen recently appeared in the New York Times and it also applies to the

IRS situation perfectly. He said, "If you don't have hope, then what's the point?" Most people in trouble with the IRS are scared and paralyzed; they don't know what to do or where to start. Some just play dead, hoping the issue will go away. The IRS never goes away.

All of my years at the IRS were filled with fear and conflict and pressure to perform. Doing the right thing for the taxpayers was not at the top of my list. During most of my tenure I have suffered in conflicts with IRS management. I am not complaining, but I am through living in fear. I just want my story to be told and I will face the consequences, but I will not fear them.

When I outlined this book I did not plan to tell this next story-because I do not want this to be a negative book. But what happened to me after I arrived in the Tucson, Arizona IRS Post of Duty was so incredible and so damaging to me and thousands of taxpayers and dozens of employees that I felt it important to share.

I retired from the IRS in December, 2013 and now have a private tax consulting practice where my colleagues, a group of retired IRS employees, and I continue to provide service to taxpayers in need. Our mottos are "We know the IRS, because we were the IRS for 150 Years," and "Helping the IRS do the right thing."

I remember during a congressional hearing listening to Congressman Douglas Barnard from Georgia, who was on a subcommittee investigating senior IRS management. He claimed "there is persuasive fear among IRS employees that reporting the misconduct of their superiors will result in retaliation against them." Congressman Bernard said "The IRS world ...is a world where whistleblowers are systematically punished and where wrongdoers are applauded. The real world is where employees throughout the IRS are afraid to come forward to report wrongdoing or to cooperate in investigations of their superiors because of a fear of retaliation. The real world of the IRS is where if you are not a team player, you are off the team."

My stories and memories may not be much different from life in any large business. Sex, drugs, fear, and harassment are probably widespread. The difference is that in some cases the IRS does not follow the law and it tolerates and even encourages bad behavior in its managers and some employees follow that example.

Why I Joined the IRS

I was one of the top tax collectors in the IRS for 33 years. I started as what I would call a "normal person," straight out of college. I somehow survived the hectic pace of the IRS. I will share what I learned in order to succeed as an employee of the IRS.

I always enjoyed my IRS tax collector job because I was able to help the Government and help people who wanted help. The IRS really is about service. But my job was also to hurt people - to make examples of them - in an effort to prevent other taxpayers from thinking about not paying taxes on time - or at all. I was not even sure what a tax collector did when I applied for the job. I graduated college with a degree in political science and had no plans for the future; there were no jobs to be found during the recession of 1979-1981. The IRS hired me on the spot. Approximately 50% of new tax collectors quit in the first year; that should have been a sign, but I had a professional job when others could not get work. I was lucky, I guess. I sort of fell into my life with the IRS.

I was a well-respected Senior Revenue Officer with 65 performance awards. I had a silver medal from Secretary of the Treasury Regan and a commendation from President Reagan. I was a classroom instructor, coach and author of a groundbreaking book on financial analysis, which I gave to the IRS. When I retired, I was awarded the Albert Gallatin Award, the highest honorary career service award from the Secretary of the Treasury. I was also a whistleblower who was punished by the IRS management for reporting cases of inequality in the application of the tax laws. I reported age and mental health/physical health discrimination, anti-Semitism, racism to African Americans and Hispanics, and abuse techniques that were being used to single out and punish taxpayers.

Sometimes these actions were so subtle, so covert it would be imperceptible to an outside observer. Many people in the IRS could be whistleblowers and it would greatly improve the customer service and procedures, but they are afraid. It was my experience that the whistleblower system did not work for me at all. My book is a living history of my life inside the IRS. Traditionally the IRS does not like truth like this to be told and it hates whistle blowers.

The IRS has a collection of employees who are trained to be of service to you, to be friendly to you and to help you out. But they always help the Government and themselves out first. They can seem like your "best friend" while they are collecting information that could result in you being audited, losing your assets or even criminally prosecuted.

Many IRS employees are good, decent people. Some are competent and some are not, some are like aggressive robots, some are (in my opinion) psychopaths and sociopaths. They can be the meanest nastiest person that you will ever meet. They will seek to destroy your life to collect money for the Government. They will poke around your life asking your friends, family and coworkers the most intimate details about you, your life, your business and your financial circumstances. They will look for money and assets they want to seize.

Many employees working in the IRS do not take anything personally. They simply don't care about anything but closing their case. They don't care if people are hurt because of their actions. They are so tired, pressured and stressed out trying to follow the IRS procedures which sometimes do not reflect the intent of the actual tax laws - that they have no time to think. They have to hurry on to the next case. The IRS service center pipeline system mostly prohibits employees from thinking or caring or using their judgment. They do a few tasks and then just move the case forward. They have no ability and no incentive to do the right thing.

The type of person you are dealing with at the IRS determines what you can expect. I was known to be friendly and reasonable, but

I was swift to take enforced collection action when it was necessary. IRS Management liked that if a person had a 9 a.m. appointment with me and failed to show up, then I would be at their bank seizing their bank accounts by 3 p.m.

Some IRS employees go to great lengths to serve taxpayers. You will see their compassion and humanity to others. I did that every day. I often paid a great price for it, but at least I was able to sleep at night.

I have worked with many people who as taxpayers do not know the system. They may lack the ability to access the internet, to read or write in English, and be unable to think about tax matters and no one at the IRS understands or cares. The tax system is complex, but at its core it is very simple. It benefits some people and corporations and punishes some people and small businesses.

Does the IRS target people in its investigations? You bet they do. This comes all the way down from National Office and there are IRS Management officials who decide every year which group they will target regarding what tax issues they seek to enforce that year. They decide who will be audited and which cases they will pursue through audits and collection efforts. They decide who will get attention and who they will overlook. The problem with this is that National Office issues broad and confusing instructions that are usually interpreted at the local office level. The application can be pretty subjective and discriminatory.

> "He who passively accepts evil is as much involved in it as he who helps to perpetrate it. He who accepts evil without protesting against it is really cooperating with it."
>
> \- Martin Luther King

2

Welcome to the World of the IRS

The History of the IRS

Taxes are nothing new to civilized society. We find records going back to Sumerian times showing that if a taxpayer did not pay he would be punished. They had a saying "You can have a lord, you can have a king, but the man to fear is the tax collector!"

In ancient Rome, the tax collectors were local men who could go up to someone and look at what they owned and assess taxes and then collect them on the spot. If they did not pay, they could be beaten or jailed and all of their assets stripped from them.

Two famous tax collectors named in the Bible are the apostle Matthew and the convert Zacchaeus, who both had connections to Jesus. Tax collectors were reviled in the land now known as Israel because Rome had power over them. So the local tax collectors – working on commission and without any oversight - would collect for the Roman Empire and also collect whatever commission over that amount that they could get. Tax collectors were rich men.

> "What have the bloody Romans ever done for us?" The people rage in a Monty Python skit. "Well, there's the aqueduct...the streets are safe at night...the fresh water is nice... the libraries are helpful, the paved roads...the criminal justice system, the sea lanes are safe from pirates, the literature, art, architecture, buildings, protection... Israel takes from Rome, but is

> unwilling to give back for the very saving of their lives. Who knows what barbaric nation would come conquering had not Rome paid treasure and blood for this fragile desert nation? No merchant could make money without a stable economy, currency, justice system, and enforceable contracts." "All this costs money!" The tax collector demands. "If Rome was so evil, why does God allow it to rule over Israel? Besides, what of the lying merchants who rob the people blind?"

I remember a story my Uncle Bob told me when I was growing up. It was about a snake and a mouse. The snake was caught in a trap and could not escape.

The snake asked the mouse to open the door of the trap. The mouse said "No, if I do that you will get out and eat me." The snake asked ever more sweetly and said no he would never hurt the good little mouse. The mouse sensed this was a trick. He had a gut feeling he should run away. But the snake knew he was a good mouse and appealed to him on a higher spiritual ground. He told him if he released him from the trap, he would go out and eat bad snakes and everyone in the village would benefit. The mouse opened the door to the trap. The snake came out and bit him. As he was dying, the mouse was mad at himself for not following his gut instinct which was to get away from the snake. He asked the snake how he could even think about biting him after he had saved his life and the snake said "That is what snakes do, we bite people and eat mice, and everyone knows that." Then my uncle said "Never trust anyone in life and you will never be disappointed. Always trust your gut instincts."

This example applies to why you can never trust the IRS. In any contact you have with the IRS, agents will ask nicely for what they want: money, tax returns, and information. Then they will use whatever they collect to come back and harm you with it. This is what I was trained to do in the IRS. This worked for me for a while, to be a "company man" who followed orders and did what I was told, no matter the mental, emotional or physical cost to me.

The IRS is the same as it ever was. It used to be called the Bureau of Internal Revenue (BIR). Tax collectors collect taxes and tax auditors assess even more taxes for you to pay. That is their role, their duty, their mission. Their role is not to be nice or understanding or compassionate. They are sent to administer the tax system and enforce the laws the United States Congress has created. The use of the word "service" in the name of the Internal Revenue Service - does not tell who they are in service to. Believe me it is the Government not the taxpayers.

The taxes the IRS collects are used to pay for programs the United States Congress debates and discusses and creates and funds. These taxes go to projects, goods and services you may or may not agree with, like war, weapons and the military, national parks and social programs like healthcare, food stamps, Social Security, Medicare, Medicaid and unemployment benefits.

The IRS does not have any official position on any of these spending programs, although its own budget has been severely reduced in each of the five previous years. The IRS is charged with assessing taxes, finding tax money, and auditing or proving what you write on your tax return. They are also charged with filing criminal charges against those who are conspicuously noncompliant and egregious in their non-filing and non-payment of tax returns.

The most amazing part of this is that the IRS is very efficient. It collects $214 for every dollar it spends to get the money. In 2014, it collected 3.1 trillion dollars to fund almost every part of the government. Even more amazing, people have been trained to file and pay income taxes and the IRS claims a 98% rate of voluntary compliance. That is what they advertise. They quietly admit this is only on 84% of the people in the United States. IRS audit and collection efforts resolves 2% more and the other 14% do not file or pay. I doubt if it is even 84%. In fact, 99% of W-2 earners report their income. Only 44% of self-employed people report their income. Only 11% of people who operate on a cash-only basis report their income. For every 41 cents the IRS spends, it collects $100 in revenue. While many people hate to pay taxes and actually hate the IRS, the IRS collects more than 90% of all the money needed to run the Government.

In comparison, China does not have a population that voluntarily supports their tax system. They have about 2/3 more population than the United States but have 600,000 armed tax collectors. They are treated very badly and often end up missing, kidnapped, assaulted, and dead. They are often bribed and corrupted by a society that is not used to paying taxes and has a mostly cash-based economy. Of course the penalties for nonpayment of taxes in China include public execution.

It is said "taxes are what we pay for a free society." But you are not free to not pay taxes in the United States. It is a system of "forced voluntary compliance."

Most people don't mind paying taxes and supporting society - but they want the tax rates and tax system to be fair, impartial and equal. Hatred of paying more than the other fellow pays is ingrained. When a tax system is arbitrary and subjective or favors a few over many, it is an outrage. We actually have plenty of money in the United States to take care of all the people all the time. Our runaway military spending has broken the backbone of the American economy. Technically the United States is bankrupt. It owes more than it has in income or assets.

President Lincoln signed the first income tax law in 1861 which created the Bureau of Internal Revenue. It was repealed in 1862 and replaced with a more comprehensive income tax law in an effort to pay for the Civil War. When I first came to the IRS (in training), the official history of the IRS was explained to me. I was told that we tax collectors had a special duty not to act like private tax collectors during the Civil War. These deputy collectors were under contract and earned commissions. We were told how these private collectors were enterprising, unscrupulous businessmen who received their authority from the Treasury Department and then went out and hired rough street thugs and gang members to actually enforce the law.

Abuses occurred and people were beat up and dealt with in all sorts of ways. Tax assessors and tax collectors had the power to enter homes and businesses and make inspection of income and assets without a writ, they were known for being heavy - handed and citizens could be jailed for nonpayment of income taxes. There were lists of suspected tax scofflaws that were posted publicly and in newspapers. In fact this was how it was when I was a revenue officer. Newspapers routinely published list of non-taxpayers. This brought a lot of public pressure on those people. But sometimes the tax information was incorrect and this embarrassed and shamed innocent taxpayers. But the IRS did not care. It never says "Sorry we ruined your good name or your reputation, or your life."

The Civil War Bureau of Internal Revenue had 4000 field assessors and collectors and was accused of unfair and uneven collection actions. Bribes and incorrect assessments were widely reported. The income tax law left collection techniques up to local collectors. These collectors encouraged the use of informers who were rewarded with 50% of the tax that was collected by the Government.

Tax collectors would smooth talk, trick and cajole their way into the taxpayer's confidence and this would result in higher collections and tax assessments.

The pay structure for assessors was between $3-5 a day plus $1 for every 100 names they assessed with taxes. Collectors got a better deal - they were paid 4% on everything that they collected up to $100,000 and 2% on sums above that amount (with compensation capped at $10,000.-$250,000 in 2015 dollars)

Millions of dollars were collected in this way, resulting in huge commissions being paid for the collections. They had strong incentives - it was written in the contract that they only got paid out of the money they collected. In 1872 Congress experimented with private tax collection where the collector could earn 50% commissions of tax collected. That program failed and the law was ruled unconstitutional. So the law was repealed in 1872.

There was no federal income tax between 1873-1893. The Government funded its operations through excise taxes, import taxes, tariffs and fees.

In 1894 Congress passed a flat income tax, but it was ruled unconstitutional in 1895.

In 1913 the modern Federal Income Tax was legally voted on and passed by Congress.

Congress passed a law which is known as the Internal Revenue Code which they keep adding to. This is found in Title 26 of the United States Code (26.U.S.C.). It is difficult to read and comprehend. It is amended every year by Congress and becomes more complex. It is filled with tax breaks for specific businesses. It never mentions them by name. Then the Treasury Department comes up with Treasury (tax) Regulations, which is the official Treasury Department interpretation of what they think Congress meant with the tax laws. In addition to this, there is the U.S. Tax Court which gives its own interpretations of the tax law, which is sometimes quite a different view than the Treasury Department. Then there are court decisions, rulings, and procedures. All of these are considered when the Internal Revenue Code is written.

The Bureau of Internal Revenue was recreated as a political patronage system which invited corruption, bribes and unfairness. By 1951 because of scandals it was reorganized into a civil service career employee organization and those old managers and employees were forced out. Then the Internal Revenue Service was born.

I knew one former Bureau of Internal Revenue (BIR) employee who was forced to resign. He was now an old lawyer. He had started as a revenue officer then became a revenue agent/auditor and admits he studied to be a lawyer while on Government time. He told how he would leave the taxpayer's file folder on his desk when the taxpayer and their tax representative came for the audit. He told them that he would go out for coffee and be right back. Then he said he would slide their file across the desk. When he came back he expected the file to be back on his side of the desk and contain money (a quiet bribe) to help the audit go their way. He said that the revenue officers did this also. They also brought in some money to the government "just to make it look good," he said. He did not express any remorse or regret for doing this. He said everyone was doing it - to not take a bribe would have cost him his job. This was because his manager got a percentage of the bribe as well. The old lawyer told me the usual bribe amounts were at least 10-20% of the balance proposed or owed.

Income Tax Rates over the Years

The first Federal Income Tax financed the Civil War, and tax rates were up to 10%. That law was repealed in 1872.

In 1916, tax rates started at 1% and went to a maximum of 7% on income up to $500,000. At the start of the World War I in 1916 the maximum rate was raised to 15%, then in 1917 to 67%, and in 1918 to 77%.

In 1936, at the peak of the Great Depression, the rate was 79%. The maximum tax rate increased during World War II from 79% to 94% and then stayed there until the 1960's. During World War II the tax rates included a larger number of citizens at lower income levels. In 1943, the Government required employers to withhold money from employee paychecks and pay the withholdings every month to the Treasury. This paved the way for employees to feel less connected to paying the taxes, more trained in receiving some of their paycheck, not all of it. It also made it easier for people because they did not have to actually write a big check at the end of the year - this can be very emotional.

So to ease the transition to withholding taxes, the Government waived any tax balances due for 1942. This might be a tool that could be used by the IRS today to limit the number of years back that the IRS will seek to collect.

President Kennedy lowered the top marginal tax rate down to 70%. President Reagan was responsible for leading Congress to lower it to 50%.

President Reagan said "We're going to close the unproductive tax loopholes that allow some of the truly wealthy to avoid paying their fair share. ...They sometimes made it possible for millionaires to pay nothing while a bus driver is paying 10% of his salary - and that's crazy." Actually the term "loophole" implies that something happened by accident or was overlooked. That is far from the truth. Tax lawyers craft the Tax Code. They put in a "tax loophole" for wealthy taxpayers who earn money from capital gains (buying and selling stocks is one example) They only pay 15% capital gains tax versus 39.5% if it was taxed like regular income. Nothing happens by accident in the Tax Code.

In the 1990's the Clinton administration lowered the maximum tax rate down to 39.6%, where it remains today. The high tax rates and the complexity of the tax laws train people on ways to find creative outlets for not paying taxes. When people owe the IRS, they figure out the IRS system and often know more than the newer tax collectors. They know how to hide assets or put them beyond the reach of the Government. They figure out how to leave money in corporations, partnerships and trusts to avoid income taxes.

Inside an IRS Office

Since my father worked for the IRS, I entered my first IRS office at the age of five and there were grey metal desks and grey metal partitions topped with frosted glass - it must have been from the 1940's. I also remember going to the headquarters office where they were still processing tax returns by hand. It was in a very old building with huge windows that were wide open to below 17 stories down. Knowing what I know now, I wonder if any IRS employees ever felt tempted to jump out the window from pure frustration. There were giant stacks of tax returns and paper weights everywhere. People were smoking and it was very hot since it was before air conditioning. The employees were all busy but were very kind to me.

Most IRS offices are laid out the same. You start by standing in line, waiting to speak to the receptionist. Sometimes you wait for a long time. In the Taxpayer Service/Taxpayer Assistance area, usually two tough older women handled every single person that came in the office. They knew everything about the whole organization. I was always respectful of them and tried to be friendly, because during the filing season they would call out revenue officers and tax auditors to help serve the public. This does not happen anymore. This is one reason why serving the taxpaying public is in decline. The IRS does not function as a cohesive unit anymore - it has been divided up and access to other the IRS units is restricted.

Taxpayer Service/Taxpayer Assistance Section is all about waiting in line. They don't let taxpayers make appointments. Sometimes you wait in line for 1-6 hours. If the office is going to close, they will send you home and tell you to come back another day. They are so short staffed and they have no control over how many people walk in the door.

When you first speak to an employee, they are required to tell you their name and badge number, like they are inmates at a large prison. Treating them like numbers instead of as individuals is demoralizing to them. I refused to give my number, ever. They called me Mr. Schickel or Officer Schickel.

Now, the new policy of IRS taxpayer service/walk in office assistance is to refuse to accept your cash. That's right – the Internal Revenue Service will not accept your cash as legal tender to satisfy your tax balance. They want checks or money orders. They do not accept credit cards.

In the tax consulting business that I started after I retired from the IRS, I take credit cards - I process payments quickly and simply through my telephone. IRS revenue officers and taxpayer service and revenue agents cannot accept debit or credit card payments. They cannot set up recurring direct debits to credit cards, only to bank accounts, and that is a detailed operation.

When you go into an IRS office today to speak with an employee about forms, tax form questions or letters you have received, you are being photographed, taped and recorded usually without your knowledge or consent. There is a small notice of this posted in the employee's booth, but most people are so stressed at this point that they do not notice. Just to get into the building that their tax money paid for they will have had to remove their jewelry, belt and shoes, they will be scanned by a metal detector, and scanned by three armed guards. This is a sorry example of where the Government is right now - afraid of its own people.

When I first started, there was the interview area which consisted of tables and chairs and partitions. There was no privacy and everything one taxpayer said or I said could be heard by the other 5 taxpayers in the room. Nothing was confidential in those interview rooms. Often they were located next to the waiting room, so everyone waiting for service could also hear all the taxpayers' stories.

After a couple of years working in the field, I was transferred into the first IRS Automated Collection Site (ACS) - a telephone call center. At 9am one day, I made the first outgoing collection call and there were newspaper reporters and television cameras recording it. That office had 150 employees who were making outgoing calls to collect taxes and take incoming calls to resolve problems and handle questions. We had cubicles and newer equipment. But the manager who designed the call site bought the cheapest floor and ceiling tiles.

It was noisy and crowded. I heard that he had saved the Government $100,000 and got an award for $10,000 because of it. This was pretty typical of how IRS management operates.

Next to them was the audit section where the auditors would have a desk and two chairs in front of them. Sometimes the taxpayers being audited would be so scared they would be high or drunk - just so they could try to handle it. I remember seeing one man who had a heart attack during his audit. He died right in front of my eyes. He was lying there on the floor and his face turned black from lack of oxygen. We all stood there staring at that man. Some of the other auditors tried to hurry up and complete their audits before they released other poor taxpayers who were being audited. After the ambulance left, we were told to get back to our desks and get back to work. That was the IRS of the old days. That same essence still is in the IRS today. It is just more covert. The IRS never ever wants anything to stop the production process which is required to close cases.

The next area was where the revenue officers sat. When I first started with the Internal Revenue Service, it was like walking on to the set of the old police sitcom, *Barney Miller.* We sat two to a table and shared a phone. Some desks had employees who were chain smokers and wore so much perfume that I choked. So you knew everything about everyone else in the office and about their cases as well. Some of my fellow employees were kind and friendly and helpful to me. I am not sure if that was because my father was already a boss at the IRS or if they just felt sorry for me because I was so fresh and naive.

The offices were strange. I can see that now, but at the time, I had nothing to compare them to. There were the Senior Officers, the Grade 12's who only other Grade 12's could talk to. They had their own tables and their own phones. They were somehow considered above the other employees. That changed over time. Many people even inside the IRS are afraid of revenue officers because they can be mean and turn on you in an instant - just like a rabid dog. Or they can be the nicest people in the world - until you don't do something that they want. In modern IRS offices, there is little security in the cabinets. They are just regular file cabinets that can easily be jimmied open when the keys are all lost. The receipt books are the same, except each revenue officer gets one in case they get cash for a tax payment. Otherwise you will have no proof that you filed your tax refund on time. The burden of proof is always on the taxpayer. The IRS loses checks and tax returns all the time, and people don't know what to do. I have seen a file cabinet stuffed with a year's worth of tax returns and checks due to neglect by some employee. It is crazy making for the taxpayer to know that they have filed or paid their taxes and then the IRS claims they did not.

I remember in the very early days of my IRS time, where each office had a teller unit and they would collect the cash payments and put the money in a safe. This worked out fine, until some people figured out that these offices were easier to rob than a bank, so some offices would be robbed every few weeks. The IRS did not pursue it, I was told, because they did not want the embarrassing publicity. So people just got away with it. Eventually IRS closed the teller units.

I remember one time when I was going to travel on Government business and it was all last minute and I was sent to the IRS Illinois Headquarters in downtown Chicago to get money for last minute travel. They brought me to a back room and there was a large safe, filled with cash. I saw really historic currency in there, silver and gold certificates. I wondered why they still had that. It was yet another mystery of the IRS. But I signed a voucher, got $1,600 cash and the next day I was on my way to the IRS National Office Headquarters for a six-month detail.

I remember the Lombard, Illinois IRS office was so bad, I was in my chair sliding over to my file cabinet and the chair leg hooked into the worn out rug and I fell to the hard concrete floor and strained both wrists. I remember that there was a raw sewage smell in the bathroom along with pill bugs, spiders, centipedes and water bugs. The doors and windows leaked. It was so cold that most people bought electric heaters and then we all plugged them in and that kept blowing the electrical circuits- so we had to use them in shifts. The office furniture was orange and avocado colored, left over from the 1960's I guess. Each file cabinet had a huge steel bar and a padlock to prevent an intruder from breaking in and getting the tax data.

Take Care of Yourself First, Best and Always

Lombard, Illinois is 21 miles west of Chicago and it rains and snows there a lot. There was a 50 foot wall where all the revenue officers desks were. It was cold and windy. The windows leaked so bad that the drywall started to get wet. After a while, green algae and black mold started to grow on the wall. As usual I complained, the union (National Treasury Employees Union-NTEU) complained. Nothing happened. So one Friday morning, I walked into the office with a crow bar and 10 gallons of bleach and I told everyone that they should go in the field to work their cases and then I smashed the wall out with my crowbar. I guess that I was mad as hell and I was not going to take it anymore. I was sick from allergies and I could not breathe in there.

Actually no one could breathe in there after I started splashing the bleach all over the walls and floor. I felt like I had done a good thing and then I left. I laugh now as I write this. I swear that I did not have a drop to drink - it was just a natural urge I had to take care of myself and take care of those around me.

I went home after that. I guess, I just didn't care what happened to me. I was just not going to be treated like dirt anymore. I had had it. I never heard a word from management and over the course of the next month the windows were replaced, caulked, the mold eradicated and the walls rebuilt and painted. Neither management nor my fellow employees ever said anything about it to me. Maybe they thought I was crazy. Maybe in that moment I was. As you can guess that moment of "acting out" led to many other moments where I played David to all the Goliath characters in the IRS or outside.

I witnessed many things in the Lombard, Illinois office. There was one branch chief/office manager who hailed from Virginia who was proud to talk about the African American employees as "those people" and he told stories about before the "War between the States" when his family had had a large plantation and owned many slaves. He told me on several occasions how he now managed the African American employees for the IRS - but it was just like his great granddaddy had done to the slaves - he managed "those people."

We all had fear and resentment of management. The union was truly my only friend so many times, because when I would do the right thing, for myself, for the taxpayers or for my fellow employees, management could be mean, vengeful, ignorant, or they could vindictively attack me.

There was also a library in each office where the tax court cases and tax books could be found. This is where the 73,854 page Internal Revenue Code could be found along with the 16,000 page Internal Revenue Manual and hundreds of Tax Court Case Books. It filled up a 15 x15 room. This was usually a good place for a nap or lunch, because it had a couch. I also witnessed a couple sharing an intimate moment on the couch one time.

Then there would be a section where the revenue agents were. They were rarely in the office. When they conducted their audits it was usually in the field at the taxpayer's home or business.

In a separate area there was the Criminal Investigation Division (CID); this had been was known as the Intelligence unit until 1978. Now that the IRS no longer has divisions it is simply called CI. You knew you were there when you saw all the boxes full of evidence stacked all over the place. Each office had a criminal section so there was always an armed agent in the office in case of disturbances.

All the desks were fitted with panic buttons which summoned the criminal agents to the area.

Around the corner was the mailroom and storage room for the many boxes of paper forms. The mail room is the most secure. It has clothes and masks and gloves that the mail clerk is supposed to wear while opening the mail. Many times there will be threatening notes or objects in the mail that they are opening. Sometimes a box or envelope will be filled with human, dog or cat feces. I have heard stories in the service center where people send in packages with bags of gasoline. Some people have sent in payments like a truck load of pennies or have written checks on plywood or wood boards. They include all the bank information so it is a legal check. One man sent in a pair of underwear and a note that said -"You already took the shirt off my back you might as well have my underwear too." Others would send in their prosthetic arm or leg with similar comments.

The Post Office puts those people who send in dangerous substances into the IRS in jail, not the IRS. But first the IRS has to take out every paper that is received in all of these letters and put on the stamp - every document received has a document locator number stamped on it. That is just policy - and the IRS loves to follow the rules.

Some angry tax delinquents put white powder like flour or corn starch into the envelopes - hoping that the IRS will think that they have Anthrax or Ricin powder in there. Don't worry - the IRS has a procedure for that too.

The mail clerk is supposed to close the mail room door and put on the protective clothing - if they had not already been wearing it and the mask. There is also a bucket and a gallon of bleach and a gallon of water in there which they are supposed to use to wash off. Then they are supposed to call the building manager and also a security agency located elsewhere. Then they are supposed to stay there for as many hours as it takes for the Federal Protective and local police to come so they do not contaminate the office and the other employees. Of course just because the IRS has a procedure doesn't mean anyone follows it. I have seen mail clerks walk around the office with envelopes that were wheezing white powder and they were asking what everyone else thought it was!

The IRS Commissioner has 2-3 bodyguards, but the poor mail clerks have no one who cares.

For a while, in a Chicago Federal Building, there was an IRS employee and his girlfriend who were homeless, and began living in the fourth subbasement in a place where the IRS stored closed files. I think they lived there for almost a year.

There were older, wiser employees of course. Every IRS office had some crusty old guy in the corner that remembered everything about the IRS for the last 40 years. Plus there was that one Estate and Gift Attorney who worked until he was 97. He was a nice guy - he just spoke very slowly.

There were some crusty older female employees who tried to seduce me when I first came on board. I just acted stupid and they left me alone after that.

The IRS used to be so cohesive. I knew everyone in taxpayer service, collection, and audit, and in the criminal division. I felt good because I had many work friends who knew anything I would want to know about tax laws. Most enforcement employees in the IRS work independently, so it was fun for me to talk to and learn from other employees. But when Commissioner Charles O. Rossotti (1997-2002) implemented his modernization plans it destroyed the IRS.

Inside the office, employees are now taught: "Don't trust your fellow employees, and lock up your computer in a drawer or cabinet when you are not around, because your fellow employees might steal it." This theft could happen even though every IRS office is secured behind many locked doors. You cannot talk to fellow employees about your case work, unless they have a "need to know."

This is an absolute obsessive compulsive attitude that has arisen in recent years and makes little sense. There is fear of being overheard on the telephone calls made on wireless phones, fear that your co-worker at the next desk might hear about your taxpayers data, fear that you will lose the confidential documents that you hold. This happens all the time, employees and contractors left or lost or stolen from them, briefcases and computers that contain millions of names, addresses and Social Security numbers left or lost or stolen at hotels and airports. In fact IRS is so paranoid about this that while traveling they advised me that if I had to leave the government computer in the hotel room, I should chain it to the base of the toilet, so the laptop could not be stolen.

My First Day at the IRS

On the first day of training some management big shot said "Welcome Aboard!" I remember having an excited feeling but also feeling a sick feeling in my gut, when he said that. Though thinking back it was like welcoming me on the ship of fear, despair and doom.

We were told that we were "in service to the Government, not the taxpaying public". We were "revenue officers, not social workers." We were told to not care about anything but "collecting money and closing cases." Some employees interpreted this as free license to threaten, scold, patronize and intimidate taxpayers. I did not.

IRS enforcement employees are trained to be mean but to smile at the same time. That's an interesting combination - mean and nice. Usually the employees just did whatever management told them to do, and the orders always came from the national office. You could find some mean and crazy local and regional bosses who applied the laws more strictly than in other places.

One day in class, I stood up and raised my right hand and said my oath of office:

> *"I, Richard Schickel, do solemnly swear that I will support and defend the Constitution of the United States against all enemies, foreign and domestic; that I will bear true faith and allegiance to the same; that I take this obligation freely, without any mental reservation or purpose of evasion; and that I will well and faithfully discharge the duties of the office on which I am about to enter. So help me God."* 5 U.S.C. §3331

Then I was a sworn officer of the United States. And truthfully I had no idea what I was doing or what was to come over the next 33 years. I sometimes felt like I was a troublemaker in the IRS. I always found something worthy to complain about. Not in a negative way but in the way of trying to make things better for myself and my fellow workers. The offices were cold and dirty. Employee morale was always poor and attitudes of management made it worse. But the most frustrating part was the IRS System - how the work is processed; it is slow, inefficient and cumbersome and that determines how the taxpayers are served or not.

IRS Training Bad Revenue Officer Training School

I think a lot of what I did in my work started when I went to revenue officer school - I learned such phrases as

- "Take no prisoners, kill them all and let God sort 'em out."
- "Kill the Beast."
- "Show me the money."
- "Enforced collection is the only answer."
- "These fucking rights letters are such a burden on us - rights? Who gave them rights? They did not have the right to take the money in the first place".
- "Seize first and ask questions later."

- "Guilty until they can prove that they are innocent."
- "Pay it and file a claim."
- "Most people don't have the money for lawyers so we can do whatever we want to do."
- "We have to draw a line in the sand."
- "We need to make an example out of this guy."
- "We have to send a message to these people."
- "Pay or we seize."
- "Pay us before you pay the Lord." (In regard to tithing)

One of the problems that I have always had was how a new employee is approved in the budget and hired. Say that $60,000 is budgeted for the hiring, pay, benefits and training of that new employee. If the employee quits or is fired, then the funding disappears also. As I stated before revenue officers lose 50% of new hires. Combine this with normal retirements and other attrition and usually the IRS only ends up with 1/3 of the new employees that they need.

The Internal Revenue Manual (IRM) is the "how to guide" for IRS employees. Employees are extensively trained on the IRM, then they end up at their desk on the first day out of training and they have no clue as to what to do. This is the area where the IRS relies on standard practice and doing what is ordinary and reasonable in their minds. This is where the new employees find out what the IRS really believes about how the tax code is applied. This is where subjectivity in the application of the tax code begins. It is all oral history.

One of the strangest things about an IRS office was when we hired new people. The new people were welcomed and then sent to shadow the old-timers for a week. Many new people left after that. That is the bad part; when a person is hired and then leaves, the money to fund their job also leaves. Many female employees left because they were afraid of knocking on doors and entering strange homes and businesses. Then the new people went away for training for six weeks. When they returned they were assigned a coach who trained them for a year as the job is very complicated to learn.

When they came back from training, the new people were always isolated from the rest of the employees like they were puppies and they were afraid that the old employees would eat them up and spit them out. We were very distant to new people because we did not know if we could trust them. We feared they were put in as plants to watch us. I know this sounds paranoid - but it is true.

The IRM is supposed to tell you what to do, but really it is the coach and other employees who tell you that makes more sense to help you do the work and close the case. I remember one coach I had after I got out of training. He never would tell me anything, just criticize me and my work. Finally I asked him what was the problem and he said "you don't raise up a chicken to scratch your eyes out." He apparently felt that anything he shared with me could be detrimental to his promotion opportunities in the future - strange! There was a lot of competition for jobs, and some of the longest range feuds were when one employee would be chosen over another. Some people would not talk to each other for years even if they sat next to each other. This sort of petty middle school behavior abounds in the IRS.

Most employees were never trained on the tens of thousands of codes on the Master Computer (IDRS). We just had to look over someone's shoulder and figure out what all the coding meant. I learned to never ask questions about how and why we did something. Invariably, I would be told "that is the way we do it and that is the way we have always done it. If you want to close your case, just do it."

The IRS training budget has been reduced from $172 million in 2010 to $22 million today - an 87% reduction. This is because the IRS was recently involved in a scandal regarding excessive training expense, because it spent $4.1 million for a manager's conference for 2,609 attendees.

The Start of My IRS Journey

I think I got off to a bad start in my career when I arrived at my first IRS office and the manager had not even been told that I was coming. He was very nervous and flustered. One day I heard a noise behind his partition. I went and checked and he was lying on the floor and his chair had slipped out from under him and was still spinning around next to him, I found that he was OK, but his ego wounded. I could not stop hysterically laughing for the next three hours. It was very bad. He never forgot that and would bring it up occasionally over the next 33 years. Maybe that was not a good start to my career.

When I was first hired at the IRS, I was fingerprinted, photographed and a background search was conducted to find out what kind of a person I was and if there were any dark secrets in my past. I also suffered my first audit. It was terrible, because the auditor was very aggressive and I had just graduated college and she was trying to force me to crack and reveal I had secret income. I said I would cash a check at college for $15 every week and it lasted me the whole week. She said no one could survive on that. I lived in a dorm with food provided - so actually I lived pretty well. But that was my first exposure to the bulldog approach to interviewing taxpayers (interrogating). All IRS employees' tax returns go to a special section of the IRS and are audited every year!

Then I entered the world of fear, anxiety, punishments and anger topped off with the negative social stigma of working for the IRS.

There was constant and unremitting stress to close the cases no matter what. We used to have contests between ourselves over who had the most dollars collected in a certain year or who had the most property seizures or the most returns collected or the most cases closed. The most aggressive employees were the ones who got rapidly promoted. I remember that the tax auditors and revenue agents would keep track of how much an hour their audits would yield. So if a tax assessment increase was $10,000 and they spend five hours on it, then that would be $2,000 an hour.

While there could be camaraderie, most of the time each person worked alone. Some employees could be cruel. The two biggest problems that I could ever have were if I lost my credentials or my receipt book. These were legal receipts that, once issued, were proof that taxes were paid - no questions asked. Sometimes, revenue officers would misplace or lose these items. Sometimes a fellow employee would see them laying on a desk top and then grab them and hide them. Or another employee might find my credentials in the hall or the bathroom floor where I had dropped them and then they would delight at watching me freak out. Lost items are supposed to be reported to TIGTA within two hours of their loss and sometimes this cruel game would go on for days. Often they would turn the credentials in to the manager, and the longer I did not report the loss, the more trouble I was in. Losing these two items meant an employee was definitely not getting promoted the next time around. An employee could also lose their job.

There was an atmosphere of wariness and distrust in most offices that I worked in. I had a few close friends and business sources of information, but this is how most people did it.

It could get especially tense in the office in the month of December, because the IRS prohibits Notice of Levies from being issued to seize cash or wages for about three weeks in December because of Christmas - a Christian custom. It does not extend this to other religions or their holidays. This made some revenue officers so trigger happy, in January they would blanket banks and employers with levies.

The employees who could not handle working under such stress used more and more of their sick leave or drank more or ate more. Most usually left in the first year. The IRS jobs provide a personality for insecure, scared people. They find a place to hide behind their persona of THE IRS AGENT.

Why I Stayed

One big job benefit is that because I survived my first year, then it was very hard for me to get fired. I remember one manager who had a secretary who was incompetent and late and high most of the time. Part of his job involved travelling. The regulations said that he needed to document her behavior every day for thirty consecutive days. That was not possible due to his travel schedule. He found it easier to hire a second secretary than to fire the first one. So he had the two secretaries sit right next to each other!

When I joined the IRS I was told that they were going to put me through hell and make me hate the job and then that feeling would force me to deal with the taxpayers in the same way. The trainers told me they were looking for people who "Just do as they are told and don't ask too many questions and don't care and don't think too much." They always told us they were paying us "the big bucks to make judgments that closed cases."

The IRS always pays slightly more than market. I was making $9,000 a year in a bank right out of college and they hired me with a starting salary of $12,154, plus 10 paid holidays, 13 sick days a year and 13 days of vacation the first year. The vacation time grew along with my salary to 26 days off a year by the time I retired. It was glorious to have 49 days off where I did not have to go to IRS. Add on weekends (104 days) and I did not have to go to work for 153 days a year, I suppose that was the reward. When they hired me, I was supposed to be paid $14,000 as a higher graded employee because of my college grades. What management did to everyone, every time there was a hiring, was to tell the new employees that they got the job and then tell them that they would have to come in under the lower salary because of budget restraints. There were no budget constraints, managers actually got cash awards for saving the Government money by screwing all the new employees.

Maybe that is why I sometimes feel that I have been angry, disgusted and afraid my whole time in the IRS.

Happy Times?

While writing this book, one of my editors said "What are some of your happy IRS stories?" So I thought – and I'm sorry if this doesn't sound typically happy - about seizing people's homes and their hidden bank accounts. I thought about how happy I was when I outsmarted some tax cheat. I relayed stories to the editor about the camaraderie I felt when all these lone wolf tax collectors got together and did enforced collection. The editor said that was not what she was looking for.

She said, "I mean positive things!" The gossip and scandal mill at the IRS always had some shocking information to hear. Then my mind did a turnaround. I thought, "She is looking for what she thinks are the dirty little secrets." So then I told her about people having sex in the stairways and parking lots (never with their spouse), and the hotel rooms paid for by the Government. I told about the marijuana and cocaine use in the IRS and how I had witnessed drugs being sold in the offices or the marijuana being smoked in the stairwell of the Federal Building. Then there were the drunken receptionists, and secretaries on psych meds, and managers and employees who would drink their lunches. I never saw a place where people would routinely fall asleep at their desks before I was at the IRS. The big part of working for the IRS is that it takes an emotional toll on you - so everyone needed to find an outlet, usually food, drinking, sex, religion, or drugs – those were the primary choices. IRS people know how to self-medicate.

The editor protested, "Richard - that is not what I was looking for at all. Now I am just confused and angry that that is what you saw happen on Government property." Then she said "OK- tell me some good things about the employees of the IRS." I said they could be wonderful and helpful or ignorant, mean and vindictive. I have always said most revenue officers would have failed a psychological test if the IRS had given it. I saw so many different personality types - so many acts of inexplicable cruelty. There was a thoughtless disregard for the law and for other people. But at the same time, I saw so many acts of kindness, where IRS employees went out of their way to help people who had messed up their lives.

Trying to understand the IRS corporate culture could take teams of psychiatrists years to determine. It is so complex, so protected and is really an oral tradition and history that makes the IRS different than any other government agency or private business. The IRS collects money and audits what people report on their tax returns. But it also gives away money through refunds and the earned income program and other programs. The IRS does not like to give money away. In fact, it is very tight fisted with the money it does receive in its own budget. The IRS has shown itself to be naïve and trusting any time the IRS wants to buy computer equipment. Some company will come along to sell old, soon-to-be obsolete equipment and then the IRS pays top - dollar and always buys high priced maintenance contracts to go along with the deal.

The stories I collected from interviews with taxpayers and their neighbors and friends and employers caused me to learn a lot and make judgments about people. I had power over people, I could use it to help them or hurt them. This affected my mind, my perception of people and of course, my ego. Sometimes I was the person who had to bring the taxpayer back to a reality check of where they and their business were right then and there. It was hard. I had to introduce the reality into their situation that maybe they could no longer afford their lifestyle or their house or private school for their children since their business was failing and they had been taking money from the tax money to fund their lifestyle. One of my mottos was it would all be easier if they could find a victory in their lives right where they were right then. That victory might be that they had filed the current tax returns on time. Or that they were current with this year's taxes. Just something to make them feel good about themselves. Because when they had a victory and then a series of small victories, great things would start to happen in their lives.

Really this is what the IRS wants anyway - people who are healthy, living and breathing and capable of making money so that the IRS can tax it, for the next 30-40 years. When the taxpayers are lost, depressed and broke, this does not make them good candidates for future jobs. So really my approach to tax collection in my later years, was I could catch more flies with honey than with vinegar. It usually worked. And it also made me feel good.

Then there was me. The guy who took risks, who tried to help everybody, who tried to be fair, the guy who saw the big picture and loved to live in grey areas, surrounded by people who saw everything as black or white, right or wrong, my way or the highway.

When you work in a place where you don't get treated very well it encourages a feeling of unworthiness. I felt it. I don't think I treated myself very well for a long time in my years at the IRS. IRS employees are always seeking approval because they rarely get any appreciation from management. I actually received 65 cash and performance awards over my career but they always felt like empty victories. Staff burnout, low morale, lack of training, knowledge and experience all contribute to that. Many errors occur in large part due to human error, attributable to lack of training and oversight by experienced employees.

Over the years I have looked at some of my fellow employees and wished they had more tact, discretion, discernment, sensitivity, wisdom, knowledge, and good manners instead of being officious, mean, uncaring, unkind, judgmental, abusive and cruel. I still keep wishing.

Who Does the IRS like to hire to be Revenue Officers?

The IRS was modeled after a military regiment, with many levels of management. Now it is structured more like a stovepipe model with high up managers directing employees all over the country. It is very militaristic in the IRS, we use terms like "Welcome Aboard", post of duty, AWOL, LWOP and we are all agents or officers. A large percentage of IRS employees have military experience, because veterans get priority hiring. This explains why some of them react as though they are fighting the enemy when speaking to a taxpayer.

Military veterans get a preference when hiring. In fact, ex-cops, ex-military police, Special Forces and Rangers and SEALS are attractive candidates that the IRS likes to hire. That could be why there is such a hostile environment between employees and the taxpayers. To some employees, the taxpayer is the enemy. The IRS also likes to hire burned out entrepreneurs looking for job security, real estate agents, ex-teachers and older people with experience in mortgage lending and banking. Let us not forget the old days when the IRS hired college graduates with liberal arts degrees; they made them feel worthless up front like they had no qualifications to find work anywhere else.

It takes a certain kind of person to be a revenue officer. Being aggressive is an important trait. Revenue officers have many tools and strategies to make a delinquent taxpayer do what they say. One of the strategies they use is to force you to make a promise to pay - like making a promise on your part is some big moral obligation. Then if you do not pay they remind you of how bad you were because you broke your promise. It was important to make the taxpayer feel guilty about not paying taxes; and it was like I was the good cop and the bad cop all rolled up in one. I was able to establish an easy rapport after I put the scare into them. I had a hunger for tax collection - well, really closing cases to please my manager. I never enjoyed the visceral lust for blood that some of the IRS employees felt or felt the satisfaction some employees felt when they figuratively ground a taxpayer's face into the gravel.

How can a powerful organization like the IRS that has so much power be able to attract people who enjoy inflicting pain... sadistic pain?

People can be good or bad, honest or lying, mean or contrite. My feelings and reactions to the circumstances that I saw and the information that I was offered helped me determine how to resolve the case. I was in a position to judge, to reward, to help or punish and hurt.

The greatest gifts I had to give were my time, my energy and my attention to the taxpayers in my inventory. I really did believe I was there to serve not only the Government, but also the taxpayers. It does say Internal Revenue *Service*, after all.

What Does a Revenue Officer Really Do?

My job as an IRS Senior Revenue Officer (tax collector) for thirty-three years required me to make cold calls to individuals and businesses that had not filed tax returns or paid income, employment taxes or other taxes. The IRS sends you a lot of letters, but eventually an IRS Officer will show up at your door. Without warning, they just show up. It is never at a convenient time. They don't care. There is a reason for that. They want to see how you really live. To see what you have so they can take it.

I was trained to meet, greet and think on my feet, and to make decisions quickly. I was trained that the IRS might one day have to parachute me into an area that had had some natural or manmade disaster, and I was to have a pen and clipboard and be ready to interview people, make decisions and directives within 20 minutes of landing. The idea was to reestablish the tax system as quickly as possible. That is what I have done my whole life - jump in, assess available information and make decisions based on what I learned. Assess, not judge. That is important because even what I believe that I see or know could be false, and then my judgment would be in error. Plus there's that word "judge" and I don't think we should judge other people. We should first try to understand them.

The biggest question was always, does what you are telling me make sense? This started in my IRS training and work, and carried over to my personal life. Combine this with Chicago street logic: "Nobody does nothing for nothing," an old attorney once told me. If they are in business, they are getting something.

While millions of self-employed people avoid and underreport their taxes, millions more do not file or pay any taxes at all. The IRS knows about it, but is limited in its ability to try to collect from those people, so it picks on the poor wage earner.

The IRS also wants to minimize the assault rate on its Revenue Officers. If we surprise you then there is less chance that you will surprise us with an angry tax protesting mob or the threat of physical danger. The Revenue Officer will attempt to talk to you and soon will be asking the most personal questions about your lifestyle, relationships and living arrangements, questions about your style of living, your marital status and your children, and will want to see inside your house and business to look for other assets, like artwork or antique furniture that can be seized.

The government gave me cases and guidelines in the law and then I alone was responsible for locating, contacting, interviewing, evaluating, assessing, judging, negotiating, enforcing, and, eventually, resolving the case. I usually had a manager who would sign off on whatever I proposed because the manager was always eager to close cases.

I tried to be fair with the people I worked with. Sometimes the taxpayer disagreed with my determination of what the right thing was for them, but for most of my career, a delinquent taxpayer had few, if any, rights to appeal what I was doing. This is scary because at one time there were 12,600 Revenue Officers just like me doing all kinds of things that were technically legal. Now there are only 4,681 Revenue Officers.

Because of this loss of revenue officers, in 1997, I wrote a book for the IRS about tax collection called the *Asset Recovery Guide*, because so many of the old-time tax collectors were retiring and so much accumulated knowledge was being lost. The book was later made into a section known as the Financial Analysis Handbook in the Internal Revenue Manual. (IRM 5.15.1) I was an IRS Instructor who taught hundreds of people how to be IRS tax collectors. I coached and mentored dozens of employees. I worked with thousands of people who did not file or pay their taxes.

In the book, I coined the term "Senior Revenue Officer" for the first time in IRS history. I just made it up. I figured I deserved something for all my hard work. This meant a person was not only their highest grade but also with the most work history and experience. Now this term is used by revenue officers, revenue agents and tax compliance officers (auditors). It is sad that the IRS rarely gives any acknowledgement to its employees. Even the most basic recognition of senior status makes a big difference.

Most jobs in the IRS make you feel stupid, incompetent, inept and frustrated. It takes so long to do basic actions that even when you really are trying to get something done and help the Government and the taxpayer, it feels like the whole system is against you. I felt that every day. Much of the Revenue Officer job involves accounting and knowledge of business practices and business markets. Revenue Officers receive very little training in accounting, business law or tax preparation.

The one constant with all IRS employees is fear. Fear that they will do something wrong, or that someone will say that they did something wrong. It is like having Big Brother looking over your shoulder all the time. It crushes your spirit and diminishes your soul. The IRS does not like or recognize star employees, it likes to herd employees together like sheep and few employees say anything about it for fear of reprisal and retaliation. I think I was just never smart enough to be afraid.

There are many things wrong with the IRS - but most employees are afraid to say anything about it. In fact, management actively turns down front line employee's suggestions on how to change and improve IRS work processes. It will pay millions of dollars to outside contractors who do not have a feeling for the tax collection business, but ignores the employees who offer better solutions.

The work of a revenue officer is so specialized and so complex that employees become dependent on the Government and think that they have no qualifications for other work in private business, and this is exactly how the IRS likes it. Of course that was not true. IRS managers would frequently tell us in group meetings that if we did not like our jobs that we should leave - that "the door is right over there." I would have been crazy to leave. In fact, IRS employees at that time were in the exclusive Federal Civil Service Pension Plan. Although I collected the money for Social Security, I was not part of the social security system. I had to stay with the IRS for 30 years to qualify for the pension. I had no Social Security Credit.

The IRS tax collector will always look for your Achilles heel, your weak spot. If you lie to the revenue officer or fail to do what you committed to do, you can expect what are most afraid - a levy on your bank or wages. Effective revenue officers are always thinking about their next action and assume that whatever the taxpayer says is not going to happen and that they will have to take enforced collection actions.

As a Senior Revenue Officer for the IRS, I was also a bill collector, psychologist, credit counselor, loan officer, auctioneer, marketing specialist, marriage counselor, financial planner, social worker, paralegal, mediator, asset evaluator, negotiator, judge, jury and enforcer. It helped that I had a natural ability to instantly connect with people. We started talking and I would jump into their lives, learning everything they wanted to tell me. My intuition would tell me everything else I needed to know to investigate their case.

You name it, I found out about it, whether I wanted to or not. In fact, many times people talked too much, telling me too much, which did not serve them well. After all I was a government agent, not a priest.

I found people who sometimes didn't want to be found and forced them to talk to me to get their financial information, negotiate installment agreements and offer a compromise for the government. I determined when people were under such financial hardship that they could not pay anything or when they were candidates for bankruptcy. I could summons them and require them to answer my questions under oath, and I did not have to offer them any Miranda rights.

How Did I Feel About the Work?

Sometimes when I would be interviewing people, I would wonder to myself who the hell I was to be listening and questioning these people, hearing their most private financial, emotional, sexual and physical stories, their weaknesses and their circumstances. I witnessed their circumstances and their emotions. In the end I figured God had put me there because I actually listened and cared. It got harder and harder to hide that, as I progressed in my career and became the IRS Revenue Officer who cared. I was able to use my position of power and authority to actually make a difference in the world and to help not just the Government, but also the taxpayers, at least those who were trying to comply with my IRS directives. But I still lived in fear that IRS management would find out that I was being decent, respectful and kind to people and I would get in trouble for that.

When you don't pay your taxes it is like you entered a bank and cleaned out the vault. You have taken money that does not belong to you. When the IRS catches up with you, you must provide a financial statement to decide how much you can immediately pay the Government and how much you can come up with by borrowing or liquidating your assets, or how much you can pay over time.

Yes, you read this correctly, you must provide a financial statement, because if you are under a summons for financial information and you refuse to provide it, you can be jailed until you do produce the information. As I write this people are being held in prisons by Federal judges on contempt of court charges for this very reason.

It is a white collar crime. People who rob banks go to jail; people who take money that belongs to the Government get long term installment agreements, settlement offers and offers in compromise.

I always told my trainees the best way to resolve cases was by questioning, listening, and looking around, then asking more questions. I became overwhelmed with the inconsistencies of the IRS. It seemed like the IRS was a real life Wizard of Oz hidden in a room somewhere who was feeding us all these stories and lies to manipulate us by fear into believing whatever he told us.

I cannot remember how many times people would spot me and know that I was an IRS collections officer and cross the street or leave a restaurant to avoid an encounter. I have been called a pig, and much worse. I have been spat upon at least twice that I could remember. Some people hated me just because to them, I was the Internal Revenue Service and I was the last straw - the straw that broke the camel's back.

Many case decisions have no basis in reality over issues such as allowable living expenses or if the IRS was going to get money out of it or not. I remember when cable TV was first coming out and managers would deny the expense as a luxury item even in far out towns that had no other TV service. Even today there is discrimination in deciding what expenses can be allowed and which cannot. For instance tithing to a church is not allowed except in Utah with its prominent Latter Day Saints (LDS) population where it is allowed. This is not written down anywhere; it is just standard practice. There are many examples of local management making up their own rules as they go along.

The Toll it Took

What happened to me physically because I worked at the IRS was that I got grey hair at 30, I got fat and old before my time. I got used to living on adrenaline and being ready to jump up and run. In fact, I still have this problem when I am sitting at a table or the computer where my legs are pulled back and I am ready to spring up and get out of wherever I am. I have noticed this with other IRS people also who are always looking at their surroundings and are ready to leap up and get away.

Time for Change

In 1997, the IRS was under daily attack and morale and production were deteriorating. I had some time to get back to the question, "Why am I here?" Many things were happening in my life. Many layers of my life had been peeled away from me and my ego was forced into retreat. Then I saw I had been living with many negative emotions for a long time: unworthiness, fear, anger, low self-esteem, and low self-confidence. Much of this I had picked up from the people who were around me, within the IRS and even my own family and friends. When I was able to distinguish that these things were not helping me, I was able to better sort them out and reject them. During the next 16 years at the IRS - I became a revenue officer who cared and actually worked to help people.

At the age of 40 things were happening in my life, the IRS was changing, I was changing and much of the old support systems were collapsing. This was when the IRS had become the subject of mock and ridicule before the public eye. Magazines, newspapers and congressional hearings all pointed out all the abuses that had been committed by the IRS in the past 45 years - since the last IRS restructuring.

Many revenue officers who had joined the IRS after World War II retired after their 30 years. So with them went many of the ideas, and wisdom on how to find assets and work collection cases. After

RRA 98 was put into the law, older revenue officers started to retire. I had learned a lot from them. All the tricks (good and bad) to getting the job done. My book was a guide to where to find assets and levy them, it also included instructions on financial analysis.

My IRS book -*The Asset Recovery* Guide, suggested that employees take charge of their office telephones and not pick up the phone or return calls until the afternoon. That allowed the employee to get most of their work done in the morning. Many people have taken this to extremes and do not pick up their messages more than once a week or twice a month or never. I admit - this was my fault. Good intention, but the IRS tends to carry things too far. That is why it is so resistant to using email to easily and securely communicate with its customers.

I worked in a stress filled environment. Many employees had emotional and physical illnesses and used their sick leave frequently. Stress is hard on the employees but also on the taxpayers. I think that I became most successful when I realized that I could do my best work every time on every case and then just let it go, not attached to the result. If I made a case decision that was overturned, at least I had made the best decision that I could and I advocated for it. I was able to release everything that was out of my control and in the IRS that is most things. Really it was not the taxpayers who were most damaging to me and others, it was management. It was like being imprisoned in a boiler room collection operation where you had to produce or be kicked out. Most people had some form of self-medication. In that stressful environment smoking, coffee, food and chocolate were comfort food and were frequently used as self-medication by the employees.

Many people have asked me how it feels to have spent so many years at the IRS. In a word, scary comes to mind. It was educational, empowering, a great drain, frustrating and tortuous. I was under constant unrelenting pressure to close cases and perform for my boss, and all the bosses above him. I was trying to please Congress and trying not to piss off taxpayers to the point where they came attacking me.

Now that I am retired, I still have nightmares and bad memories. Many of my retired IRS friends feel the same way. Sometimes I think I should open a PTSD group for IRS employees.

Who is a Typical Taxpayer?

The IRS calls people who do not file or pay "Delinquent Taxpayers." This promotes a negative connotation. The word delinquent usually means a person or situation that is bad, failing, or a person who is an offender or guilty.

Most of the reasons why people owe taxes came down to my unofficial "D" list that I compiled over the years. Many people experienced death, depression, divorce, drugs, drinking, deception, dumb choices, or dumb behavior. Add to this some non-D words such as illness, a gambling addiction, adultery, bad luck, stupidity, and incompetence. Some people say they are too busy, or too afraid to open the IRS letters. They are so overwhelmed with their daily lives and the whole tax filing system that they try to hide. Sprinkle greed and deliberate tax evasion in, and it makes for an interesting cast of characters. There was always plenty of blame to go around as well. Blame the economy, the market, their competitors, their partners, their spouse, their employees, the President, Congress and the IRS. Rarely did they blame themselves for having any part in their financial collapse.

It seemed like many of the taxpayers I was working with did not just set their sights on "Keeping up with the Joneses," they wanted to surpass them, living very high in the moment without regard for making provisions for the future. Some taxpayers seek to leave the whole tax system because they figure out that they work all the time, and just keep having to pay and pay and pay for houses, cars and other "stuff." They never get ahead and taxes can take up to 50%

of income. So they decide the small rewards of being in the Social Security system and receiving Medicare insurance are not enough for them. This is often a short sighted decision, but I am just reporting what I have heard from my taxpayers.

Then there was the talking to the taxpayer part of the job. I would go out and demand money and they would tell me the reasons they did not file and pay their taxes. The following list is from an old training guide I had. We used it to teach new employees what they were up against. It still applies to the IRS today.

- I don't want to pay the tax.
- I thought I could get away with it.
- Self-employment tax or income tax is too high.
- I don't have the money to pay.
- I thought I beat the audit lottery.
- Big guys cheat all the time; I wanted to also.
- My friends cheat every year.
- My expenses equal my income so I don't have anything to report.
- I don't want to pay for Government spending.
- I don't want to pay for government programs that support (insert some program directed at minorities or poor people)
- I am going to have to wait 40 years to get my Social Security - I may not live that long.
- Tax laws are unfair.
- I will not support the military or nuclear weapons or…
- Tax laws are un-American.
- Tax laws are unfair.
- I am selfish and greedy.
- I don't care about other people.
- I needed the money to support my extended family.
- I needed the money for my gambling habit or drug habit or alcohol habit.

I remember another case a friend worked that had a 21 year old man who won the lottery. He chose to receive the money over 20 years and spent most of it in Las Vegas. He bought a $500,000 house for cash and then borrowed his future year's income and spent that also. One day his mother asked him to pay for a new kitchen at her house and it was $40,000. He agreed, but did not have the money. He went to a bank and borrowed $40,000. He did not have money to pay for the loan, so the bank took the house away from him and sold it a public (almost secret) auction to the president of the bank.

The lotto winner had never filed income tax returns, so he owed the IRS quite a bit of money. The IRS found out about the house sale and came in and seized it from the bank. The IRS paid the bank the $40,000 plus costs and took it back. Then the IRS had a public sale and the energy at that sale was very high. That is not a good thing for potential buyers to be in love with what they are bidding on. So the IRS was selling the house for $300,000. The bidding went up to $440,000 and the house was sold. The lotto winner got tax credit toward his tax balance. Last I heard he was living in his mother's house, and it will be years before he can borrow against the winnings again. This is a case of easy come, easy go.

IRS sales sometimes offer great financial opportunities. See: http://www.Treasury.gov/auctions/irs/

It is interesting to note that IRS tax sales are a great place to launder cash, because the IRS does not report cash transactions over $10,000 as is required for banks, and others who are required to report cash sales or deposits over $10,000. One purchaser told me all of the money that he used was "hot". I did not care, I was more worried that I would not be able to sell what I had seized. I was just grateful the purchaser had come and bid on the property.

3

The IRS Computer System

AS YOU READ THIS BOOK, it will seem like I am obsessed with the IRS Computer system. I guess I am. IRS started planning for it in 1957, the year I was born. The mainframe master computer went online in 1961 and it is called the Automated Data Processing System (ADP). It contains information on every person, business, trust, partnership, estate from that time to the present, it is a huge database. This is called the Master File. It is like a large file cabinet that has data on every American citizen alive or dead since 1961. Not online access, but all information can be located either from the computer or from earlier microfilm records that are said to go back into the 1940's. It is another mystery about the IRS. The computer contains many of the secrets of the IRS and the IRS does not like to talk about its secrets. The IRS wanted to automate earlier, but was delayed because taxpayers were not required to use their Social Security number on their tax returns until 1961. So using names to index tax return data was too confusing.

The computer system started as an IBM 360 and was later upgraded to an IBM 370. These systems use large magnetic disks to record and save data. The language the IRS uses was created by Admiral Grace Hopper of the United States Navy in 1957 and was known as Flow-Matic. It later migrated to BASIC (Beginners All Purpose Symbolic Instruction Code) which is still used today. Hopper later created COBOL, a language that the Master File Computer also still uses today. Both the hardware and software are antique and rarely used in the business world today. The IRS has thousands of these old computers with different machines and ad hoc solutions to keep the system operating.

The computer was state of the art when it went online. Those were good times for the IRS. Mortimer Caplin was the IRS Commissioner and he appeared on the cover of Time Magazine where he was described as "a highly respected tax expert." In fact President Kennedy was the first and only president to ever visit the Internal Revenue Service Building. It was the best of times for the IRS.

Terminal operators typed IBM cards that contained information line by line on the return. The programmers told the computer what to do and what information to display. What the computer could do was very limited. For instance, in those days it was unusual for a wife to work, and there was not enough room to list both a husband and wife's income or social security numbers on the computer. That was later modified.

The master computer is located in a cave in Martinsburg, West Virginia. That was appropriate for the time as they were trying to keep the tax information safe in the event of a nuclear war. Just to make sure the records exist no matter what there is also reportedly a backup system in a former salt mine in Utah.

The information is contained on magnetic disks and is stored as a binary system. The processing is what they call batch processing where consolidated transactions are stored to be processed at a later time.

The computer disks were shipped from the service centers to the cave to update the Master File. This update took 3 full days, because every account had to be checked and validated, whether the business was still open or closed and for every person who had ever filed a tax return - living or dead.

At one point they had planned to use the secret Federal Telephone Service (FTS); a system that was secure and hardwired outside the United States Bell Telephone Network phone system. This was a predecessor of the internet system. That plan did not work out. I was always so fascinated by the computer system that I asked the IRS computer technicians detailed questions of the IRS computer and its history.

Now this is the important part: these data disks were shipped via the United States Post Office and later by private carriers to West Virginia every week. In 2005, the IRS rented wire services to transmit the data. The security of the data disks is essential. Yet, the IRS rents a data line from a private company. I was never able to determine if it is a secure line or not, but there are many cracks in the armor of the IRS computer system and I believe that confidential tax data is leaking out and causing or contributing to a $21 billion identity fraud system. The IRS is very proud of how secure the system is. I am just questioning the security of the data disks. Just one disk contains the private financial information of millions of people who pay or have paid taxes. It would be the best source of information to be used in false refund claims.

Some outside contractors working for the IRS have downloaded millions of taxpayer's names and Social Security numbers, addresses and other data and there is no overview. They have also lost confidential tax data stored on laptops and CD's that were lost or stolen.

Under this master file system, in 1970 a less cumbersome system was created to extract data from the Master File and use it for collection and open audit cases. This system went online in January, 1970. It is called the Integrated Data Retrieval System (IDRS) and it is still in use today for collection and audit cases. It does not use direct computer entry either.

The computer is 54 years old and that makes it unable to respond to current demands that would save the Government at least $50 billion a year. Any employee who has access to the master computer

(IDRS) has unlimited access to the tax records of every business, trust, partnership and small business and every United States citizen, *every one*. This includes sensitive personal and business information. This information could be used for industrial spying or personal retribution. Some employees see how much income some taxpayers report and compare it to their own salaries and are tempted to steal. The IRS has had cases where IRS employees have used this sensitive data in identity fraud schemes.

In one employee's case, $400,000 in tax refunds were deposited into one IRS employee's bank accounts. There is an internal audit procedure that will make sure an employee gets caught if they do this but that could take six weeks to six months to six years for an employee to get caught. But it can be manipulated and has been known to fail before. Much of the information the IRS has is proprietary and highly confidential. Business secrets and funding strategies are very valuable, especially to industrial spies.

The IRS is losing tens of billions of dollars because of its antiquated master computer system. In the year before I retired, I was outraged because the IRS and its old computer that cannot keep pace with modern demands reported that it had paid out $5.2 billion in false/fraudulent refunds in 2011 and paid out $3.6 billion in 2012 and $6.5 billion in 2013. In fact the IRS has announced that it expects refund fraud to rise 223% to $21 billion in 2016. The IRS proudly announced this and I could not believe it.

The old computer did not pick up on the fact that 5,500 fraudulent returns were filed by a single tax preparer for refunds totaling $27 million and a payout of $490,000 to a single address in Bulgaria that filed 700 returns. This was the result of an old computer, reduced and inexperienced staffing, and poor internal controls.

I was so distressed about this that I actually wrote a letter (as a private citizen) to billionaire Warren Buffett, asking him to make a significant impact in the tax system for the next 40 years by buying the IRS a new computer system. I am still waiting for a response.

Needless to say, the IRS is not able to attract or pay the best and brightest computer programmers because they would die from boredom and frustration. The IRS hires college graduates who clearly are not in the top half of their class, and then teaches them the old COBOL based system. The IRS pays a $25,000 bonus for new employees who know COBOL and FORTRAN programming languages. The IDRS system is not friendly to other computers. So there are hundreds of other computer systems that extract data from IDRS. This system is great for establishing relationships that the suspected delinquent taxpayer has with other people, employers, and dependents and makes it easier to set up a genealogy type search. In my experience, when one person is doing something illegal and making money they usually share it with family and friends. So there is rarely just one person who is in trouble.

Eventually the computer system grew to include 10 service centers located around the United States. The service centers do indirect data entry. There is no direct access online into the Master File. The computer system which had once been state of the art, is now old and obsolete - an antique unable to complete its original job.

The IDRS system connects into 200 different software systems and there is no one system that does it all. Years ago, I heard that IRS used over 680 programs that tied into the IDRS computer.

Many tax returns are still manually input into the IDRS system by data entry operators, just like in the 1970s. They are not scanned like in modern businesses.

Some IRS service center employees, who were unable to keep up with production quotas, destroyed tax returns. They put them in the garbage or in backpacks to throw away later. I know of one employee who even flushed tax returns down the toilet. Another hid them in a suspended ceiling which worked for a while until the weight of the paper caused the ceiling to collapse! Service center jobs are all about production statistics.

There is much information on business tax returns and audit papers that is very valuable to a business's competitors. This includes business plans, business strategies, asset and inventory lists, tax returns, compensation records, future business plans, financial resources and customer names and details. This makes the IRS ripe for industrial espionage attack. But the IRS has no audit control on the closed paper files and security is non-existent. Thousands of boxes are shipped off to caves and former salt mines every day that have this data. The boxes of closed cases contain the most valuable information. Business plans, marketing strategies, customer and vendor lists, past and future corporate goals and strategies as they impact the tax situation. All obtained during the course of the audit process.

Many billions of dollars have been spent trying to replace the system over the last 30 years, without much success. In part, this is because the IRS promotes from within and rarely hires industry experts. It has been said that "The greatest problem is that the IRS relies on its own people who have come up through the ranks to lead new computer initiatives. In fact, the first IRS Chief Information officer, Hank Philcox, was an IRS insider who had risen from the ranks after beginning as a revenue agent."

I have seen this many times in my career. Revenue officers or revenue agents, who liked to play on their home computers in the early days, were quickly promoted to jobs in information technology and they had no clue what they were doing. They had only a smattering of computer knowledge and computer speak, no formal knowledge, education or experience.

The worst time was in 1985. A long awaited new master computer system was scheduled to go live online on January 1, 1985. The new system had not been tested. Whoever set that target date - must not have known that that is the busiest time for the IRS in the whole year. So whoever was in charge chose to turn on the new system and turn off the reliable ADP/Master File and IDRS systems. The software was shut off and the hardware disabled and removed. The IRS was fully committed to the new system; it crashed in the first week, simply overwhelmed by the magnitude and volume of the work. I was at my post of duty working my cases and helping during the filing season with the large numbers of people who just show up at the IRS office in response to a letter or IRS seizure action. It was a disaster!

We had no access to the computer records. We had to use the paper cases that existed at that time. We kept posting checks and tax returns we received but no one posted them to the Master Computer - because there wasn't one.

No returns were processed. No letters were sent from the computer. No refunds were being issued.

No one could get anything done, they could not look at account transcripts, do audits and collection correctly (or efficiently).

This is 2015. The IRS is at least 20 years behind in technology integration. For instance, the IRS uses Exchange and Outlook for email, and still uses Windows XP as it has since 2003. Although Microsoft no longer updates Windows XP, the IRS made a special contract with Microsoft to provide extended support until it can upgrade to Windows 7. One IRS computer manager I spoke with last year said that because the IRS laptops were so old another $30 million was needed just to buy computers. Otherwise he said half of all the IRS computers would crash if Windows 7 was installed. Like everything else, the IRS laptops and desktops are not on a regular update schedule either. It was supposed to be every 3 years. Now it is closer to 6 years. They are only replaced if they break. But first they use salvaged parts from other broken computers to construct what we used to call a Frankenstein Computer. They hardly worked. Once my computer was down for 34 days, I just stopped working on the cases. It was good times. Management and Computer Services did nothing. No one seemed to care. But I read many books during my hiatus. Then of course I was backed up in my case inventory for the next 6 months.

The more I tried to understand the systems operating in the IRS, the business model became blurred into a mess of hurting people and being without sufficient resources to do my job. There was always a push to close cases. Sometimes there was a push to collect money, but that was never the important part. It was closing cases, no matter how that happened.

4

The Mission of the IRS

When I started, the IRS had a Collection Mission Statement posted on the wall that said:

> To collect delinquent taxes and secure delinquent returns through the fair and equitable application of the tax laws, including the use of enforcement tools when appropriate, provide education to customers to enable future tax compliance, and thereby protect and promote public confidence in the American tax system.

That is what I was supposed to do. But that not is what the job is actually is all about. As an IRS official, I hurt people and destroyed their names, their reputations and their lives, not just then but often years into the future. At the time, I accepted the philosophy that they (the delinquent taxpayers) were somehow bad people to whom the IRS needed to teach a lesson.

At a core level, I knew the Mission Statement was a mission headed for disaster. That disaster came to a head in the Senate hearings of 1997 and 1998 which effectively destroyed collection techniques based on stories of taxpayer abuse that may or may not have been true. As a result, the law changed and was called Restructuring and Reform Act of 1998 (RRA 98). This was supposed to be a law that refocused IRS efforts on customer service and was supposed to transform it into a modern financial services organization similar to the private sector financial institutions. The IRS transformation was a massive undertaking that required changes to virtually every aspect of the IRS, according to a TIGTA report. RRA 98 required the IRS to change its organizational culture, restructure, modernize and improve taxpayer protection and rights. The IRS was supposed to change from an enforcement driven environment to a more customer service oriented environment. This never happened.

They should have retired the entire IRS in order to remove the old ideas about tax administration. Instead, the IRS blindly went forward, being forced to apply a law that they neither requested nor respected.

The IRS was effectively crippled from doing its primary job - to collect taxes. Life at the IRS changed forever. I did not know what to do. We as an organization did not know what to do. It was like some great incestuous secret had been discovered and no one could believe it.

When the collection tax law changed so dramatically with RRA 1998, it was the first time that I saw that the IRS was afraid to act, like it had been caught doing so many bad things that it was afraid to do anything more. It was like a giant that had been attacked and was wounded and was wandering around unsure what to do, if it could not seize and slay taxpayers who had no rights previously.

Then IRS changed the Mission Statement to:

> Provide America's taxpayer's top-quality service by helping them understand and meet their tax responsibilities and enforce the law with integrity and fairness to all.

Needless to say this has not happened. When taxpayers are calling in and not getting an answer 60% of the time, that is just another frustrating abuse that is being pushed on people who are calling with questions about how to comply with the tax laws, or responding to the mounds of letters that the IRS computer continues to spit out at the rate of 130 million a year.

So, I had to make my own mission statement for my own life. This is what hung over my desk for many years. A large poster that said:

> *Do what you can with what you have where you are.*
>
> Teddy Roosevelt.

Then on a smaller paper I wrote:

> *Start by doing what is necessary, then what is possible, and suddenly you are doing the impossible.*
>
> St. Francis of Assisi

Additionally, one day while attending an African American history month party at the IRS, I learned of a freed black slave who was a Civil War rights activist. His name was Arnold Bretonneau. A speech he made changed my whole life. He said:

> *Every man shall stand equal before the law.*

He did not actually get to witness that in his lifetime, but it was inspiring to me. I added that to my personal mission statement.

Then I looked around at the mess I was involved with in the IRS. I saw gross inequalities based on disparate treatment of employees and management, people discriminated against for speaking out and trying to do the right thing, people who were African American, or Hispanic or female or homosexual. There was the old boys club and sexual harassment was always in play. I witnessed so many instances of this. People were getting hurt by "friendly fire" if they did not follow management's expectations. People were mocked and belittled, sometimes publicly in IRS meetings. This happened to me all the time. But I guess that I was too slow or too stupid to care. I just trudged forward seeking to do the right thing for the Government and the taxpayers whose lives I was involved with.

I realized that in order to help people, I needed to learn the law; every nuance of the law. I needed to look at the intent of the law found on the white space between the black printed lines, the same with the Internal Revenue Manual (IRM). I looked for the real mission of IRS Collection in the secret "official use only" documents and the hidden IRS Policy Statements. The IRM was not even available to the public until sometime in 2003, as I remember.

But there were always other missions that the IRS did not prepare for. There are a number of programs that pay out money to encourage people to work such as the Earned Income Credit, a type of welfare program for the working poor. Other programs the IRS administered were the Economic Stimulus Payments in 2007, a giveback of tax dollars to stimulate the economy, followed by the First Time Homebuyers Credit in 2008 that consumed a lot of IRS resources, because it involved big tax payments to encourage people to buy homes.

Since 2010, the IRS has been charged with administering the Patient Protection and Affordable Care Act (Obama Care) which is completely unrelated to collecting taxes, but individuals who do not have health insurance will receive small fines that the IRS is charged with assessing and collecting. But the amounts are so small the IRS would not even issue cases that small if they involved income tax. It is estimated that the IRS would need another 16,000 employees and an additional $10 billion budget to administer the plan.

The IRS also collects delinquent child support and has agreements to collect delinquent student loans, Social Security overpayments, delinquent separate maintenance, alimony and state income tax.

How I Felt Doing This Job

In the Internal Revenue Service, I suffered abuse and pain from a few managers who were psychotic, mean, obsessive/compulsive and had sociopathic tendencies. I worked with people who delighted in punishing and abusing delinquent taxpayers, and generally treating people like crap. I had to make many unpopular and unpleasant decisions that affected the lives of thousands of people. I did not enjoy it; it just needed to be done. I was the abuser and the abused depending on your viewpoint.

The IRS uses its powers to abuse the taxpaying public and its employees. Many of the actions of abuse I saw were actually legal at the time and, in my opinion, were immoral, cruel and unethical. The power of the IRS is the power of FEAR.

Many people in the IRS get a little power and authority through their jobs. Then they think they are better than other people and they hurt people in large and small ways because they received some power. Power can drive a person crazy, corrupting basic human ideas that we should love other people, not destroy them. This does not represent most IRS employees, but the ones who have the most authority and power are often in control of hundreds, or even thousands, of employees.

The IRS is all about fear and intimidation. Owing the IRS is different than owing a private creditor. With taxes you have already taken the money. It's kind of like you have loaned it to yourself by *not* paying the taxes. This is why you can never truthfully claim you did not have the money. Income tax is based on the fact that you received the money and had it in your hands at some point. The fact that you chose to do something other than pay the Government the taxes you accrued was your choice.

It Flows Down Hill

Congress makes tax laws, not the IRS. The IRS just decides how to apply the laws and has the absolute power to do that. Absolute power corrupts absolutely and the IRS is no exception. Prior to 1952 there were agents who solicited and accepted bribes for failing to enforce the tax laws. That is why the IRS had a massive ethics overhaul in 1952 and again in 1998 when many laws were changed to give the taxpaying public more access to rights they already had in the U.S. Constitution but were not receiving from the IRS.

Many decisions are left up to the Group Managers and individual Revenue Officers and Revenue Agents. Some of these managers are obsessed with collecting statistics that show they are working the cases, not statistics that show they collected any money or tax returns, because that is illegal for the IRS to monitor at a local group level. Each Group Manager has complete discretion in how they interpret and apply the tax laws. Some Group Managers harass their employees if the employee follows the Internal Revenue Manual when the Manual doesn't match the Group Manager's intent. But at the same time, the Group Manager is berated and harassed by their Territory Manager who is in turn berated and harassed by the Area Director.

I have known some managers who are focused and just, but they are few and far between. When you work in the IRS you see many cases where something is offered to a taxpayer if the case is being worked by one Group Manager, and then right down the aisle another Group Manager is denying the same thing to some poor taxpayer.

I know it is hard to feel sorry for the IRS or its agents, but that is one of the points of this book. They are just people trying to do the right thing and provide service, but they are often at a crossroads even with their own managers.

One of the problems I have found with the IRS is they approach every situation like a big bully. They ignore the fact that most people get stuck in a tax problem and try to respond to what the IRS wants from them, but they are overwhelmed with fear. I am reminded of this in J.R.R. Tolkien's book, The Hobbit, where the wizard Gandalf explains why he has selected a small hobbit like Bilbo to accompany the dwarfs to fight the enemy. He says, "Saruman believes it is only great power that holds evil in check, but that is not what I have found. I found it in the small everyday deeds of ordinary folk that keep the darkness at bay. Small acts of kindness and love."

There is a widespread "collective spirit of inadequacy" with IRS employees. They are constantly berated by IRS Management that they are not good enough, smart enough, productive enough, or have any value. They are told that they are disposable.

They look at the tax returns of people who have great wealth and the very poor and wonder how they ended up in a job where they can never get ahead moneywise. These perceived inequities make them angry so some employees lash out at the taxpayers of America.

I felt I had a directive to close cases, and I had many tools that I could use to do that. I learned that in the IRS, I had as much power as I could take. If I claimed the power, I could exercise the power. That got me tons of recognition as an aggressive tax collector; a leader among my peers. It also got me some nick names, like" Wild West Cowboy Collector" and "Loose Cannon on Deck." No one, including me, knew what I would do next to show innovative and effective ways to close cases. The reaction among the tax professional community was mixed. One tax lawyer who earned $675 an hour said at a public meeting that "Mr. Schickel is the Prince of IRS Collection. He gets it." I was tough, professional but also reasonable.

It really did not matter how I closed the cases. If I did the right thing or an action that damaged people, just as long as the cases closed. I was in a continual state of frustration for 33 years, because I never had enough time to do anything completely, or correctly or with the best result for the taxpayer or the Government. I always felt like a fire fighter with a hose too short to reach the fire.

I always did what I defined as the "right thing", although my definition of "right" changed over the years. Doing the right thing came at great cost to me both professionally and personally.

Sometimes, I was not sure what to feel when I was the Officious IRS Guy knocking on someone's door, but I secretly was naturally empathetic to the needs of other people. I felt conflicted every day.

I often felt a sense of loss and loneliness after I had acted on major cases. I did my duty, but lost part of myself in the process; as if I lost part of my humanity and my sanity but still got the case closed. The case closures where all that mattered. Overage cases were the bane of my existence. Those cases were usually over one year old. I could do whatever I wanted on the newer cases with little management scrutiny but when the cases got old they reviewed the cases all the time. This took away the power and control that I had over the cases. It was not a good thing.

One quote from the Bible was particularly troubling. It said,

Keep my commandment.
Love God, love your neighbor and love yourself.

A lot of the actions that I took against my neighbor would not seem loveable at all. Rather they could easily be interpreted as destructive. But then the other line in scripture is what my ego/mind was more comfortable with. It said "*render unto Caesar what is Caesar's and render unto God what is God's.*"

I liked this, because it made me feel like I was doing good work in collecting the taxes for the United States Government (Caesar). It was years before I discovered that forcing people to pay taxes as determined by some people in distant Washington D. C. who claimed to represent me and my best interests, was not a government of the people, by the people and for the people. It was a government that promoted war and rewarded the rich and corporations.

I was under so much pressure in my early years to just "get it done" and move on to the next project that it became a miserable, joyless experience. I was not having the fun I used to have seizing peoples bank accounts, wages and assets. This slowly evolved into the place where I could administer the tax law, fairly, compassionately and mete out punishments as appropriate. This happened midway in my career and changed my life. I became a human being tax collector. The IRS does not like tax collectors like this.

I was not alone in trying to do the right thing. I know of at least a dozen people who worked with me that were promoted by management and then did not follow the directives to hurt the taxpayers and they ended up back in the field as a bag carrying revenue officer for the rest of their careers. Doing the right thing while employed with the IRS comes with its own penalties.

In my many years at the IRS, I learned how to read people: body language and facial expressions; how to think while listening; and how to talk and act in high pressure situations. I learned "meet and deal" skills which allowed me to talk to just about anybody about anything. I learned how to establish a common ground where I was able to not only communicate, but also how to read the person I was talking to.

I was naïve when I came to the IRS, but I still had gut feelings when I suspected someone was lying to me. This made it very hard for me to believe a person when all of their financials and tax data looked alright, but I had a bad gut feeling. So I just kept digging and usually was surprised how much more information I could uncover. It was the result of the taxpayer lying to me and trying to put assets beyond the reach of the United States Government or not reporting income.

The more I was open, not just at work but increasingly at any time of the day, the more information came to me about not just financial aspects of the delinquent taxpayers, but also the circumstance of their personal lives. Sometimes this revealed the cause of why they were being investigated by the government. Sometimes I was able to perceive the reasons for their drug or alcohol abuse - the real reasons why they lost their businesses.

The IRS trained me to *"Do the right thing, at the right time for the Government and the taxpayer."* Sure I had facts and figures in front of me, but I trusted my gut as to how to interpret it. Did they intend to run up big tax bills and then try to get away with not paying, or did they just screw up out of ignorance, and other circumstances?

The IRS taught me how to discern the truth but also how to manipulate the truth and the facts of a situation to benefit me and the Government. My goal was to get enough information to close my cases - however that happened. I learned how to read people well enough to have them come into my office and tell me everything I wanted to know, effectively letting them transfer all control and decision making over to me in regards to their financial and tax lives.

Opposite that, I learned from the very best of bad taxpayers how to lie. Now let's get this straight: I do not ever lie, because I tried it in grade school and found that in order to be a good liar, you had to remember what you told each person that you had lied to. I am not good at that. I learned the saying *"Oh what a wicked web we weave when first we practice to deceive,"* was accurate.

Everything in the IRS is sensitive and confidential. Everything is classified as "need to know," "official use only," or "secret," or "top secret." All return information is "need to know" and some celebrities or politicians, suspected criminals and grand jury cases get a higher rating. Grand jury or criminal projects that cover a larger number of taxpayers have high levels of security. Anything related to computer data or statistical sampling is top secret.

The Queue is a Wonderful Place to Be

Another place cases go is called the Queue. The Queue is a hold file between the IRS Service Center and the Automated Collection System (ACS) and before a case is assigned to a revenue officer. A story in the Washington Post on April 8, 2015 reports that in one affluent IRS District, cases less than $1 million are being held in the Collection Queue and will probably never have contact with an IRS officer. This is because of the retirements, attrition and lack of new employees.

Sometimes I have seen taxpayers and their representative request a case be transferred from ACS to a revenue officer- which is a right that they have - only to have the case sit there for years not being assigned to the revenue officer. The fall back to this is also by law, the IRS issues a letter once a year reminding people of their balances due. But since no one can work the case it just sits there quietly growing large with interest and penalties. This is new since I started at the IRS. We used to have to touch every single collection case if it was issued to the field. Now many cases sit in the Queue and the statute of collections quietly expires there, never having been worked by an IRS employee.

The IRS did not start using eFax systems (your fax message to the IRS goes directly into an employee's email) until about two years ago, but they are not routinely found on bank or wage levy notices or notices from the IRS or its employees. There is no central list for employee's names, office addresses, and fax or eFax numbers available to the taxpaying public. That list is also classified as need to know. Unfortunately this list cannot be published here either.

When I was trained, we could never talk about an individual's taxes. But we could talk about a copy of a Notice of Federal Tax Lien that had been filed with the County Recorder and show a copy to a taxpayer's neighbor or employer. That way we were listening and questioning them. I realize now that that was a form of intimidation. But now there is an absolute paranoia that covers everything that the IRS does.

Looking back, I think what I did mostly enjoy about my job was listening to people and figuring out how I could get them back on track with their taxes. I hated the incomprehensible forms that were required for even the simplest actions to be taken.

My thirty-three years with the IRS have shown me that most citizens are satisfied to pay what they regard as their fair share of the burden for those in society who are unable to work, are ill, elderly, or living in poverty. Income taxes also support the government, our military and every program the Federal government has. Taxes, when they are regarded as fair, make people proud they are taxpayers, but most people want all of us to feel the same burden that they feel. They want fairness, and defining fairness is what causes so many problems.

The IRS, the President and Congress

Congress does not like the IRS, because when the IRS knocks on doors it usually includes the doors of people who are friends or supporters of the elected officials who expect special treatment from the IRS. They usually get it, too. The IRS is very afraid of inquiries received from the White House and Congress.

The IRS has been in a curious financial relationship with Congress since its inception; Congress gives them money. It must also rely on the president to advocate for its funding. This is budgetary abuse and harassment and the IRS suffers from it every year. The IRS budget for 2015 was cut again by 3%. The budget was cut to $10.9 billion, which forces cuts of $346 million over the remaining 9 months of the fiscal year. But it is really $600 million due to inflation and the mandated, but unfunded costs related to Obama Care and other programs. This is the lowest funding since 2008 and the lowest since 1998 when inflation is considered, according to IRS Commissioner Koskinen. Congress has cut the IRS budget 17% in inflation-adjusted terms since 2010 while the population has risen by 7 million people. Every dollar that is not being budgeted to the IRS results in thousands of dollars that may never be collected from delinquent taxpayers. Reduced funding and staffing will result in 46,000 fewer individual and business audits and 280,000 fewer collection cases being worked.

I often saw how much IRS management fears Congress when they received a letter from a Senator or Congressman questioning some action that I was talking. Most of the time, I would be forced to back off.

J. Edgar Hoover, longtime Director of the FBI, routinely requested that people be audited. It is said that he hated John Steinbeck and had him audited every year because he believed him to be a communist. He was also responsible for the FBI program called COINTELPRO, which targeted Dr. Martin Luther King, John Lennon, peace activists, and union and church leaders in an effort to discredit them.

I heard stories over the years from older employees that Presidents Hoover, Roosevelt and Truman used the IRS to investigate and harass their political enemies. There is an unwritten dialog that goes down through the ages in IRS employee's communications. Employees tell stories they have heard over their careers to the new employees. I always thought it was very interesting, how much my IRS life was like so many other tax collectors over the ages.

President Truman was involved in a corruption scandal with the IRS; there were reports of bribes of mink coats and deep freezers being given to top officials. In 1950, 166 top officials of the Bureau of Internal Revenue (BIR) along with the Commissioner of the BIR, the Secretary of the Treasury and an assistant attorney general were all implicated in tax evasion. Truman allowed a system of rampant corruption, bribery and influence peddling. That led to the Bureau of Internal Revenue being reorganized into the Internal Revenue Service in 1952 and the Inspection Service being put in place to oversee the IRS. The Inspection Service is now known as the Treasury Inspector General for Tax Administration (TIGTA).

It is reported that President Kennedy used the IRS to investigate right wing organizations, extremist groups, and political groups that were hostile to his programs. He instituted a program called the Ideological Organizations Project in 1961 to target those who were in disagreement with his policies. President Johnson is said to have promised favorable tax treatment to wealthy contributors for votes.

President Nixon is forever remembered for his extensive use of the IRS to investigate and punish political enemies, left winged groups, African American activists, communists and anti-war activists. The second article of his impeachment claimed that he and his subordinates sought to "obtain from the Internal Revenue Service, in violation of the constitutional rights of citizens, confidential information contained in income tax returns for purposes not authorized by law." President Nixon was later audited and assessed $400,000 in additional income taxes.

President Nixon was responsible for establishing a special group inside the IRS called the SSS (the Special Service Staff), whose job it was to select and monitor "extremist organizations and individuals" that the White House identified in lists that they provided to the IRS.

Nixon's Vice President, Spiro T. Agnew pleaded guilty to one count of failing to report $29,500 in income. He had also been accused of accepting bribes, extortion, bribery and conspiracy. He resigned but later alleged that President Nixon had used the IRS to make up charges against him. He had been involved in other illegal activity as well.

President Bush had his own scandal with the IRS allegedly being used to investigate a church he did not agree with.

In 1996, President Bill Clinton said "We say to America's taxpayers, when you deal with the IRS, you also have privileges and we respect them. You have protection and we will help provide it. You have rights and we will shield them."

In 1998 due to reported abuses of the IRS Collection Division-many laws changed giving taxpayer's new rights and responsibilities. The IRS was also reorganized to mirror private sector financial services business models. The Revenue Restructuring and Reform Act effectively crippled the tax collection system.

The IRS Congressional Hearings in 1997

In 1998 the IRS Collection and Exam/Audit Divisions were attacked by a few individuals and the media drummed up circumstances based on half facts. Congress held hearings that sickened me, because in every single case the IRS was asked to comment on the cases in question. But the IRS can only comment when the taxpayer gives them approval to speak. So it was very biased and one sided. The IRS was vilified for doing what they were supposed to do, which is to audit tax returns and collect taxes. Laws were changed that practically prohibited the IRS from doing their job. No one reported that the accusations were all unfounded, or that all the charges were investigated and found to be false and contrived for the news media.

Because the IRS cannot respond publicly on cases, it quietly exacts retribution on a case-by-case basis. In the case of the Tea Party Scandal of 2014, this was based on the intent and purpose of the organization. The amount of press that resulted from the Tea Party situation also hurt IRS employees and the compliance effort. Delinquent taxpayers have said things questioning the employee's personal integrity and whether or not they could be trusted with the information that they are being given by the taxpayer. The negative publicity has caused great emotional and mental fatigue to IRS employees and it is not fair and it continues to occur, according to my sources.

Some employees may have done things that stretched or exceeded their legal authority. Look at the current IRS versus the Tea Party Scandal. If someone did something wrong it would have come down from a higher level. IRS employees are very good at following orders. Most employees follow directions. They are expected to do what the law says or what policy statements or orders of protocol dictate that they do. That is how it is set up.

RRA 98 offered taxpayers a Taxpayer Bill of Rights. They are:

1. The right to be informed about how to comply with the tax laws;
2. The right to quality service;
3. The right to pay no more than the correct amount of tax;
4. The right to challenge the IRS's position and be heard;
5. The right to appeal an IRS decision in an independent forum;
6. The right to finality (how much time the IRS has to increase your taxes or collect balance dues);
7. The right to privacy;
8. The right to confidentiality;
9. The right to representation;
10. The right to a fair and just tax system.

After working for the IRS for 18 years, I found the law was extremely cumbersome; however it was good for the taxpayers. The Collection Due Process and Collection Appeals Program are examples of that. Appeals Officers are seasoned and trained professionals, in the IRS; they have the authority to make settlement agreements. I always recommend that if a person is offered Appeal Rights that they file an Appeal.

The IRS Organization

The IRS is divided into five parts:

Audit/Assessment - Field Revenue Agents and Office Tax Auditors (aka Tax Compliance Officers).

Taxpayer Assistance - Incoming telephone and mail and walk in offices.

Collection - Field Revenue Officers and the Automated Collection System telephone call site (ACS).

Criminal Investigation - Special Agents.

Appeals – Appeals and Settlement Officers, they negotiate and settle cases. They have broad authority to negotiate.

The Treasury Inspector General oversees both with internal audit and provides security and armed escorts for employees, and investigates bribe attempts and employee misconduct.

The IRS Demographics

The IRS is down to 81,279 employees from its high of 122,000 employees. Twenty five percent of the employees can retire in 2015 and up to 40% of the employees can retire by 2019. Fifty percent of IRS employees are age 50 or over. Only 3% are below age 30.

The IRS has 25% (29,699) fewer employees than it had in 1992 and has not hired in five years. The IRS has less employees now than it had in 1980, although the population of the United States has risen by 27% since 1980. The armed forces in 1980 were at 515,408 and are now at 1,458,697, an increase of 35%. Sixty percent of all U.S. Government employees are 45 years and older. Between 2010 and 2015, 17,000 full time IRS jobs were lost.

The IRS has 34% men and 66% woman. They are 56% Caucasian, 26% African American, 12% Hispanic, 5% Asian and 1% Native American. Eleven-and-a-half percent of IRS employees are disabled to some degree.

There are 12,212 Revenue Agents who do the field audits, down 12% since 2010. There are 4,681 Revenue Officers (tax collectors), down 21% since 2010. There are 2,539 Criminal Investigators (down 2%). Because of attrition and retirements, this is expected to drop to only 1,600 IRS Criminal Special Agents. Of that, 400 are in management. So that leaves only 1,200 to do all the criminal investigations. There are 1,496 Office Auditors down 11%. There are 10% less revenue officers (tax collectors) and revenue agents (auditors) than five years ago, and they are the front-line field enforcement employees. The number of IRS employees assigned to answer tax-payer telephone calls fell from 9,400 in 2010 to 6,900 in 2014 - a 26% decline. The IRS announced that it also expects to lose another 1,800 enforcement personal through attrition this year

The IRS has not done any major hiring to replace attrition and retirement in 6 years. The staff that it does have is new, inexperienced, inflexible and insufficiently trained to meet the demands of the Internal Revenue Code and the many tax law changes that occur every year. Twenty five percent of existing staff can retire - today.

Most employees are paid on the General Schedule Pay. Most of the service centers hire lower graded employees and pay them little better than minimum wage. Most IRS employees make $22,000 to $55,000 annually. Higher level employees make up to $120,000. Criminal agents make the most. Because there is a shortage of criminal agents they automatically get paid for a 50 hour week. They can retire after 20 years. Many make in the low $100,000's.

The IRS has 174 Managers and Senior Executive Staff (SES) that make between $100,000 and $230,000. They would likely be paid more, but federal law states they cannot make more than the salary of the Vice President of the United States; which is currently $230,700.00.

5

What Do You Really Pay in Taxes?

FORGIVE ME, THIS CAN GET very confusing. You probably already think that you pay a lot in taxes. You do, but some of it is hidden. Tax systems are designed to be confusing. Otherwise people would truly understand what was going on and revolt.

If you are an employee, as of 2015, you are paying 6.2% for Social Security plus 1.45% for Medicare - and your employer pays the same. This tax only applies to the first $117,000 you earn. A person earning $50 million a year pays the same amount as you. Senator Bernie Sanders claims that "if we lifted this cap on income above $250,000, we could extend the solvency of Social Security for another 47 years." Plus unemployment insurance is paid for you through your employer. That varies but I estimate it to be 1% in most cases.

If you are self-employed you have to pay 12.4% for Social Security and 2.9% for Medicare. That equals 15.3%.

Then you also have income tax withholding. In this estimate we will say 20% is being withheld for the IRS and 5% to your state of residence which will provide you with a tax refund.

Depending on where you live you also have state income tax (average 3%) and township, county, city income tax. Plus taxes for local school districts. In some places there is also a real estate transfer tax that you pay just for buying a house. State income taxes are all over the board and vary widely. They range from no state income tax in Alaska, Florida, Nevada, South Dakota, Texas, Washington and

Wyoming to the highest tax rates of California 12.3%, Hawaii 11%, and Massachusetts 12%. I have also heard it called Taxachusetts.

So just for going to work, for every $1000 you earn the Government takes approximately $297. You are left with $703. Less if you contribute to an IRA or pension plan.

OK, so you got out of your office with what is left of your check. Then you get into your car, which was already taxed with a sales tax when you bought it. Then you have licenses, stickers and other fees from the Government (they can be 6-10 %.) You look at your tires; they seem worn out. There is a special excise tax just for tire sales. Then you put gas in the car and yes, gas is taxed at the Federal, State and sometimes local levels. Federal excise taxes are 18.4 cents per gallon for gas and diesel. The State of Arizona also adds 18.4 cents per gallon. In California state tax is 39.5 cents per gallon. There is also the LUST Tax which is 1 cent per gallon. Sounds exciting right? This is paid on Leaking Underground Storage Tanks. (This applies to old gas stations that have closed and left their rotting tanks in the ground.)

You get in the car and turn on the air conditioning and you have already paid a tax on the Freon gas that is used to make the system work. If you stop at the store on the way home there are taxes on your food and non-food items, sometimes at different rates. You are taxed on your cigarette and cigar purchases; this is a separate excise tax over the sales tax. You also pay the Federal Liquor Tax on your spirits, wine and beer. There may also be a tax from state and local liquor agencies. Actually, the truck that brought all that food and liquor and supplies to the store had to pay the Federal Highway Use Tax, just to get what you need to the store.

If you stop and buy a gun, bullets, a bow and arrow or a fishing rod you pay a special excise tax. When you go home your real estate taxes might be 3% or more of the value of your home. If you rent, these taxes are included in your rent. Sometimes your landlord will also have to pay taxes for the right to rent to you, which is also included in your rent.

These taxes are built into the price that you pay for the goods and services you want. If you buy an RV for traveling you pay a recreational vehicle tax. There used to be luxury taxes on furs, diamonds, jewelry and other luxury items. You pay a tax on all of your utilities, and on watercraft registration.

While you drive and talk on the phone you are also paying federal excise taxes, federal universal service taxes, and well as state and local telephone taxes. In some places you pay taxes on internet and cable access. Airplane tickets have a federal tax of 7.5% of every ticket plus $4.

Federal and state governments have other taxes that you pay indirectly, like corporate income tax - this is usually passed along to the consumer as a higher cost to the item.

On top of all this you pay other taxes when you are required to get a building permit, a driver's license, a vehicle license plate, tolls and fees for toll roads, bridges and ferries.

The spread of taxation and the complexity of it is overwhelming and terrifying. But people are trained by society to just try to earn more money to get the things that they want.

I have read stories that at the end of the day, you may only have 40-50% of your paycheck after you have paid all these taxes.

This seems a strange byproduct for a country that was founded after protesting the taxes of the King George III, the last King of North America. That argument was about being taxed without representation. In the United States today, we have a Congress that represents some of the people all of the time. I don't think this is what the Founding Fathers had in mind when they created the United States of America.

The United States has the largest standing military in the world. The USA spends $729 billion a year which is 39% of all military spending for the whole world. The United States spends more on military spending than the next ten top countries in the world. What are we so afraid of? China only spends $188 billion and Russia spends $88 billion. I have worked with many taxpayers who like to help people and support national parks. They do not want to pay for weapons, bombs and armies. So they simply stop filing and paying taxes.

It seems like a pretty simple deal to spend less on the military and more on the people and infrastructure of the United *States.*

6

The IRS Culture

Lead Us Not into Temptation

FEAR is what motivates taxpayers in their dealings with the IRS. Many people want to do the right thing and pay their fair share of taxes in support of their country and provide for the welfare of less fortunate people. But some taxpayers look at the tax system and life in a different way. There are many emotions that come to people as they think about taxes or having anything to do with the IRS. The IRS is the most hated government agency because it causes its own United States citizens to live in fear... fear of getting caught, fear of loss and fear of punishment. These emotions are accompanied by anger, greed, worry, anxiety and depression. Even talking about the IRS can suck your energy away.

They evaluate the situation with these factors: Will I get caught? Will I get punished? How badly will I get punished? Then they make a risk assessment based on the answers. This is a very small percentage of the delinquent taxpayers that I worked with over the years. Then there are those people who may pay the least amount of tax that they are legally entitled to pay (tax avoidance) which is legal, versus those who do not want to pay taxes at all - or pay less than the legal amount that would be due (tax evasion) which is illegal.

The Internal Revenue Service has many employees who are trying to teach a lesson to all the taxpayers that they think are all cheaters and liars, thieves and scoundrels. They take the position that the actions of the taxpayer were deliberate, planned and were to their personal benefit. Like I said, I saw many taxpayers like that who had the expensive cars, the awesome homes and vacation homes, the jewelry collection, the gun collection, the stocks and bonds, and fat bank accounts. The people who were living large, mostly on the Government's money. But I personally know many people who also have a lot of taxed money who have these same possessions. That is why some IRS employees need an attitude change.

But I would have to say that 80% of the people were just people who were pursuing their dreams and trying to make the best of their lives and then bust! They not only failed, but they had lost everything. I tell stories from both sides in this book. (Those people who bragged to anyone who would listen about how they pay little or no taxes and are part of fancy clubs, travel around the world, and are in the money.) The strange part of this is it never seemed like the taxpayers who were burning through huge amounts of money stolen from the Treasury were happy. They just had more worry and fear.

Many taxpayers use corporations to not pay taxes. They hoard money and then pay out huge bonuses and salaries to their executives. In the IRS, the squeaky wheel always gets the grease. I have been involved in many cases where wealthy and politically connected people screamed the loudest and I was ordered to back off - or make payment arrangements that were the least amounts imaginable.

With the IRS, it helps to look to the past to see why things are as they are in the present, and how they will be in the future unless the IRS is completely reformed.

While cleaning out a cabinet I found a copy of an old memo from the Director of Field Collection; it was from August 1, 1967. It addressed **Revenue Officer Morale and Attitudes.** It was surprising how little has changed. I am quoting from the memo but unable to read the signature of the approving official. It appears that the employees were surveyed and this memo gave the results.

The header is:
Internal Revenue Service
Collection Division
Washington, D. C.

- Most Revenue Officers and many Group Managers feel that there is too much emphasis on production and unnecessary pressure to meet statistical goals. They feel that managers go overboard in trying to meet standards and benchmarks; simple goals are too often interpreted to be unquestionable musts.
- The Revenue Officer occupation is physically and mentally demanding more so than even other IRS positions. Revenue Officers do not receive recognition or reward for their work.
- The report states that there is a large disconnect between upper management, lower management and employees. Revenue Officers and Group Managers feel a kinship but both feel estranged from upper management. They believe that communication is poor. Nearly all the Revenue Officers and managers felt that they are being over managed. (In 2015 IRS employees use the word micro managed)
- Most Revenue Officers believe that they are too many checks on their integrity. They questioned the need for "off limits areas" and mandatory checks of their work was a harsh supervisory response that was applied to all employees, arising from the misdeeds of a very few employees.
- Revenue Officers stated that the evaluation system is overly negative and places too great an emphasis on what has not been done instead of the good things that have been done in a timely manner.
- Revenue Officers felt that their jobs were becoming more dangerous and that they were being exposed to more hazards and management had done nothing to protect them.

- Revenue Officers feel that the promotion process is unfair and the "best qualified candidates do not often get promoted. Those promotions go to high production employees who are mobile." (Ready to move where needed and who have outgoing and forceful personalities.)
- Revenue Officers thought that the Inspection Service (now TIGTA) was production motivated and looked for insignificant issues and picayune errors. They believe that IRS management overreacts to the Inspection reports.
- Most Revenue Officers were dissatisfied with one or more features of office space and equipment. There were too few telephones, interview space that does not afford adequate privacy for taxpayers and the lack of and age of typewriters, adding machines and calculators. They were also dissatisfied when they had to use government cars that did not have radios or air conditioning which was standard for the time.

This memo covers 19 points and then it stops. No solutions are proposed. No acknowledgement of the problems. This is the way the IRS always works. The manager did not make any empty promises or state that he would try to change the work environment. He did not respond at all. This memo could have been written in 2015; conditions are the same as they were 48 years ago. I know that nothing was ever done on any of these issues because when I started, 14 years later all the same situations continued to exist. The problem is that it the same people and ideas live on from the past. The IRS needs fresh blood, new people, new methods and new technology. When I retired these problems still existed.

This is how IRS Management is. They let employees air their grievances and then do nothing about them. Because employee's problems are not management's problems, management's problems are how to make you close more and more cases, faster and faster.

I discovered the IRS is consistent with how they treat employees who raise similar issues anywhere in the United States. They back the manager and send a psychologist into the affected group and do personality tests and listen to the stories and then they deny that their manager has done anything wrong and it is all the unbalanced employees who are causing the disruption of service delivery.

This ties in perfectly with a statement made by Nina Olsen, the IRS Taxpayer Advocate. She reported "the IRS Collection process is the same as it was 30 years ago. It relies on bulk processing of correspondence and systemically generated actions - letters, etc." She reported that "The IRS system is unproductive and inappropriate to the taxpayer who simply cannot pay."

She continued, "The IRS collection strategy appears to assume in far too many situations that delinquent taxpayers have made a conscious decision to not comply with tax obligations. They use the 'full force of the law' to correct problems in a manner that is premature in many cases. The IRS should adjust this mindset and achieve a better balance between the use of enforcement tools and other collection tools, including reasonable payment agreements and offers in compromise. Collection treatments should be tailored to the needs of each taxpayer, with the goal of not only addressing the delinquencies at hand, but also promoting future compliance."

What the IRS Does Well

The one thing that the IRS does in a modern and efficient manner is to issue employer identification numbers (EIN) over the internet with about ten minutes of work. No need to talk to IRS employees. The number is issued and a letter confirming it is available to be printed at that time. Or it says that you can get the letter mailed to you by the IRS but it advises that that could take up to 4 weeks.

As mentioned before, the IRS can be an efficient and effective tax collector and is able to monitor a very complex United States

Tax Code reasonably well for 86% of the population who choose to file and pay their taxes. But to me, we the people means all the people, not just 86% of the people and includes corporations. The IRS mostly deals with people who file and pay their taxes in a system supposedly based on voluntary compliance, but it always seemed to me like all the wage earner (W-2) employees are caught in a box, with the IRS frequently sticking a hot poker to stir up fear. The fear of the IRS coming and putting you in jail or taking your house, car or bank accounts is enough to keep most people in this system of enforced compliance.

IRS Management Stories

The IRS is too large, too powerful and can be abusive to the taxpaying public and its own employees. Too few laws govern how they can collect taxes, or about what information they can collect and use for what purpose. No other government agency has as much access to your personal information and the power to seize and sell everything that you own, without a court order. There is very little oversight of IRS Senior Management, which sets up all the programs and decides how they will be carried out.

One manager admitted to me that he was so powerful because he often rode the elevator and listened to people talking about people, policies and procedures. He was a tall man and there was a manager who was another level above him, but he was short and heavy like Louie Depalma (Danny DeVito) from the show Taxi. This manager would sometimes pat him on the top of his bald head and say "How you doing Little Louie?" He knew what was going on - everywhere all the time. When he later had a rough spell with his alcoholism, and senior management wanted him to retire, he had 30 years of service and would have received a nice pension. But since he knew so many secrets, he was able to negotiate to receive 43 years of credit towards retirement and the IRS paid in the extra money to buy him an additional 13 years of pension credit to get rid of him quickly. It is important to know and always remember that the IRS can and does do whatever it wants to do when it wants to do it. It is always the 600 lb. gorilla in the corner of the room. You can say or do whatever you want, the gorilla can still crush you.

Another IRS manager got involved in an embarrassing episode with investigative reporter Geraldo Rivera. The Hotel Lexington in Chicago, which had been owned by Al Capone, had a secret vault that had been bricked over. Geraldo Rivera claimed that Al Capone had hidden money and treasure and maybe old cars in that vault. He was very good at publicizing the event. Over 30 million people are said to have watched the live TV show. The IRS fell for it, hook, line and sinker. They even refiled Notice of Federal Tax Liens and tax judgments and had the IRS Collection Division Chief for Illinois present to seize anything that was found.

Then workman broke down the wall and found...exactly nothing. I personally found this embarrassing. It made it look like the IRS never lets anyone ever go. Even the Bible suggests that we forgive those who owe us money every 7 years. Al Capone died a very rich man on his palatial estate on Palm Island, Florida from syphilis. The Government missed the mark on collecting his treasures when he was alive. But I mean come on, he was convicted 82 years ago and he died in 1947 and this TV program was in 1986 - 39 years later. Let's forgive and forget. The IRS is still bragging about outsmarting Al Capone and convicting him of tax crimes, when no other law enforcement agency could get him. How did they do that? Why are they still talking about it today?

Capone's accountant gave the evidence they needed to show the vast amount of income that passed through his hands was not reported as income. This was from illegal activities such as labor union racketeering, prostitution, gambling, and drugs. IRS Criminal Agents are also tax accountants and everyone at the IRS loves a story where the accountant does well in the end.

Past History of IRS Management

Some of the Commissioners of the IRS were very colorful characters and faced public censure, as well as imprisonment because of it.

Edward A. Rollins was Commissioner from 1865 to 1869. He was charged with tax evasion, bribery, corruption and black mail.

Alfred Pleasonton was Commissioner for eight months in 1871. He was forced to resign after he lobbied Congress for the repeal of the income tax and quarreled with the Treasury Department over enforcement of the tax laws.

During Prohibition, Commissioner David H. Blair was in charge of prosecuting people who manufactured, distributed or used alcohol. He is reported to have said that "every bootlegger should be stood by the wall and shot to death." He issued a leaflet that encouraged all citizens to spy on their neighbors and use telephones outside their neighborhoods to report Prohibition offenders anonymously. The famous Elliot Ness worked in the Treasury Department's Bureau of Prohibition which was connected to Mr. Blair and the Bureau of Internal Revenue. He is responsible for gathering evidence from Al Capone's accountant that led to his conviction for income tax evasion. Mr. Ness died at the age of 54 following years of heavy drinking. So the man who used abstinence from alcohol to make his career was in the end a victim of alcohol.

Joseph D. Nunan, Jr. was Commissioner from 1944 to 1947. He was found guilty of income tax evasion for the years 1946-1950 and sentenced to a prison term of five years for each count. He actually served about one year in prison.

George J. Schoenman 1947 to 1951 was Commissioner at the time when the Bureau of Internal Revenue was ruled by political patronage, corruption, and bribery. During this time the Truman White House faced allegations of wrongdoings by political appointees, specifically friends of the President who worked within the Internal Revenue Service. James P. Finnegan, Collector of Revenue in St. Louis, had failed to report $103,000 in income. After his subsequent conviction for income tax fraud, nine other senior political appointees in the BIR were indicted or resigned in the face of fraud allegations. This included Commissioner Schoenman and the head of the Justice Departments Tax Division and the President's Appointment Secretary. Commissioner Schoenman was accused of failing to pay taxes on income of $176,000, but was never indicted. Up to that time he was also accused of soliciting a bribe from a lawyer who previously represented Al Capone. All Bureau of Internal Revenue employees were political appointees. Commissioner Schoenmann and his Assistant commissioner both resigned due to "health reasons" at that time.

This led to the reorganization to root out fraud, waste and corruption in 1952.

I read an article in U.S. News and World Report dated May 25, 1956 about T. Coleman Andrews who was the IRS Commissioner from 1953-1955. Commissioner Andrews was known for instituting the TCMP audits where agents blanket a town or neighborhood and just go door to door seeking returns, filing information and payments. It was very effective at bringing thousands of non-taxpayers into compliance. Mr. Andrews left the IRS and changed his mind on a lot of things. He said that the income tax was slowly destroying the middle class. He said that he "disagreed with Congress using the income tax to enforce social reforms to reduce everyone to the lowest common denominator economically". "I don't believe in using tax legislation to force social reforms upon the people or to punish sin." He said that most income tax legislation was "conceived in vengeance to get the rich people." He said that he did not think that the income tax laws "should be used to punish success. "He said "I think everybody is overtaxed, but I think the middle class is being especially discriminated against. I think the discriminatory manner in which tax rates are graduated is unfair. "

He advocated mailing out tax forms to each taxpayer during his term. But in this interview he said that the tax code is socialism. He said that socialism is "from each according to his capacity and to each according to his need." He said "Maybe we ought to see that every person who gets a tax return receives a copy of the Communist Manifesto with it so he can see what's happening to him."

He said that the complexity of the tax laws favored the rich and powerful and confused the common man. He said that the complexity caused people who could to finagle their way out of paying taxes on their full incomes though the use of trusts, estates, and corporations.

Commissioner Randolph Thrower (1969-1971) was appointed by President Nixon and was fired by John D. Ehrlichman "for resisting White House efforts to punish its enemies through tax audits."

Roscoe Egger was Commissioner from 1981-1986. He was only the second tax professional (CPA) that has led the IRS. He is remembered for the 1985 computer replacement disaster, where the old system was disconnected and the new system failed immediately. Under him, hundreds of thousands of tax returns disappeared - many destroyed by employees who could not process them because the computer was dead. Tax evasion rose during this time and he brought public attention to the fact that the IRS computers were out of date and inadequate for doing the tax work.

He was successful with getting increased funding for the IRS and I was hired as a result of that. He also advocated that the IRS prepare tax returns and just bill the taxpayers, because it already had all the data needed to do so. This would have eased the taxpayer's burden. But I was told at the time that this was strongly challenged by tax preparing businesses like H&R Block.

Anti-Semitism and More

When I arrived in Arizona, I found out that IRS Management here (and in fact management in charge of tax collection for the 13 Western United States) was not following the Internal Revenue Code or the Internal Revenue Manual, I was shocked. Some managers and employees in the Tucson office were making decisions based on the race and religion of the individual taxpayers. It was taking actions against those who were exercising their constitutional rights. It was identifying and targeting certain people because of their accounting methods or their lack of business/tax knowledge.

I was outraged after the various bizarre cases surfaced where I was directed to take actions against Jews, African Americans and Hispanics all because of perceptions that some IRS managers had about them as a class of people. Old ideas of hate and division are still being presented in a modern day IRS. But the stories could have been told in the 1920's, or the 1950's or at any time when hate was preached to groups of people. I will not write about these stories as I do not wish to perpetuate the ideas that they represent.

I saw cases where rich people were afforded special treatment because of their connections with Senators and Congressmen or the White House. I have seen people targeted because they were gay, anti-war, anti-nuclear weapons, anti-government. I have seen people jailed because they got an IRS agent mad at them because of their presentation or lack thereof, of documents that they were being forced to present. The IRS has the power to summon people to present testimony and documents. I have a problem with this, mostly because the 5th Amendment to the Constitution gives citizens the right to not be forced to incriminate themselves. So a person cannot be forced to tell on themselves. This is a 5th Amendment right. Some summons are so broad that they amount to a fishing expedition. These appear to violate the 4th Amendment against unreasonable search. When a person appears under a summons it is very rare that they are offered *Miranda Rights*. If they fail to appear or do not provide all the self-incriminating documents or testimony, then the IRS will ask a federal judge to jail them indefinitely based on contempt of court charges, creating fear, confusion and conflict.

The IRS tried to fire me after 27 years of exemplary service because I spoke up and protested the ways things were being done. I did not play the game they were playing. I know some people think that the IRS screws people. But I think that the Tax Code should be equally applied throughout the United States.

Back to my story, IRS Management did not try to attack me directly because what I was saying was illegal and wrong - they are not that delusional! They knew that would be like throwing gas on a fire. After documenting and sharing my complaints with the first three layers of management, I found that management always protects management. They turned a blind eye to what was happening. It was so bad one manager had gone through 33 employees in 10 years. That was a manager who only had 6-10 employees at any given time. I was talking to and writing letters and emails to management officials at higher and higher levels to find someone who would and could do something about the way IRS employees and the taxpaying public was being treated in Arizona. They knew they could not publicly acknowledge these actions, let alone defend against them.

IRS Management is pretty consistent when it comes to strategies on how to fire employees. The number one method is travel fund fraud, when management alleges that an employee adds extra mileage while in the field or claims to have been in another town but is not. Second, they look to see if the Government credit card is being used to pay for personal items, alcohol, online sex or escorts. Third is the envelope full of cash that an employee finds in his mailbox, and fourth is what they call integrity issues, where they say that an employee is not managing their finances or personal affairs ethically or competently and that is in line with what the public would think an IRS agent should be doing.

I have witnessed revenue officers opening envelopes that were filled with cash from unknown sources. Just to see if they would report it or just take it home. I know of one who decided to take the money home and he was arrested on his way out of the building. This was a form of entrapment that allowed the IRS to quickly fire someone. I received one of those envelopes once myself while sitting at my desk and by instinct $2,000 went flying through the air as I screamed I had received cash and did not want to touch it. I know how the IRS works. I have seen them destroy people's lives. I was more like a team leader not a team player so I was always attracting trouble.

IRS Management attacked me on various bizarre issues. One time I got a one day suspension without pay because payment on my Government credit card was 3 days late (it was mailed on time). A second time they suspended me for three days because my government credit card had a non-payment over 90 days. Later it was shown that the credit card processing company had cashed my check, and then applied it incorrectly.

Then there was a suspension for 7 days, I believe because I showed someone a publicly filed copy of a Notice of Federal Tax Lien in an effort to collect a tax debt. This is what I had been trained to do. As you can imagine it is difficult to even write this, because I just want to put it all out of my mind.

The last suspension was for 14 days. I think that was where they claimed that I had accessed over 100 names on the IRS Master Computer illegally. I did access them and it was in support of a large tax evasion scheme with a large number of parties. It was legal and customary. I witnessed TIGTA agents conspiring with IRS management to build cases against me.

Manager Madness

I never worried; I knew I always did the right thing. We were always amazed by a certain group manager who seemed to know more about our cases than we knew. When that manager would go in the field with us, he seemed like he had already been to some of our field calls, like he had already studied the case and knew it better than we did.

When I went into private tax practice I was shocked to discover that there are witnesses who claim that this manager actually spoke to their friends, family and business associates seeking tax and income and asset information to build a case against the taxpayer. He was also seen to do surveillance work on at least one taxpayer's house and business. This is illegal. A revenue officer group manager is supposed to manage the revenue officer and does not have the authority to make field calls, speak to third parties or do surveillance. A group manager can go in the field with the revenue officer, never alone.

Finally, after all my suspensions, I was a wreck because I could not find anyone to listen to my story about the bad things that were happening. I had tried the Whistleblower Program and letters to members of Congress and other options available to federal employees and found they were all slanted in the favor of management. They attacked the complainant as well as the complaint and I got no action from them. I wrote to the Commissioner of the Internal Revenue Service and I think the suspensions followed after that. They must have wondered if I was stupid. After the 14 day suspension, I would have gotten fired. That is how the process works. Thank God I worked for the Federal Government. In a private business I would have been fired long before that.

Then the National Treasury Employees Union (NTEU) which had represented me in many actions over the years when I had protested management and system abuse, decided to invoke binding arbitration. It was an administrative trial - the IRS attorney flew in from Washington D.C. and the administrative law judge from New York City. In attendance were local witnesses, my union attorney, and even the president of my local union chapter. Thank God for NTEU! They saved me and have helped thousands of other employees over the years. It is the only organization that can effectively challenge the IRS. In fact, NTEU was founded by IRS revenue officers in the 1930's. The more things change apparently the more they stay the same.

So to begin, the charges were read against me, then the IRS outlined its case. But there were so many irregularities that kept coming up when witnesses were to testify. One of their chief witnesses refused to come to testify and in fact had refused to be interviewed except through a closed door at her home. Another high level manager who had retired after the news of the initial scandal of my case broke and was then working as an outside contractor in Washington D. C. could not answer any of the questions asked by the judge. At one point the judge asked the former high level manager if he had been drinking or was having a reaction to prescription or illegal drugs.

The judge asked the TIGTA agents how they could present a case without credible witnesses. The woman who refused to testify was in fact formerly married to a man who was a drug lord. The three managers who were called to testify all appeared to be confused at the whole process. They had collectively fired dozens of employees and caused many other people to quit, transfer or retire early. They had destroyed many employees' lives as well as many taxpayers' lives through their casual arrogance. They seemed genuinely confused that I was not only responding but also that I was fighting back and had gotten the union to support my effort.

When the union attorney and the judge asked the managers those questions, it was almost like they were belligerent at someone questioning their authority. One manager bristled when asked if he had made field calls after hours or spoken to my taxpayers directly without me being present. This made for an entertaining though stressful day.

When the charges of discrimination based on race or religion were brought up, the judge was very interested in the testimonies given. When I listened to his questions trying to make sense of my situation, I knew by 11:19 a.m. that morning that I was going to win my case.

I won the case and all the back pay from the suspensions along with sick leave and vacation pay that was given to me in cash. The Government spent over $80,000 trying to get me. In fact they had to pay my union attorney $30,000 because they lost the case. I never received an apology for the damage done to my reputation. One of the upper level managers who appeared to hate me just because I was not kissing her boots admitted that she had called back to Illinois and told my old managers that I had suffered a nervous breakdown and that is why she could not approve my transfer back there. Evidently that is why after applied for 24 jobs in Illinois and did not get one. I guess the fact that I had an appraisal when I arrived in Arizona of 4.8 out of 5 and it was reduced to 2.6 out of 5 contributed to that situation. My appraisal indicated that I was a failing employee.

Management at all levels seemed incredulous that I was causing trouble for them. They just could not seem to get it. Because they had been doing bad things that went unquestioned for so long, they were confused. One manager was very confused. He used to call National Office and tell them that the Internal Revenue Code (IRC) (the tax law) or the Internal Revenue Manual (IRM) (the how to do this job guide) was wrong. He often told employees about those errors and in order to close cases he made up the ways that Tucson would work cases. He said "I know what's in the manual, but it is wrong so this is how we will do things in Tucson." I found this also at the statewide level (made up protocols with no oversight)!

Sometimes I was worn down, but I was not washed up, yet. Sometimes I would be depressed and when I walked into the Federal

Building in Tucson, Arizona I wished that someone would shoot me in the line of duty so that at least I could have the Federal Building named after me. The stress of working for the IRS causes many strange thoughts.

The managers who had fought against me, did not fare so well. Each was forced to retire on the day they qualified, according to my source.

I often thought working in the Tucson IRS office was like being trapped in hell. I could often hear that Eagles song *Hotel California* playing in my head - the one line - "*You can check out any time you like, but you can never leave*" resonated with me. But I survived. Life should not just be just about surviving.

Al Capone Lives On Forever at the IRS

The Official IRS Historian - Shelly Davis captured in her book *Unbridled Power: Inside the Secret Culture of the IRS*, exactly the feeling that happened in my life. She wrote - "In my official capacity as IRS historian, I was often asked questions about Al Capone's extensive cat-and-mouse games with the IRS, a struggle in which the IRS ultimately triumphed. One might imagine that the IRS, even in its paranoia, would not object to being glorified in the press. One of the most popular IRS recruiting posters features a close up of Al Capone's mug shot, under the tagline: "Only the IRS could get Al Capone." But when I checked with the IRS attorneys regarding Disclosure under the Internal Revenue Code Section 6103, they advised me that "I would be violating the law if I even told someone *that Al Capone went to prison* for failure to file his tax returns."

She continues - "But that's common knowledge! I would protest. It's in your books. It's out there. It's in the public domain! It's even disclosed by your own recruiting poster!"

Fear powers the IRS and a closed minded application of the laws causes extensive government waste.

Alphonse Capone
Only an Accountant Could Catch Al Capone.
Infamous mobster Al Capone wasn't easy to catch. But when Special Agents of the IRS stepped in and charged him with tax evasion, this crime czar's career came to an end. Proof that sometimes only the accountant can apprehend the criminal. If you'd like to put your accounting skills to work in a challenging and action oriented job, IRS Special Agent may be the ideal career for you. If you'd like to learn more about an exciting career as an IRS Special Agent, go to http://www.jobs.irs.gov, click on Careers. You'll find Law Enforcement information located in the Careers at IRS on that site.
Be an Accountant With Conviction.
The IRS is an equal opportunity employer.
IRS
Department of the Treasury
Internal Revenue Service

Sexual Harassment and Discrimination

Sexual harassment was rampant at the IRS because of the old boy's network. The IRS crucifies employees caught doing this, but it protects managers who do this, with transfers and promotions. The IRS pays out millions of dollars in damage awards to those who have been sexually harassed.

I remember one story of an old revenue officer who went into a bar with his girlfriend on a Friday afternoon and he said that down the bar was his manager with his girlfriend and across the bar was his branch chief with his girlfriend; they were on government time. He said they never acknowledged each other in the bar or after and this was in 1984.

If a person is identified as being disloyal to the IRS, their future quickly deteriorates. I have seen men who had extraordinary temptation thrust upon them when a younger woman suddenly was interested in them. This helped to later build sexual harassment charges against them. Things like this happen often in the IRS. A manager may have a younger girlfriend who is working under him, the affair goes cool and the subordinate employee files a sexual harassment/ discrimination suit against the Government. I have watched the manager who did the harassing get protected and switched to other jobs. Then the "girlfriend" can count on a $75,000-$150,000 settlement from the IRS if she does not pursue the matter in court, plus a nice promotion - sometimes into management, if they just settle the sexual harassment out of court.

The way employee sexual harassment was handled was quite different. I have been the victim of sexual harassment as well by a very confused female and a very confused male at different points in my career. In order to resolve the cases, management simply transferred the offending employee to another group. One person was very creepy - he would take pictures of employees without their knowledge and add little cartoon phrases that had sexist, crude and offensive comments. There's a strange collection of people at the IRS.

I saw discrimination in job assignments and promotions. It seemed like minority employees and disabled employees always had to work twice as hard to get the same promotions.

The one idea that many people have trouble understanding is that for a tax collector, good is bad and bad is good. In a good economy there is less money for IRS hiring, because money is freely flowing through the Treasury. But in bad economic times, it is good for the IRS - because there are more people who cannot pay their taxes so the IRS hires thousands of new employees. That is how I came on board because of the recession of 1979-1981.

7

The Big Seizure

I WAS IN THE CAR again. It seems like I spent half of my 33 year career in the Internal Revenue Service driving around looking for people and their possessions so I could seize them. I was driving to meet my Revenue Officers and a few dozen tow truck drivers. We were going to the biggest property seizure the IRS had ever done in Northern Illinois.

A corporation (my delinquent taxpayer) owed the United States Government $1 million in withholding taxes, which are the taxes taken out of their employee's paycheck. The employer is supposed to hold these taxes in trust for the Government. This is how the Government collects money to pay your income taxes, your tax refund, your Social Security check, and Medicare or unemployment benefits. The Government will pay these benefits to you whether it has collected the money or not, so the IRS is very tough on collecting these types of taxes. Nonpayment of these taxes can come with penalties and interest as high as 65%. This is where almost all the money comes from to run the Government.

This case started the way all my cases started. I knocked on their door, looked around and demanded that the delinquent taxpayer pay the IRS the money they took from both their employees and the Government. The IRS required me to make a legal "Final Demand" for the payment of the tax money. Simply said, the officers of this corporation and I had talked many times, but they were belligerent and refused to cooperate, as if they were somehow above the tax laws.

They were disrespectful and abusive to me, the IRS Tax Collector! This was not a good idea, especially not in the 1990s, when this incident happened. I had so much power at my discretion which I used to collect taxes.

All I had to do was write up a report, swear it was all true, and have a secret meeting with a Federal Judge. Then I had the legal right to seize everything and anything the corporation or the corporate officers personally owned.

The 4th Amendment of the U. S. Constitution states:

> *"The right of the people to be secure in their persons, houses, papers, and effects, against unreasonable searches and seizures, shall not be violated, and no warrants shall issue, but upon probable cause, supported by oath or affirmation, and particularly describing the place to be searched, and the persons or things to be seized."*

The Federal Judge agreed to seizure of assets just based on my word. He gave me the power to destroy these people, their business and their lives, at least temporarily. It is lucky that this is a form of white collar crime so at least they did not have to go to jail. It was years later before I questioned the ethics or legality of this.

I arrived at the parking lot of a shopping center at about 5 a.m., to see that it appeared that everyone was inhaling coffee. The stress of the moment was palpable. The IRS runs on coffee, chocolate, donuts and stress.

At 5:40 a.m. we left the staging area and drove to the industrial park. I led the strange parade of tow trucks with their bright yellow emergency lights flashing, their engines belching diesel fumes, and government cars containing my fellow Revenue Officers. We drove down the quiet, suburban streets. We all parked about a block away from the business, just waiting for the sun to come up. The

Judge said it was very important that I did not disturb their sleep and should not contact them before sunrise.

Another part of my team was heading to the Corporate President's home where they would seize two vintage automobiles stored in the garage and some other vehicles and equipment as well. These people were lucky. I was only seizing the equity they had in the house. They could still sleep there until it was sold. In other instances, the IRS was more heavy handed and would seize the house and all its contents. This happened a lot in Florida and Texas, as I remember.

From down the block we saw the first employee arrive and open the business at 6 a.m. At exactly 6:07 a.m. (sunrise) I gave the "Go Order." I pulled up in front of the building, blocking the exits from the parking lot and yard.

I knocked at the rear door. The very startled employee opened it and told me the company was closed. I held my Official Internal Revenue Service Credentials out in front of me, a brown cardboard folder with shiny gold embossing on the outside and my picture stating who I was. My credentials said that I had the authority to investigate nonpayment of taxes and then do what the law allowed me to do. At that time, a delinquent taxpayer had no rights. He could not go to court to protest what I was doing. He could not do much but try to survive on whatever I left them with. Some people did not survive, and suicide was a common way to finish things up on the taxpayer's end.

I told the employee who I was and who the dozen federal officers behind me were. I gave him the papers from the Judge and said we were coming in. Funny, you would think that in a job like mine, where I was confronting people and demanding things, I would have a weapon, a gun, a bullet proof vest, maybe even pepper spray, but no, those were all prohibited for me to carry. I just had the small cardboard credentials. It was me and God and the full United States Government behind me. That morning, it felt like they were way behind me.

The day before, I took all the money from the company's bank accounts and put a block on the wire transfers and credit card receipts. I also sent levy/seizure notices to all of the people they did business with, based on information gathered from all of their telephone calls I had tracked for the previous 60 days.

The employee was freaked out and let us in after I handed him the Judge's Writ of Entry. Now this corporation, its officers and all they owned and cared about, was under my control as an Officer of the United States Government. Just like that. There was a lot of adrenaline pumping that day. The employee asked if he could call his boss. He was breathing real hard and said, "I really need this job." He called his boss and explained to her what we were doing. He asked her if he would still get his paycheck. The lady who was the corporate president demanded to talk to me. She was screaming and cursing into the phone. We really did not have much of a conversation. I hate when people "talk at me." I had warned her that this was what would happen if she did not make an installment agreement and keep current with tax deposits.

Although I had seized all the money in the corporate bank accounts the day before, I made sure that all the employees eventually got their full pay checks. Plus, I told them how to apply for unemployment. Thirty employees lost their jobs that day.

It costs the Government less money if it pays unemployment to the workers rather than having them continue to work for an employer who takes out taxes but does not pay them over to the IRS.

When I first started with the IRS, I used to feel responsible and feel bad that people lost their jobs because of actions that I was required to take. Then I remembered that I was just the guy sent to clean up the mess. The owners of the company were the ones who actually were responsible. I also realized that if, when they needed their Social Security benefits and I said, "Sorry, we did not get that money from your employer, please go talk to him about it," it would not be long before a group of those employees would string the employer up on a tree in front of his house.

When I was a janitor in college, I was the person sent to clean up after people had parties and events. I just had to clean up. I did not get to attend the party. The same thing applied in my tax collector job; I would come in after the money had been used, lost or stolen and I was forced to make decisions to clean the situation up.

After a while I was indoctrinated into the mindset of the IRS and I started to lose my feelings of concern and compassion for my fellow man. I remember some of my fellow tax collectors calling the taxpayers dirt bags and scum. I never let it go that far, but I often was reminded of the saying, "Absolute Power Corrupts Absolutely." The IRS is much insulated from the real world and pretty much does whatever it wants with little resistance and offering no explanations. The Internal Revenue Code prohibits the IRS from commenting on specific cases. Technically you have the right to due process and your 1st Amendment rights but to get those through the IRS requires so much money in lawyers and court costs that it rarely occurs.

Sometimes, because I seemed like a calm, friendly gentleman, people were later shocked when I seized everything they owned. They told me, "I can't believe you did that to me! You seem so nice." I could be nice if you were doing what I demanded you to do. Otherwise my other half, the tax collector, took over and demanded justice. I believe I was always fair.

I invited her to come down to her old business site to verify our inventory of everything. I don't know how much of it she heard as she was screaming and cursing so loudly at me over the phone. She asked me how the hell she was supposed to get there since we had seized all four of her cars. I told her that that was not my problem and maybe she could get a ride or take a bus or a cab. I told her that she did not need to come at all. Everything was under my control now and I was handling things. The screeching started again so I ended the call.

I later learned my other team of Revenue Officers had endured a lot of yelling and name calling by this woman and her husband when they seized their house, the two vintage cars and two more sports cars, but the couple had finally allowed the IRS access into the garage to have the vehicles towed. It required local police backup, but when they saw which way it was going, they let the seizures take place. The local police saw the Writ of Entry from the Court and told the woman and her husband to back off and not disturb the IRS or they would be arrested for disturbing the peace.

When the IRS seizes a house, it is different from other government agencies doing seizures. The IRS seizes the equity you have in your house, subject to any mortgages so you can continue living in your house; you just don't own it anymore. That way there is no eviction done by the IRS, so no bad publicity. The IRS is very sensitive to bad publicity because the IRS likes to destroy lives quietly. The highest bidder at the sale can evict you, if need be.

I had explained to her before what we were planning to do and what she could do to prevent it. I explained she had certain rights (before a seizure) and responsibilities and that she could seek legal counsel. It is always a big mistake not to talk to the IRS guy when he knocks on your door, or to ignore what he suggests you do to resolve the tax matter.

As we moved into the business building, we located financial records, computers, cash, guns and the boss's desk with an overflowing ashtray and a bottle of Scotch. We secured the yard and found 42 tractor-trailers and other trucks on the property. The United States now owned everything. When the corporate officers arrived, they brought the local police with them. I showed the officers the Writ of Entry and they said, "We don't mess with the Feds," and offered to remove the owner from the building so she did not interrupt my work. I said no, she had the right to be there.

By 7:30 a.m. the building and the yard were secure and the tow trucks were hooking up the trucks and towing them to a military base that offered the IRS free storage. It was going very well. But the paperwork, the bills of lading and the seizure papers took me days to figure out.

We did not just get the trucks and tractor trailers but everything that was inside the trucks as well. The IRS did not get ownership but they had the right to collect for the shipping, handling and storage. I started getting calls from freight dispatchers across the United States asking where their freight was and how to get it reshipped to its destination. You should have heard the truckers' CB radio talk that day in Chicago. The IRS made a big impact on truckers in Northern Illinois that day!

In the weeks to come, I saw that we had a big effect on the surrounding communities also. When people see that the IRS does seizures, it helps them to stay in compliance with the tax laws. The Internal Revenue Service operates on FEAR.

Following the seizure, I appraised the vehicles and advertised the public auction. On the day of the auction sale, over 100 potential bidders showed up. I had all the trucks started up and they were belching diesel fumes after having been idle for several weeks. I auctioned off the trucks and the Government netted over $200,000, to be applied to the delinquent taxes. Auctions are always exciting because we would do cash only sales. Many people in the crowd waiting to bid on what they liked would have bulging pants pockets with tens of thousands of dollars.

Never Ignore the IRS

The best advice if you are in trouble with the IRS is to never stop talking to them. I suggest you hire a tax attorney or CPA or Enrolled Agent who knows exactly how the IRS Tax Collection and Audit

System works. The IRS does not think or act like any other business. It is all very specialized.

Not talking to the IRS can lead to increased investigation. IRS agents have been known to have your post office mail monitored, your phone calls traced and sometimes monitored, and on rare occasions, they will sort through your garbage, or pick up your garbage bags and take them, looking for information. I have seen cases where information was overheard in restaurants and bars and then developed by the agents into tax evasion cases. I have seen where agents take photos of license plates to develop possible tax evasion leads from those who attend political meetings, sporting events and events such as weddings and funerals of suspected mobsters.

Delinquent taxpayers have written me letters thanking me for being caring, compassionate, honest and respectful. I used to share the letters with management in hopes of getting a higher annual review, but IRS management does not welcome positive information like this. I got in trouble many times for doing the right thing. The fact that someone in a position of authority took the time to listen and respect another person meant cases could be resolved with much less drama and stress.

In another case, a business taxpayer had suffered from mismanagement and embezzlement and owed the IRS $400,000 in employment taxes. The IRS and other creditors were demanding and threatening the taxpayer, so they closed the business which included over 50 trucks and pieces of construction equipment that were all free and clear.

They contacted me and were very cooperative. They wanted to sign over the titles to all the trucks to the Government so that I could seize and sell them, and apply the proceeds to the tax balances. This involved a lot of paperwork, and I did everything I needed to do. However, this was at the time when I was being abused by IRS management for not discriminating against Jewish, African American and Hispanic taxpayers in my work. Even though seizing and selling the equipment was the right thing to do, a series of managers repeatedly denied my request over the course of two years.

Sometimes the IRS attacks its own and forgets about collecting the money owed the Government. At that point in time, making me look incompetent was more important to my managers. In the end, no seizure occurred and all the vehicles were lost to other creditors who took them because the IRS did not act first. The owners of this company were the kindest people and thanked me for caring and listening, and, in the end giving them peace of mind.

The owners of the company had tried to respond to the IRS and kept calling and asking for help. They wanted to comply with the law. They were willing to do everything they could to protect the interests of the IRS, but they did not understand what to do or how to do it. This is true of most taxpayers; they want to cooperate but the IRS is not designed to respond to people who are calling. In fact, the IRS only answers 40% of the incoming calls.

The part that was so much fun for me when doing a financial review was asking questions that should be very simple but were so hard for some people to answer. Like how it is that you file your taxes and claim income of $36,000 a year yet the mortgage payments on your house are $48,000 a year - just the mortgage, mind you - not food, clothing or anything else. I asked, "How do you do that? Do you have a big pot of cash somewhere? Did you inherit money, did you borrow it? How do you live on so little money?" Questions lead to more questions. If they don't have good explanations, that is how the IRS can make a Federal case out of a person's life.

As you may have guessed, people lied to me all the time, or at least tried to lie to me. They tried to hide money under other people's names, hide homes and vacation homes, cars and trucks. The IRS advertises that the tax system is "voluntary" but if you do not file or pay taxes, you should expect the IRS to come after you. Technically, it is possible to never pay taxes and get away with it. I met people who did this, but you can never own anything in your name, or stay at jobs for very long, or have bank accounts or any assets. It is like living on the run all the time and it must get very tiring. Actually almost 47% of people in the United States do not pay any Federal income taxes at all, because they do not make enough money, or qualify for credits that make them have no tax liability. But every worker does have to pay the Social Security tax or self-employment tax. That provides for them when they qualify for retirement. It sets a sort of minimum income level.

8

Field Calls

When I would knock on a taxpayer's door, I was the Internal Revenue Service; I was the whole Federal Government making a house call to you or your business. At least that is how one taxpayer described it to me. Many taxpayers would get angry when we met and yell and scream and curse, some would cry and beg, some just quietly collapse inside, having been quietly tortured by the long wait for a field revenue officer to be assigned to the case.

It is common for an IRS agent to write down or photograph all the license plate numbers on autos, trucks, campers, trailers, or RV's and note other assets when making a field call to a home or business. They would later run the plates to check who owns what. Expensive or antique cars are a great area of emphasis. They also take pictures of business assets and personal residences with the intention of later seizing and selling the property.

When making field calls I always knew exactly which house was my taxpayer's. It was usually the house with the untrimmed bushes and weeds all gone to seed, where the shades were broken and there was a broken car in the driveway. It was a land where dreams had died and now I was viewing what was left. Sometimes the garbage cans would block the front door.

Since I would usually live in the same town where I was knocking on taxpayers doors it would be uncomfortable for me to see the delinquent taxpayers when I was out in my off time. Later, I figured out that I should not be embarrassed, I had done nothing wrong. But I did not like that feeling. It was uncomfortable and awkward.

When I made field calls I was always trying to look around every corner for my personal security and peeking in windows looking for stuff to seize. I have seen revenue officers "fall" against mail boxes and then review the mail inside looking for the name of a bank on one of the letters (This is illegal). I used to carry dog biscuits to bribe dogs to get away from me so I could run back to my car in hostile situations. I know some revenue officers would carry mace or pepper spray - just in case. It was not legal but they really had no other protection. I have seen some revenue officers who would have beautiful new cars and then have large travel vouchers every month whether they needed to travel or not, just to pay their big car payments.

This is a job where I was out in the field driving around making field calls much of the time. Field calls are dangerous; you don't know if a convicted criminal or mental case is going to answer the door or just shoot through it. Then when I entered a house I would see the lifestyle, the furniture, and the screaming kids. Mostly I went to houses that looked more like they should be on the Hoarder TV show. They were stinky, nasty and disgusting. My eyes were scanning everything, never losing sight of the door I came in, in case I had to leave quickly. I would make notes of any valuables I saw, and write down any information from calendars, mail or bills that were spread out on tabletops. I learned to read upside down fairly quickly. It was like invading the house of the delinquent taxpayer. I would look at the jewelry they were wearing, the artwork on the wall. If it looked expensive I would complement them on it and then they would brag about what it was and its value, the same as they would with antique furniture and other assets, never thinking that they were talking to the IRS guy who could and had taken artwork off the wall and sold it before.

The most awkward moments were when I went into a business and said I was from the IRS. These were the longest waiting times I have ever encountered. Even if my wait only took a few minutes, employees would stop what they were doing and look at me. In fact, they would not only look, they would stare and gape at me as well. I would be there reading whatever I could see, looking for the names of banks, jobs or customers of the company. Then some shocked bookkeeper or angry corporate president would come out and I would present my credentials and again loudly announce who I was and why I was there. The facial expressions that I saw ranged from shock to sadness to confusion and dismay. Anger usually came shortly thereafter.

Going into a business is always risky. It is very psychologically intrusive. That is one of the parts of the field call. Then I would demand to be shown the business again, looking for assets. I would talk to employees about the machines and other equipment. I would write down serial numbers, model numbers and other information with the intent of coming back and seizing the equipment later. I also looked at finished product, work in progress and raw materials as other items I could get some cash for if I seized and sold them. I was always talking fast during the field call interviews, because it is such a stressful situation and I have seen many taxpayers freak out and get very angry and then yell and get physically aggressive. I did all this without a search warrant.

People who have any issues with the IRS are stressed out. They often feel fear, worry and anger. Even when they are trying to resolve their issues they report that they feel frustrated, inadequate, defeated and see the whole situation as being hopeless.

Sometimes the biggest part of my job was just to listen to them, before we could get anything done. I always listened and they always talked about the cause of the IRS problems or problems in their lives. I got better results just listening for a few minutes than other employees who were officious or mean and abusive. Some actually sound like robots.

Just like in that movie *Network* - some people were at the point where they could say *"I'm Mad as Hell and I'm Not Going To Take It Anymore!"* Now a person at this place is unable to listen or think; they only want to lash out and react. My job was to get people loaded back on the taxpaying wagon so we could get money from them for the next 30-40 years. Sincere listening skills go a long way. I would not allow bitching sessions or lectures on how the Income Tax was illegal, etc. I just redirected them. One man said that he had lost so much in his life and the part that he really resented about the IRS was that although he was poor now, the IRS made him feel small and like less than a person. He felt disrespected by the IRS and like a victim.

I found that by clearly explaining about the IRS collection process, and how long they would owe their tax balances and describe their appeal rights, and then counseling them on what would be best to resolve the case, it was like I was giving them their power back. I was giving them hope. Hope and respect go a long way.

Bribe Attempts

I was trained to listen for bribe overtures, because the presentation is very subtle. I had to clear up what the actual intention was of the taxpayer up front. The taxpayer might use a phrase like "What can we do to make this go away?" "What can we do to make this a closed case for you and get it off the books?" "What do you want to make this case go away?" I would say full pay and then they would say – "besides that." I always asked them what they meant.

The only bribe where money actually crossed my palm was for $5,000 on a $50,000 balance due case. Little did the taxpayer know, that I was undercover? The conversation was being recorded and photographed. The taxpayer came to a conference room at my office and handed me the envelope for the amount that we had agreed on and then I counted it out bill by bill and then said OK so this is $5,000 and you are giving this to me, not as a payment towards your taxes but for me to make your case go away off the collection computer. Right? Then the person shook his head up and down he was so happy. He said that was such a load off his mind. Then the two Special Agents came in and arrested him on the spot. He actually had a stroke after that, so he avoided any jail time.

Another bribe attempt was from a prominent lawyer who was running for Congress. He made a dollar offer the first time I went there and then the next time I went back, I was wearing a wire which in those days was taped to my back and was as big as a box of Kleenex and I went in wearing a jacket and he came over shook my hand and patted me down - so much for that bribe offer attempt.

At least later he did not win in his bid for Congress. Or maybe he would have fit right in there.

Another time, I had a man who was from India and he owed about 3 million dollars in employment taxes. He offered me a bribe of $300,000. I told him I would go home and think about it. I went back to the office and called TIGTA. We arranged for a series of telephone calls where we discussed the bribe. Figuring that he had me on the hook now, he started telling me that he was having business troubles and could only give me $250,000 then $200,000 and he kept lowering it until he was only offering me $50,000. Every time I talked to him, I had two agents in the room listening into my telephone calls, sometimes trying not to laugh hysterically. Finally when we got down to $50,000, I broke character and I said "What the hell - you cheap son of a bitch - I am not going to take a bribe of $50,000. Why would I risk losing my job, my pension and jail time. I make more than that a year." He quietly said, "Mr. Schickel, you will take the bribe, because I have been tape recording of you agreeing to accept the bribe and I can go to the U.S. Attorney with this information. I own you." I told him I would think about it.

Of course, I went to the U.S. Attorney first and they brought him before a federal judge. Except when he came to court he was wearing clothing that a man would wear in India and he claimed that he only spoke Hindi. He brought a translator with him. Even though the tape I had made was played, his attorney pretended that I must have been talking to someone else, because his client barely spoke English. His attorney also allowed that bribing the Tax Inspector was common in India - so if anything had happened, it was only because this man was afraid so he felt forced to offer a bribe. That lawyer had all kinds of defenses, except for the truth.

Somehow the judge fell for it. My bribe case fell apart. I was admonished by the U.S. Attorney to never bring another bribe case with a person from a foreign country into his office again.

I Got a Feeling

Speaking to the many taxpayers I worked with over the years, I had a sixth sense that told me when a person was speaking the truth, telling a lie or hiding something. Early in my career when people were lying to me, I would get a bad feeling in the pit of my stomach.

Sometimes I would drive for 150 miles through winter snow and cold to make a single field call and the person probably would not even be home. I was going to post offices, courthouses, county recorder's offices, and banks looking for information or even gossip about my taxpayers

Sometimes the best source of information would be an ex-spouse or a neighbor. In small towns, the Postmaster always knew exactly where everyone was at all times. They would tell me directions to the taxpayers house - which I needed to see and leave a card, but then they would add that the guy I was looking for is probably over at his mistress's house at that time of the afternoon, or other such juicy information.

I have seen the IRS do something called "cold canvassing." This might involve targeting one side of a busy commercial street going door to door asking for tax information and demanding business tax identifying information, to see if the businesses were in compliance or not. Word of these projects spread fast in the local community. I have heard of cases where certain industries were targeted, such as CPAS, attorneys, real estate agents or certain types of businesses. The formulas for figuring out who will be audited and on what issues may be secret, but the process is very apparent every new tax year.

I was taught that when I would feel sorry for a person it was like turning over control to them. That they would try to control and manipulate me. I was taught to find out the three C's – ***Cause*** - why did they owe the money, ***Cure*** - how were they going to pay the money, and ***Compliance*** - how could we get them back to filing and paying their taxes again. I learned that the person who cares the least is in control of the case and in fact the life of the taxpayer. Some employees like this cheap thrill. It makes for a formal cold feeling. That power trip starts to grow on them.

I think a lot of tax problems happen because people want to fit in and be cool. To look cool and live cool but they lack the financial resources to pay for it. So they borrow and steal and mortgage their future for the pleasures of the flesh and toys of the present moment. I think our culture promotes this, so we don't have a lot of people waking up all at the same time and realizing that the rich people and their corporations are in control of the government and the economy.

One of the last things I used to tell my taxpayers when closing their case as an installment agreement or as currently not collectible or even as a full pay was "If anyone from the IRS calls you, call me or let me know immediately - I don't want to see you back in my inventory." This is because at the IRS the right hand does not know what the left hand is doing. There is no coordination of efforts.

But in later years, the IRS said I could not do that anymore, because if I talked to someone who was no longer in my inventory, this was disclosure and snooping on the computer. Bizarre and crazy! I tried to provide service to people and was told this.

I provided world class customer service and was reasonable to deal with. I had a great rapport with tax professionals and taxpayers - even if I had seized their bank account or wages. Once we came to the table - I treated them with respect. I did not torture them with fear. I did not talk down to them. I explained where they were legally, how much they owed, and I offered them hope by telling them that they would only owe the tax for 10 years and then it goes away forever.

Unless they did an offer in compromise, bankruptcy or appeal - then the 10 years gets extended and what sounds like a good thing can turn into a nightmare. In the case of an offer, if they filed it to settle their taxes at the end of the collection statute - the IRS is still going to keep the case open for the next five years and if you do not file or pay any new tax balance then all the old taxes, penalties and interest all come rolling back to you. So, sometimes offer in compromise is not a good way to resolve a case.

9

Greed, Abuse and Loss

Throughout the course of my IRS career, I worked with an array of people, mentally unbalanced, narcissistic with greed; from the rich and the famous, to the poorest. Mostly, I worked on cases of people that used to have money but it had all slipped through their fingers. Greed is an important part of the lives of many people I have worked with. I asked many questions pertaining to this when I talked to delinquent taxpayers.

Most of the people that I worked with through the IRS were very wealthy. I say this in the past tense because by the time I was talking to them, they had little or nothing left. I remember one man who inherited $57 million and enjoyed spending it all over the next 25 years. When I met him, he was broke and happy living in his sister's gatehouse at her estate. He said he was so much happier poor than he was when he was rich. The money was a curse to him. It is really all in the attitude of the person. You can be rich and happy or unhappy, or you can be poor but happy or unhappy. The thing is that you make all the choices. If you think being poor will bring you an empty, bleak future, then that is what you will get in your life. Life is all about your attitude, about how you perceive it. But some people felt freedom when they did not have the burdens of managing a business, the employees, the money or the image that they projected to their community.

After 33 years working in the IRS, I have known some amazing people and some mean, psychotic people. I learned about greed, lying and thievery from some masters of the art, both in and out of the IRS. I am here to show you the human side of the IRS. It is not a fear machine. It is a group of people who mostly want to help other people. Service is not just in the name. But there is also the other side of the coin.

At this point in the book you may despise me for my actions during my IRS career; or maybe you are angry at how the IRS system works. Please read on - it gets better, in so many ways.

In my life as a tax collector, I dealt with people who lost hope after their dreams died. They may have survived a death in the family, disease, divorce or losing everything they had, but the awful fear of having to deal with the IRS caused some people to go into shutdown mode. I often asked myself, "Why do bad things happen to these otherwise good, hard-working people? Why have they invested everything they had into this business and lost all their money plus a lot of the Government's as well?"

IRS work suited me perfectly. I could be close to people but at a safe distance as well. I could drive around and enjoy the fresh air even if it was freezing or sweltering. I spent many hours in libraries and forest preserves and cemeteries, anywhere where I could find a shady spot and silence so I could write the many pages of case history that were expected. I was almost my own boss, but it was not a 9 to 5 job. The stories people shared about their lives and circumstances, and the sometimes horrible living conditions they endured were enough to wake me up in the middle of the night. Other times, trying to do the right thing for the taxpayer and the government was difficult because the IRS is so hostile to settling cases in a simple manner.

ATAT Group

Many IRS managers think that they have to prove something to the world in every individual's case. A further example of this is the special and secret Abusive Tax Avoidance Transactions (ATAT) Group where a large number of highly paid federal officers go after small individuals who do not want to file or pay taxes ever. The IRS has bound itself up paying so much attention staying engaged in this guerrilla war with these people.

My personal philosophy and one I think held by most businesses is that you get in, work the case and get out with as good a deal as you can get. I think that more money should be spent on a broader effort of compliance – lets go after all those who do not file or pay at all and have cash businesses. "Big Bang for the Buck!" This is not the IRS philosophy. IRS might be more like "cut them - watch them bleed - they deserved it." As long as it closes your case - it is OK. They work on hunting people down who have used the tax laws to avoid or not pay taxes. Some are very sophisticated tax protesters. The cases are very complex and involve not only personal risk, because here some of the taxpayers will fight back and strike back if they can. Regular front line revenue officers can also use pseudonyms. The ATAT group firmly believes that its customers are guilty until proven innocent. In fact, all the revenue officers there that I have ever known are so afraid that their customers will follow them home that they use made up names and identities to hide. This pseudonym program is officially approved by the IRS.

The IRS Does Not Follow the Law

Newly installed IRS Commissioner Koskinen said under oath in a congressional hearing. "We follow the law whenever we can." Maybe that works for the IRS, but try saying that to your tax auditor or the criminal agent who comes after you for tax evasion. Ignorance of the law is no argument either.

One example is under the RRA 98 which effectively neutralized the IRS Collection Division - the law said that taxpayers should have online access to their own records and that taxpayers must have a way to see and review current and past returns by 12-31-2006. The IRS ignored this and again this is because of the fear that the IRS has of any online transactions. The IRS does not use email at all for taxpayer contact or to respond to questions. Yet every major corporation has secure sites that allow online account reviews and inquiries. This is one reason why customer service is so poor at the IRS.

A second reason is because of the antiquated IDRS master file system. There is no internet accessibility and in this day and age that is abuse of the taxpayer. I mean you can securely see your tax records on Turbo Tax programs - a private company. Why can't you see them on www.IRS.gov?

According to a TIGTA report the IRS does not follow its own rules regarding the law on issuing a Final Demand/Notice of Intent to Levy Letter warning a delinquent taxpayer that their bank account or wages might be seized shortly. They found that this happened between 60-90% in the IRS collection systems.

In fact the IRS does not follow other laws either, like when the Tea Party Scandal happened. They lost emails. There are two parts to this story. First, computer crashes and data loss happen often on laptops used in the field, because they are 3-6 years old. Second, there is a limited amount of space for how many emails that can be saved. Third, when I would erase an email, it would be taken out of the main computer system and the disks eventually reused or destroyed. This is just how the IRS works.

The National Archives by law is supposed to notify when data or records are lost. But the IRS does not care, it never turns over data to the National Archives as it is required to by law. It stores records in the secret vaults located around the Internal Revenue Service Building in Washington, D.C. I have seen the vault doors and talked to people who described the records held there, records about rich and prominent people, presidential and congressional records, records on communists and subversives (as defined at the time) like Dr. Martin Luther King. It is like the records exist and they are too afraid to destroy them, but don't want them seen by the National Archives and they use this IRC 6103 section to justify that.

Sometimes, the IRS thinks it is above the law and bristles under any scrutiny of its methods.

The IRS was warned by Congress in 1998 to not use Records of Tax Enforcement Results (ROTERs) in evaluating employee performance. This means the employees cannot be evaluated on how much they collect, how many returns they audit, or how many seizures they make. IRS talks a lot about this. But behind closed doors - these are all used to evaluate employee performance. The area that helped me the most over the years was a ROTER - called "*Number of Fraud Referrals.*" Since I had a sixth sense about tax fraud and evasion cases, I could identify a fraud case on my first meeting with a taxpayer. I knew the way around the ROTER's law was to look at what they could use to evaluate me. In the past, dollars and tax returns collected were ROTERS. Then they could not do that anymore, so they made up some new ROTER's like how quickly I closed cases (resolving overage cases and potentially overage cases) and how many referrals I made to criminal investigation and audit to instigate investigations, or how many summons or subpoenas that I served.

The same applied to the auditors. The cases that were closed as a refund or a no change to the tax amount owed were negatives on their evaluations. I often wondered why audit spends so much money on auditing people and businesses who have no ability to pay the increased tax assessment. Cases worked quickly and with minimal taxpayer protest or contact were the types of cases that got people promoted quickly.

The bottom line for all of these cases was how aggressive the IRS employee could be, because believe me the cases do not close themselves. Employee evaluations, appraisals and yearly cash performance awards are all based on subjective standards designed to reward employees who are mindlessly shuffling cases toward closure.

When I was under pressure to close cases - I was very aggressive and that got me promoted and recognized with dozens of cash awards.

It's Nothing Personal

IRS managers would always say don't let this case get personal. That was such bullshit - of course it was personal, my evaluation, my promotion and my raise all depended on how I worked cases.

After a while, it was emotionally hard on me to have to do my job. I could not share what I did with my family or friends because they could be critical and just did not understand the stress I was under. My IRS family as broken as they sometimes were, were who I could turn to for understanding.

The IRS loved when I enforced promptly. If you had an appointment with me at 9 am and failed to show up, I would drive to your bank at 3pm and seize whatever cash you had.

With the IRS, nothing is ever what it appears to be. The IRS looks for something that they can use as a quantifiable data and then assesses and judges its employees on it. The IRS loves to keep score - no matter what the subject area; it is always accumulating data, testing and measuring it. There is the spoken and written word and the law that the IRS pays respect to, but the actual fact is that what really goes on is that the IRS is an agency full of bean counters. That is why they like to count cases closed, seizures made and fraud referrals made.

The funny part is that after I made the fraud referrals I did not care about the case anymore. I got credit for the referral. That was all I cared about, that was what was important. Likewise Criminal Investigation had quotas that they were to receive a certain number of fraud referrals from Exam and Collection and open them as criminal cases.

A recent IRS TIGTA report verifies this dark secret. It claims that the IRS continued to use quotas to launch investigations and seizures. It may not look like you are being evaluated because you made a seizure - but actually just under the table that is what happens. That is how much of the IRS management operates - under the table. The report also states that management is not stopping employees from using discrimination and intimidation in their dealings with taxpayers.

Some IRS Managers are just ignorant, mean, vindictive and incompetent. The IRS through its automated computer actions and its employees can be vindictive to both taxpayers and its own employees. I tried to do the right thing, follow the law and shake up the system but it only led to reprisals, harassment, suspensions and attempts to terminate my employment. When the IRS employees are not being abused by TIGTA then there are many levels of management that do the same thing. Your direct manager can be a tyrant, demanding case closures without regard to issues of the cases. The system does not work anymore, if it ever did. IRS Management comes up with policies and procedure that favor certain employees and programs. The Treasury Department and IRS Top Management also have a history of looking more closely at certain groups of taxpayers. We saw this in the Tea Party Scandal, where there is abuse and the pursuing of certain taxpayer groups due to political motivations. This is nothing new for the IRS. President Nixon used the IRS to dog and pursue his enemies also.

Some IRS Managers and employees embrace the tentacles of power and use them to abuse people and their rights. When they review cases they offer decisions on how to discover and exploit weaknesses in taxpayer's situations. I sometimes felt that people who were attracted to IRS management went for ego and more money. But the ones who lasted the longest sold their souls to the manager just above them.

10

IRS Employees Doing Bad Things

IRS Employees Caught and Jailed

The vast majority of IRS employees I have met are good, decent and honest people. Many will also follow orders without question. But there are some who give the Service a bad name. Thousands of IRS employees have been investigated by the Treasury Inspector General for the IRS and they publish the results of their investigations. Tens of millions of dollars have been stolen from the Treasury by IRS employees.

Some IRS employees use the data to which they have access to rip off the Government. A recent example of this is a Tax Examining Technician who was sentenced for aggravated identity theft and mail fraud.

She used her access to taxpayer's names, Social Security numbers, date of birth and addresses as well as information about tax professionals. Together with her co-conspirators she used this private information to steal the identities of taxpayers. She changed addresses and bank information so that she could deposit refund checks into her own account. One man working with her had a check for $595,901 on him when he was arrested along with three pages of IDRS data on more identity theft victims. In fact, one of her co-conspirators impersonated a tax practitioner and called the IRS regarding the tax refund and to change the address. She offered to split the proceeds with the co-conspirators. She said that she would give them all the information that they needed to get addresses changed. She said "All of this money is just sitting there for the taking." Another of her co-conspirators received a refund of $961,779.00. She is now serving a 50 month imprisonment, followed by 5 years of supervised release and was ordered to pay the IRS restitution in the amount of $501,048. Many other IRS employees have been arrested for this also.

Internal Revenue Service employees have been indicted and in some cases been found guilty of:

Murder for hire scheme of a fellow employee
Operating a prostitution ring
Trading tax data for sexual favors
Accessing and viewing pornography on a government computer
Accessing and storing child pornography on a government computer
Theft-An IRS employee who processed checks made out to "IRS" changed the checks to read "Iris Smith" and then deposited them in her personal account.
Theft of government property
Theft of government funds
Wire fraud
Mail fraud
Obstruction of justice
Unauthorized access to tax information for private financial gain
Conspiracy to defraud the United States
Conspiracy to commit passport fraud
Unauthorized access and inspection of tax returns
Conspiracy to commit fraud
Bank theft
Embezzlement
Fraud
Travel card fraud
Theft of government computers

Money laundering
Destroying official records
Aggravated identity theft
Distribution of controlled substance (methamphetamines)
Counterfeiting 115 Revenue Officer official credentials with the intention to sell on the open market
Government credit card fraud
Murder for hire of an ex-spouse
Stealing a government car
Impersonating an FBI Agent
Accepting a bribe for disclosing secret grand jury information.
Threatening two state police officers with an audit as they were arresting him for drunk driving
An exam manager threatening to audit people that bothered him.
Witness tampering
Stealing money from the IRS
Gambling on government time
Possession of alcohol in a federal building
Drunkenness while on duty in a federal building
Perjury
Lying to a grand jury

The IRS Got Caught

There is a disturbing U.S. Court of Appeals case Dixon v. U.S. 91 AFTR 2d 2003-569 (9th Cir. 2003) where IRS attorneys were found guilty of intentional acts of fraud, perjury, witness tampering, secret IRS Payoffs, and secret IRS deals that favored some taxpayers and damaged others. IRS counsel entered into secret agreements with certain taxpayers in exchange for false testimony and cooperation in the government's case.

I have witnessed some of this in my dealings with IRS Criminal Investigation cases. They make their case better by targeting one individual and then have other co-conspirators turn government witness for a better plea agreement deal.

The Dixon case offers important insight into the day to day operations of the IRS. Every office has a secret cadre of employees and managers that think they "know what is best for the IRS" and develop their own vigilante style of enforcement. They have no qualms about bending or distorting the law, to accomplish in their view "the real mission of the IRS." I have witnessed this many times in my career. I was a mover and shaker but I always followed the law.

Attempting to Corrupt Tax Administration Is Big Business for those Outside the IRS

There are many scams that come from outside the IRS to steal money from the taxpaying public. They come from the atmosphere of fear that the IRS has created. The IRS never uses email to contact taxpayers for collection, audit or criminal matters. The IRS always sends a letter to you before they begin audits or collection actions. The IRS never calls you on the phone requesting a balance due and demands that you pay that day or they will come and seize your wages, bank accounts, car, or your children. They never say that they have a judgement or arrest warrant for you and that they are going to send a police car right over if you don't send them money or prepaid debit cards.

If you are ever contacted in this way - call the IRS number directly (1-800-829-1040) and ask about activity on your tax account. If some fraudulent scheme is happening to you, report it to TIGTA at (1-800-366-4484) or online at www.treasury.gov/tigta/contact_report_scam.shtml.

TIGTA reported that in 2014, 154,000 taxpayers were contacted by individuals impersonating IRS employees. More than 1,600 taxpayers have provided their Personally Identifiable Information number to these criminals and paid them more than $9 million.

The IRS System Business Results-Abuses and Benefits

The IRS systems operate in a constant stressed condition due to lack of resources and employees. The Automated Collection System (ACS) is one example of this. This system is a call site system with many locations around the United States. Its purpose was to make outgoing calls and receive incoming calls to collect taxes and resolve cases. Years ago, due to short staffing, they stopped making outgoing calls, because the income call volume was so great. This is because the IRS is always better at issuing letters than at responding to the phone calls of those trying to respond. This is a frustrating abuse to the taxpayers who are trying to get answers or make payment arrangements with the IRS. It is also an abuse to the other taxpayers who do file and pay on time.

According to a TIGTA report, the ACS workforce has declined 39% due to attrition or reassignment since 2010. Part of this is because 3-4 ACS sites have been "repurposed" to now work identity fraud cases. Identity fraud does not yield any uncollected funds to the IRS.

The IRS Rewards Employees Who Do Not Pay Income Taxes

There was another IRS embarrassment when it was revealed in 2013 that between October 1, 2010 and December 31, 2012, 2,800 IRS employees who owed Uncle Sam money had received 2.8 million dollars in cash awards and 675 weeks of paid vacation awards; and 175 of them received pay promotions that will automatically award them a bigger paycheck over the next 10 years. All of this is perfectly legal. These employees all had conduct issues, including fraud, travel card fraud, fighting, drinking, reprimands, and suspensions and leading up to some being removed from the IRS.

Additionally, 1100 IRS employees had tax compliance problems. They neglected to file or pay their tax returns. They received $1 million in cash awards and 416 weeks of paid vacation awards and 69 got the long term pay promotions. This is another example of the right hand not knowing what the left hand is doing. Some of this information was not known to IRS management due to disclosure restrictions or the facts came out after the rewards were paid.

Actually many Federal employees owe money in taxes. According to an article in Forbes dated May 23, 2014, a total of 318,000 Federal employees and Federal retirees owe tax delinquent balances of $3 billion.

IRS Employees Who Are Now Convicted Criminals

There are IRS employees who have illegally accessed Social Security numbers - in bulk – providing them with names and addresses of inactive accounts of people who do not need to file or pay because their income is too low or they are retired. Employees have been convicted for criminal tax identity fraud in Kentucky, Georgia, Missouri, Pennsylvania.

Temptations in Tax Administration

When some people think of the IRS, they think of power and money. With great power there is often the temptation to use that power as ordinary man would, arbitrarily and unfairly for some personal gain or feeling that they derive from treating people in a manner that is not what the Bible would call - “Loving Your Neighbor”. Some of those people are attracted to the IRS. I suppose any big business has its share of sociopaths and psychopaths, but I have noticed that they appear to congregate in the corridors of power at the IRS.

The goal of the IRS should be the blind administration of the tax laws, which are already subjective enough. But instead the IRS is like some hidden Wizard of Oz directing a massive effort towards compliance. Sometimes that massive effort is focused directly on you.

Chasing the Bad Guys

A tax preparer in Riverdale, Georgia was charged and found guilty of filing false refunds and claiming over $20 million in refunds as well as filing false tax returns. She obtained the names and Social Security numbers of more than 1,000 Identity Theft victims. She got 16 years in federal prison. Other tax preparers have searched and found the names of dead children and filed returns in their names also.

Temptations within the IRS

IRS employees are bound by many laws. One of them is that they can be suspended or fired for "harassing "taxpayers.

Some employees will sit outside homes and businesses and stalk the taxpayer. They are ostensibly looking for income or levy sources, but really it is harassment.

TIGTA publishes regular reports about IRS employees who have gone "bad." In IRS we called it "the dirty list." It contains details about IRS employees who were fed up with their current circumstances and decided to use the IRS system, or their position of authority or access to confidential tax records, to enrich themselves, their family and friends.

I have seen IRS employees try to gain favor with police who had stopped their car for speeding. One kept his driver's license inside his IRS Credentials. Another left his credentials on the dash board of the car. Twice I saw them get tickets because the police officer had been audited and screwed by the IRS. So much for that.

But some employees have solicited bribes, taken bribes, cheated on their own taxes and stolen money from the United States Treasury.

TIGTA has all sorts of computer matching programs to try to catch IRS employees doing wrong. When they suspect someone, they will monitor their telephone at home and work, their mail, collect and review their garbage, search their personal internet access, work computer access and put them under surveillance - until they find what they are looking for.

But the systems don't appear to work that well. But it is OK -because most IRS employees live under a cloud of fear so they are terrified of getting in trouble.

One time, I was on the master computer looking for some guy with a common name and on a summary screen - I saw 6 names like his name, one name was the President and First Lady with their address at 1600 Pennsylvania Avenue and their Social Security numbers. I could not get off that page fast enough. But I was never questioned about it.

The Snoop

One IRS employee (and he is not the only one I have heard of who did this) was caught snooping on 202 celebrity and sport figures private tax records between 2003-2008. So much for internal IRS controls - which are supposed to discover these incidents. The IRS employee said in court, it was because "he was curious." He looked at the tax data and tax returns of actors, actresses, directors, screenwriters, singers, sports figures and other well - known people and their spouses. Each person who was spied on was notified. The employee lost his job, his pension, received 3 years of probation, a $1,000 fine and 60 hours of community service. This makes me wonder what he eventually used all that confidential tax information for. Was he planning to sell it to a tabloid? The information that the IRS has is very valuable in the wrong hands.

TIGTA said that "it analyses the computer audit trails to look for unusual or suspicious access by IRS employees." But it appears that this system did not work for six years in this case.

Credit Card Abuse

One field officer used her government credit card to purchase a new Cadillac automobile for $25,000, two months before she retired. It took the IRS a year to figure that out and eventually she was forced to repay the Government in interest free payments for the car. I am not aware of any legal action taken against her.

More IRS Employees Arrested

If an IRS employee is arrested they are required to call their manager first and inform them. I don't know how often that happens. But I do know of employees who have been arrested in their private lives for drunk driving (DUI), domestic abuse, domestic violence, suspicion of arson, harassment, drinking in public, public drunkenness, under the influence of illegal drugs, possession of marijuana and drug paraphernalia. I know of employees who have so mismanaged their personal financial affairs that they have had autos repossessed, been evicted from apartments and houses, (this included one IRS Bankruptcy Specialist who filed personal bankruptcy, which was much to his advantage at that time.)

When an employee illegally accesses personal or business tax data on the master computer this is called Unauthorized Access of Taxpayer Records (UNAX). This is a criminal act. The IRS is required to inform all the taxpayers whose accounts were viewed illegally and they can sue the IRS employee personally and the Government also.

It is hard to remember when TIGTA called me in years later to ask about cases that I had accessed on IDRS, because it was so long after the fact. IRS procedures required me to get rid of all records on a case, when I closed the case, and then I had no access to any of the information. In fact I could not tell you the name or address or any of the cases I remembered when writing this book. That would be illegal disclosure and I never do anything illegal. This is like asking you what you had for lunch on June 18, 2010.

In IRS offices posters on the wall say:

UNAX-Don't Go There! 2,320 IRS employees have been terminated, suspended, resigned, fined or jailed. Stop. Be smart. Keep your job. Don't commit UNAX.

(Document 12800 Rev 32012)

UNAX
Privacy, Governmental Liaison & Disclosure
IRS
Don't Go There!
2,320
IRS Employees...
Terminated,
Suspended,
Resigned,
Fined,
Jailed*
For more information,
ask your manager
or search UNAX on IRWeb.
Stop. Be smart.
Keep your job.
Don't commit UNAX

The poster on the previous page will give you some idea of why the IRS Agent you are speaking with might be in a bad mood when you speak to them. This is what employees see when they first walk in the door, not exactly a warm greeting.

A TIGTA report also said that some of the employees of these outside contractors who were hired without background and criminal investigations accessed IRS computer systems and had access to secure facilities and illegally reviewed tax returns, law enforcement information and tax information. IRS employees have been jailed for these offenses but the outside contractors got away with it. Some had tax data on non-secure CDs that included up to 1.3 million taxpayer's names, addresses and Social Security numbers.

I have seen at least 10 employees who were handcuffed and arrested and escorted out of the building by armed Treasury Inspector General Agents (TIGTA). One man was protesting, so they put him in leg irons as well. In all the cases the TIGTA Inspectors suspect that the employees had done something wrong or illegal and pursued and harassed them, forcing them to resign under threat of criminal action. Mostly it is a big bluff, because they already know that the crime will not be prosecuted by the U.S. Attorney. I saw one man kicking and screaming as he was dragged from the building. Then the remaining IRS employees went quietly to their desks and the whole office was quiet. There is so much fear - all the time, everywhere in an IRS office.

I remember one time a regional commissioner and a district director and some staff analysts kept a hotel room near the office paid for by the government where they were found to take their girlfriends and hookers. They eventually got caught - not for their behavior, but for fraudulent travel vouchers that were used to pay for it.

I saw or heard about IRS employees having sex in government buildings, elevators, offices, meeting rooms, store rooms and parking lots. I remember one warm summer day, I pulled up to my office and saw a friend of mine sitting in his station wagon with a newspaper propped up on his steering wheel. I went over to talk to him and then I saw that one of our female colleagues had her head bobbing up and down on his sex organ. Since they were both married (to other people) they were spotted having sex in other places as well. One Saturday, we were given overtime and they got the key to the Branch Chief's Office. We were all working, but we saw them go in there and then surprise! The Branch Chief showed up - he had not been scheduled to work. He caught them having sex on top of his desk. I can still remember the screaming, then the couple exiting the office half clothed, still sweating from their romp and with red faces. They were both reassigned to distant offices.

I worked at the Automated Collection System (ACS) call site 30 years ago. I was as usual barely scraping by on what the IRS paid me. There was a soda pop machine and it cost 35 cents a can. One fellow employee walked over to me and pulled out a large wad of cash (he must have had $600) and asked if I could buy him a pop because he did not have anything smaller than a $50 bill. So I did. But I thought that it was strange. Then over the next few weeks I would walk around the corner or by the water fountain and see him passing small packets of white powder to different employees. I quickly figured out what was happening. So I reported it to TIGTA. I found out later that they had parked a white van in the parking lot with a camera in it and had installed cameras in the ceiling throughout the computer room and office. I later saw a video of some of those scenes that they had recorded. I do not recall how I got access to that - but it showed drug sales, but also something I did not expect. People having sex in the office, in the manager's office and in the computer room.

It's Nothing Personal

IRS managers would always say don't let this case get personal. That was such bullshit - of course it was personal, my evaluation, my promotion and my raise all depended on how I worked cases.

11

Seizures

Never Seize This...

When I was trying to figure out what to do in a case, the top four cases I did not want to seize were:

- Pet stores, farm animals, kennels, fish farms, horses or cattle. Live animals need to be fed and cared for and can die. In fact they have died while under IRS seizures in the past.
- Nursing homes, nurseries and day care centers. Again, because people have to be fed and they can be injured or die if the IRS takes over a facility or even cuts off the cash flow of the business.
- Any residence or business that has had chemical, gas or oil spills in the past, or has underground gas tanks. The IRS is terrified of the EPA.
- Funeral homes, mortuaries and labs.

I went to seize the contents of a funeral home and crematorium once and I thought this would be a simple seizure, taking the furniture, equipment and inventory - such as coffins and urns. So I had served the papers to the owner and then was walking around doing an inventory of the property. All was fine until I opened this large refrigeration unit. I found three human bodies. The owner of the funeral home said that he had lost his license because he had a drinking problem and had complaints about other funerals where the bodies were smelly during the services and bloated, because of improper embalming and storage. His electricity had been shut off twice in the past two months. He was supposed to bury these three bodies - they were indigents he received under a county contract. That small room stunk so bad it made me want to vomit. I grabbed my seizure papers back from him and raced out the door.

Pay Me and Then you Can See the Doctor

It is difficult to collect from chiropractors, hairdressers, dry cleaners and others who have cash businesses. But I found that if I stood outside of the business and handed every patient a Notice of Levy then I quickly either put them out of business or got them into compliance. Some doctors and dentists are also difficult to collect from, because it is hard to find out where their income comes from. Again this is because they might do business under one entity but be billing under another entity.

A Smelly Seizure

Once, I seized a 50,000 square foot warehouse from a man who ran up a large tax bill. A few weeks after I talked to him, he sold the profitable business to a friend who used his life savings of $20,000 cash to pay for it. The warehouse had a large dock and was used for transferring shipments and storing items to be shipped later. The purchaser told me that he felt he was so lucky to get the business so cheap. I asked if he tried to get clear title. Did he hire an attorney? Did he check for liens that were filed? "No, No, No!" He said. "I knew a good deal when I saw one." He bought the business and even showed me his receipt. But I explained to him that the other man did not really own it, so he could not sell it. He was very confused as to why the IRS was taking it all away from him. When he figured it out - that his friend had swindled him - he arrived one morning carrying a tire iron and started threatening me. I told him I was just doing my job, but he kept banging on things with the tire iron. Many hours of discussion finally allowed him to understand that the seller had ripped him off. He was so angry that I had to have the local police remove him from the building.

Again, just like the first seizure I talked about, my actions disrupted the flow of goods to other businesses owing money for shipping, freight and storage. That was the money that the IRS was going to collect. I hired four employees, rented lift trucks and we started to empty out the warehouse that had everything you could imagine stored in it.

As the warehouse was clearing out, I started to smell a slightly pungent and familiar odor. Finally I found 100 barrels of hazardous ammonia leaking into the municipal sewer system through the warehouse drain. The angry truck driver called the Environmental Protection Agency (EPA) and told them that the IRS was dumping toxic poison down the sewers. An EPA Inspector came out and told me he was going to ticket the IRS for this offense. Believe me, I caught hell. Finally higher-ups settled this matter and I got out of the warehouse business.

The IRS collected over $100,000 from the business. The man who sold the business to his friend was found dead about six months later. Someone had pounded in the back of his skull.

I Make Full and Final Demand for Payment

Demanding things like money and tax returns was in my job description. I made demands and expected people to do what I said. I could be the nicest guy in the world, but I carried a big stick in my back pocket - the power to seize and sell your possessions if you disregarded me.

During my first 18 years at the IRS, I was required to make at least one "seizure of property" a month. I made over 100 seizures during my career. These could be a cash register, safe deposit box, house, business, car, truck, boat, RV, any assets, vacation house, stocks or bonds. Some were in the best interests of the taxpayer and the Government. They helped people realize that their businesses were losing money and no longer feasible. Some were, what I would call now, made for the purposes of intimidation and harassment. Everything I did was approved by management and was done under the direction of management. Still, I was the IRS guy doing it.

The problem after the laws changed was that people at the IRS did not change. They just had to find more ways to discreetly hurt people. Rudeness, arrogance and talking down to people are all abuse. Working the cases like you are a robot is another way. IRS Revenue Officers have a huge amount of power, judgment and discretion. At least the old Revenue Officers knew this, but today they want a more homogenized employee which allows for abuse on a whole new level.

I advise people having IRS issues to be patient and in constant contact with the IRS. Don't trust the IRS to do the right thing! Most IRS customers are average people who can't figure out the tax laws which now total 73,854 pages in the Internal Revenue Code, the Regulations, the Revenue Rulings and court cases. It is confusing, contradictory and complex.

Revenue Officer Schickel and the FBI, IRS Criminal, ATF, and DEA

(The Right Hand Does Not Know What the Left Hand is Doing)

Sometimes, I would get into scrapes with other federal agencies who were also working on my cases, unbeknownst to me.

One time, I was going to seize a pizza parlor and it was very routine. I handed the owner my seizure papers and DEA agents stormed in and in the back room found a large quantity of pills and marijuana. They had him under surveillance and were doing an asset forfeiture case. I refused to give the property back, (because remember I was being evaluated for how many seizures I did). So I called in and got an official seizure number and then got the credit for the work and then I turned it over to the IRS attorneys to decide what would happen (The IRS gave it to DEA).

Another time, I was seizing a fleet of trucks and IRS Criminal also wanted the trucks so they came and tried to claim what I had already seized. I was involved in many of these disputes over the years. Once I had a DEA agent running a fake business and I was doing collection action. The fake business had employees and they were not paying the payroll taxes which gave them money to buy drugs that they used to lure (or entrap?) people to buy their drugs so I got into trouble on that case also.

It seems like I was forever being called into a room to meet with FBI, IRS Criminal, ATF, DEA or EPA agents and told to back off. But I never knew any of this beforehand, because that is how the Government works - no one tells any other agency what is going on. The right hand does not know what the left hand is doing.

Competition is fierce during cash or asset seizures, because in the case of forfeitures - the agency who takes it gets part of the money for their budget. It is like a bonus.

IRS Collection never prevailed in these cases. I always had to give stuff back. But I always made sure to get credit for my seizures.

Don't get me wrong, I am lucky to be alive, especially with some of the organized crime figures and their businesses that I was dealing with. I just made field calls. I did not know who these people were or how dangerous they could be.

12

IRS Abuse of Taxpayers

Collection Abuse

I admit, I was one of the abusers. I did not like to think of it at the time. I was working and had bills to pay and I really believed all the training that I had received, that we were doing our duty as citizens to find, pursue and punish delinquent taxpayers. My job required me to violate taxpayer's rights. Those rights were violated because the taxpayers did not know how IRS Collection worked. They did not have the education or money to hire a tax professional and they kept thinking the IRS was going to try to do the right thing in their case. These were horribly naive ideas and they proved to be false. Worse yet, in my official duties, I violated the United States Constitution which calls for due process under the law. And under the Internal Revenue Code at the time, it was all perfectly legal. I hurt people and I am sorry for that now.

Only rich people received due process and then not easily. The judicial system was stacked against the individual or business taxpayer. A friend reminded me of this when he talked about his experiences as a bill collector that repossessed veteran's homes. He said, "I justified what I did then because I had a family to support, bills to pay, and had been promoted into middle management positions, with a dozen other people just waiting to undermine me and get my job. I stopped being a bill collector when two of my customers committed suicide, in the same week. Their worlds were falling apart."

Seven of my taxpayers have killed themselves, dozens more suffered mental breakdowns, attempted suicide or experienced health issues like stroke and heart attacks and some just died. I always liked the cases where the person died, because then I could quickly close my case. I was not the only one that caused their problems. I was just the last one. The last one to take away their money, their home, their business and their pride. I rewarded them with fear, worry, despair and anger - the weak ones did not survive.

When I look back on it now, I see how badly most taxpayers were treated by the IRS. Then I remember specific circumstances where some taxpayers were treated horribly and cruelly by the IRS. Sometimes for no other reason than just to make an example out of them.

IRS Fear

Many times we allow people and institutions such as school (fear we will fail a class), the government, or the IRS (fear that we will be audited) to attract our energy and then they live off of our fears. These institutions have some power over us by law and custom, but we give them even more power with our worry, fear and anger.

Just the thought of the IRS strikes fear and causes illness in people. Sometimes they take it to extreme and unhealthy levels. They develop physical illnesses instead of confronting their tax problem.

I remember one case where a man's mother died and he became depressed, so he stopped filing tax returns. The next year he was afraid because he had not filed the year before, and so on it went. It was ten years before I tracked him down. Again there was a Substitute for Return huge dollar tax assessment. I went to his house and left my card. Very soon afterward he called me in a panic.

He was a high-level manager and he told me he was afraid of the IRS. He did not know what to do and pleaded with me to have mercy on him. He told me in those ten years of his fear of the IRS, he thought that he might be convicted of tax evasion, or put in jail, or that the IRS would seize his house and car and wages. He told me that this fear had destroyed his life. He had developed high blood pressure, Type 2 Diabetes, and back problems. He had had several surgeries and was getting worse. He said he barely slept at night and his sex life was a thing of the past. The fear consumed him. He had a large stack of IRS letters, some certified, that were neatly bound with a rubber band. Yet all the time he held the keys to his release. If he had filed the tax returns, he would be free from the fear. All those years as an employee, he had income tax withholdings that would more than pay for whatever taxes he owed. In fact, when he went to the CPA he found that he had over $120,000 in tax refunds, but because he had not filed within three years of the due date, he lost $90,000.

This man loudly proclaimed how wonderful and amazing I was to just talk plain talk with him about his tax situation. He had allowed it to fester into a huge dark cloud that brought depression, despair and illness to him. He said that talking to me was as if I had arrived in his dark room and lit a match which exposed all his troubles to the light, and it instantly began to dissolve them. As he talked, stories about his late mother came out - about their oppressive relationship and how he was never good enough. When his mother died he allowed the IRS to transfer into her role and belittle him, just like his mother had done.

He said that the unconditional love and understanding that I had shown him overwhelmed the darkness that he had created about the IRS. He was Christian and he was happy that God and the IRS had sent me to work his case because he had been praying for that for years. He said that this work I had done with him also allowed him to forgive his mother and turn her over to God. I heard from him years later. He became very successful and had been promoted several times.

Another man told me after I worked on his case, "Mr. Schickel, I don't know if you believe in Jesus Christ or not, but I have been praying for someone like you to come into my life. I do not eat well, I do not sleep well, sex is just a memory and I am sick from half a dozen ailments. When I would open a letter from the IRS, I would actually vomit. I am blessed that you have changed my life."

Change is also hard because you have to ask. Imagine that you are driving your car on a muddy dirt road and you get stuck in the ruts of the road. You cannot get out of it alone. You need help and support; you need to let someone else in to help you get out. The hardest part is that you will have to trust yourself and you have to decide to trust another person. If you can, in this moment, put out the signal or the intention, you will find that help and support will start to come to you in the form of other people.

I have spoken to many people who are scared and feel abused after their contacts with the IRS. Case decisions have no basis in reasonableness in many cases. They have more to do with teaching a taxpayer a lesson. The thought of collecting money does not come into the equation at all.

Special Classes of Taxpayers

Being labeled an illegal tax protestor (ITP) (a US citizen who refuses to pay taxes based on their own interpretation of the US Constitution and the 16th Amendment) creates another special class of taxpayer that is discriminated against. People who disagree with the Government are heavily penalized and face heavy-handed enforcement. Another designation is Caution on Contact (CAU) which indicates that the taxpayer is hostile and may be physically violent. But you have to remember who is making these reports - it is an IRS employee that may be biased in their viewpoint. There are people who are mentally ill, even deranged and present a physical threat to IRS employees. But the IRS spends a disproportional amount of time working on their cases. By giving so much time, resources and energy to these cases they are actually empowering these tax resistors and their causes. Egregious cases should still be followed, but only in cases where they are actively promoting non-compliance in public forums.

An inaccuracy related penalty can be 20%, (Internal Revenue Code 6662), Civil Fraud Penalty 75% (IRC 6663), and erroneous claim for refund 20% (IRC 6676). Late filing of a return regarded as being frivolous can be another 75% in penalties (IRC 6651 (f)). The IRS has a list of what it describes as frivolous tax positions at www.IRS.gov. If you claim that the Income Tax is illegal or you don't have to pay - that will earn you the penalty. So much for freedom of speech.

Wealthy People Suffer Too

The IRS has a special program that targets wealthy people. It is called the High-Net-Worth-Individuals Audit (HNWIs). The IRS Global Group works on cases involving individuals with income of $10 million or assets over $30 million. The audit begins with the individual's income tax returns and then they look at gift taxes and complicated investment partnerships, businesses and trusts to determine where all the income is coming from and where it is going. This is modeled after the very successful business programs the IRS uses when they assign revenue agents to be in high income businesses year round. This program uses the DIF scoring, but also looks at lifestyle and tries to create a mathematical model and then analyzes it statistically. These audits can go in any direction, depending on what information is requested.

I have had cases where people who are wealthy were discriminated against simply because of their wealth. In one case I had a man who had a penalty of $80,000 simply because his CPA did not follow the law and gave him bad directions because he had been having an affair with the taxpayer's wife and she broke up with him. I had all the documentation needed to abate this under reasonable cause criteria. I wrote up a narrative and then my manager who was not a giving sort of person acknowledged what I had written and approved it. I was a grade 12 and he was a grade 13 - so we are fairly high up in collection. Then I sent it to the service center for the abatement to be processed and I considered it resolved.

A few months later I heard from the taxpayer and they had gotten another balance due letter. Another case of the right hand not knowing what the left hand was doing, I thought.

I tracked the case down and found that supposedly a rejection of the penalty abatement had been sent out - except I, the CPA and the taxpayer should have all received a copy of the letter. No appeal rights were given. I finally talked to the grade 4 employee who took this action and then apparently suppressed their rights - she said "they should pay it just because they are rich already." It took him 3 years to get this resolved to his satisfaction.

I have seen this recently also with another wealthy person asking for abatement of a penalty for $150,000. The request was summarily denied by the Automated Collection Employee, solely because "he is a rich guy he should pay it, no one is giving me a break."

Make an Offer that the IRS Can't Refuse

The Offer in Compromise Program (OIC) has practiced age discrimination for years and has used medical information regarding physical and mental disabilities to determine who would be offered a settlement agreement under this program to set up special classes of taxpayers who benefited from the laws that were used to settle their cases. This means that if you are old or sick, the IRS was more likely to accept an offer from you - without regard to your actual financial situation. Later laws were supposed to change this. One was that they would accept an offer to settle your tax debt, but then if your income went above a certain amount over the next 5 years (future income collateral agreements) or if you did not file and pay your future taxes on time, you would immediately default your offer in compromise settlement agreement and owe all the taxes you originally owed and all the penalty and interest that came along with it.

Future income potential was also attached to these agreements. This actually was a way to make the taxpayer not want to earn anything over a certain IRS approved amount or they would have to pay it all to the IRS. This lead to other forms of tax cheating and hiding income.

The OIC program is chronically mismanaged because the IRS does not endorse the idea of accepting offer or settlements. When I worked OIC cases and wanted to accept them, IRS Management was repelled by the idea. They used to reject 90% of them. We could always find some reason to reject them. This was just mean spirited.

The OIC program is supposed to raise money for the Government - usually money that it otherwise would not have access to. The IRS can take your wages, bank accounts, stocks, bonds and your home as well as other assets that it has filed a lien against. But it cannot take something that is not there. My experience showed that most people had employers, friends and relatives who would loan them money to make the offer so the IRS matter would be resolved. The good news is that the acceptance rate for OIC's in 2013 was up to 41% from 30% the year before.

I had one taxpayer, a reputed mobster with a gambling and drug problem, who owed the IRS $1 million. I was able to negotiate a settlement for $70,000 mostly because he was dying from liver cancer. I suspected he could have paid the whole thing, but he admitted most of his money had gone to gambling, liquor, cocaine and prostitutes over the years. So he borrowed the money from his brother, another alleged mobster. Then he took the $70,000 cash loan to the race track and made large bets and lost all the money.

I was mad, his brother was mad, but he still did not get it. He thought that he would go to the track and double his money through successful bets and then have enough to pay the IRS and give him a new start on life. Never mind about paying his brother back. I learned he died from liver cancer later that year. But it showed me an important message about his perception about money. It is easy in and easy out. He had confidence that more money would always come his way and it always did at least for a while.

IRS Scares Contractors

Sometimes I would have a case with a taxpayer who was a craftsman or construction contractor and it was hard to find out where they were working. So I would watch their house and then follow them to their job site. I would go into a new housing development with my credentials open and look for the guy and it would always be the same. I would hear people just putting their tools down and running out of the half-finished homes and getting in their trucks and getting the hell out of there - word of the IRS arriving made this happen. Another revenue officer would write down the license plates of all the contractors who left and we would track them down and open cases on them also.

Chasing the Bad Guys

The IRS does not always look too hard if they are looking for delinquent taxpayers. In 2012, the IRS closed 483,000 tax accounts because they claimed that they could not locate or contact taxpayers who owed $6.7 billion. This seems like a high number of people that disappeared from the tax rolls. TIGTA thought so too; they said that the IRS did not do their jobs in 57% of the cases. They did not research or use all available information to try to find and contact these people. In 7% of the cases they did not even file a Notice of Federal Tax Lien against them, a very powerful tool that would affect the delinquent taxpayer's ability to get credit, buy a car and hold a job. These people won the IRS Lottery. Sometimes a credit report is ordered, but using an online service like www.peoplefinder.com can find more people than the IRS case investigation does. But all social media sites are blocked from IRS computers, even free resources like www.Zillow.com which provides valuable and free real estate information. But this is how it works – the IRS is cheap - they are penny wise and dollar foolish. They do not order credit reports for cases under a certain dollar amount. They cannot use the free private services found on the internet to find people - because if they even search for them (under this new confused way of thinking) that is disclosure and if they paid for a search that would be illegal procurement.

This happens in part because the IRS does not want to pay for standard searches that most collection agencies pay for. They want to go through each boring task to try to find a person. Just like they used to do before the web and computers came along. One of the requirements before I could close a case was to check a local telephone book. When was the last time that you saw, let alone used a telephone book? You might think this is a good thing. It sure is if you can get yourself lost. But it is not fair and equitable to the other taxpayers who get found and go through the stress of having to deal with the IRS.

This can also happen based on the address that you have on your tax return. If you live in a remote, under-populated area of the United States there is less chance that you will be audited or contacted by a revenue officer. IRS employees call these "tax free zones." Some states only have a couple of dozen employees and cannot drive 5-8 hours just to make a field call. They simply don't have the resources. The IRS has greatly reduced its enforcement presence in these areas and the local people know it. They see neighbors who stop filing and stop paying and nothing happens to them. So they stop filing and paying. When the taxpaying public does not believe that the IRS can hurt them, they tell their friends and neighbors and noncompliance grows exponentially, especially with self-employed people.

It has become more acceptable to not file your taxes or to owe taxes, just like filing bankruptcy seems to carry no stigma anymore either. It is morally acceptable to take what is not yours and then not make amends. Income taxes are taxes on income that you earned and held in your hand at one point.

The Boston Globe in an article dated April 1, 2015 states that "sophisticated tax cheats see the odds improving that they won't get caught. The non-partisan Tax Policy Center says today's IRS is "hopelessly outgunned, especially when it comes to complex areas of the law where aggressive entities can marshal armies of lawyers." In 2014 government enforcement actions brought in $57 billion from dishonest taxpayers. Activity is starting to slow down in IRS Collection, due to lack of employees.

- Notice of Levies (bank and asset seizures) were down 63%
- Notice of Federal Tax Liens were down 15%
- Property Seizures were down 25%

The IRS pays for itself and more - it is one government program where cuts would actually increase the federal deficit."

In the beginning of my career, I was assigned to certain zip codes and towns and I knew people, the bankers, the postmaster, the lawyers and accountants in that area. They helped me find and resolve cases and I helped them by my recognition. The best tax system has local agents and a strong local presence. This is not what the IRS does now. It just sends piles of threatening letters and hope that people pay without any questions asked. Face to face meetings with skilled IRS employees have been replaced by unresponsive employees, who when you can get them on the phone, are officious and act like robots - and are unable and unwilling to help you. Sometimes they don't even know how to help you if they cared to. The IRS is like an unbridled stallion. It is out of control and harms many taxpayers who are trying to resolve their cases.

The longer a person owes a tax, the less likely the IRS is ever to be able to collect any of the balance due. The farther away from the year a tax return is filed, the harder it is to resolve audit issues and to provide records to support your tax return. Many people do keep receipts, but many do not know that most receipts will fade after one year and become unreadable - then the IRS does not allow them in an audit situation.

The IRS has tools which could be used to resolve more cases, but because of institutional and local assumptions, based on prejudice it does not. When managers direct employees to take enforced collection actions based on their bigotry and prejudice it results in the oppression and suppression of rights that each citizen is supposed to have, it is just wrong.

Sometimes, people in the IRS would feel challenged or get scared and forget about civil rights. They would just keep moving forward trying to close their cases. It is one thing to run the tax system based on fear - that is bad, but when Government exploits that fact - like the IRS has, it is a crime.

Managers are well known for doing whatever they can to manipulate inventory statistics. I have seen them create phantom revenue officers to add to their groups to lower their bad case statistics and raise their good statistics.

There were a lot of IRS actions that were abused, like the Notice of Levy before 1998. I would drive to a bank and hand them the levy. Then the banker would freeze their account and type up a check for whatever was in the bank account. This caused great harm to taxpayers and their families and businesses and their employees and the taxpayer had no knowledge of it until days later; no chance to appeal. Sometimes I did this and the account had already been paid and not updated on the computer.

I remember when we went on seizures, it was a time when everyone was pumped up. In the late 1980's they required us to take a portable government telephone with us, in case of emergencies. This phone was in a bag that was as big as a large lunch box. We were all afraid of it and never did get it to work, even when we needed it. It was easier to drive off and find a phone booth. We also carried a tool box called "the Seizure Kit." This contained chains, hammers, chisels, wire, locks and hardware needed to secure a home or business and to rekey its doors. It contained the signs that we would hang on the property that we seized. That sign said in bright red letters:

Warning
United States Government Seizure

This property has been seized for nonpayment of internal revenue taxes due from John Doe by virtue of a levy issued by the District Director of Internal Revenue. Persons tampering with this property in any manner are subject to severe penalty of the law.

I remember two personal residence seizures from tax protesters. I had one and another officer had the other. In his, the taxpayer burned down his own fully furnished house to prove a point. He also cancelled the house insurance. I told the other officer he should buy a fire insurance policy on the house in the Governments name. But his manager refused. The IRS can be very short sighted. So the $165,000 dollar house went up in smoke and so did all the equity that the IRS had seized.

In my case, my taxpayer was also a tax protester. He burned down his house after I seized it, but then I issued a levy to his insurance company and collected a nice check for $79,000.

Some revenue officers preferred to use very large and heavy tow chains. They would go into a restaurant or dry cleaners or other retail business and put the chain through the front doors and then chain them together and not let anyone leave until they had paid their bill to the IRS officer. I was always amazed at how much cash we would collect on these - we would call cash register seizures "milk runs" and save them for Fridays as a special end to the week. I remember the business owners pulling cash out of false panels in the floor, ceiling and wall and from hidden safes.

We were under some pressure regarding our seizures before the laws changed in 1998 regarding what we called "perishable goods sales." This meant we were selling something that had to be sold quickly before its value was lost, this would apply to livestock, food, frozen food, flowers etc. We would secretly go to the neighbors or the competitors in the business and tell them that we would be holding a public auction and that if they came and had cash they would get a good deal. There was never any advertising, it was all done in 1-3 days; no rights to observe. No people to get in the way of the powerful IRS seizure machine. Thinking about it now, I can't believe we did that. Setting up secret "public" sales to people we chose at fire sale prices.

When we did seizures of automobiles, the taxpayer always wanted to get back into the car and jam the keys in the ignition and race to get it out of there. That is why I always had the tow truck on one side and my car on the other side to block it in. One day a man told me he had to get his "personal items out of the car." Those included a gun and some marijuana. I caught him and made him drop it on the seat of the car. Then I got the police. That was when we still could, and I did not need to argue with the cop over him trying to seize it. Another time, I remember a man who was connected to organized crime jumping into his car that was under seizure and started it and bumped the tow truck out into the street and drove away. I never did find that car, I always wondered if there was something in the trunk that he did not want me to see - like a body. After that, I always retrieved any of their personal items out of the car myself.

I do feel bad about another man who loved his brand new, paid for in cash, red 1984 Cadillac Coupe DeVille. It was a beautiful car. I arrived with my team and the tow truck driver. This man appeared to be on drugs or something and he was screaming and finally he spit on me cursing me in Italian. The car was parked on a long concrete driveway, about 40 feet from the street. I had the car blocked in and got police back up. Then I put the parking brake on and I had the tow truck driver stay in the street and then I had him drag the car down the driveway leaving a thick layer of those rubber tires on the driveway for him to see day after day. It was just easier than calling TIGTA and complaining that I had been assaulted. I guess I fell under that spell of IRS Magic that what happens in the field stays in the field and is never discussed. When I almost got in trouble I blamed the tow truck driver. I feel bad about that now.

Restaurants were always hard to collect from. So what I trained new revenue officers to do to collect was to have a friend go in and have a meal and then pay by credit card. This allowed IRS to track the credit card processor the taxpayer used. Then we would levy the credit card processor and cut off 50-70% of his receipts; very creative and very effective and also legal.

The IRS was and perhaps still is culturally insensitive. In my initial training class, the only Spanish we were taught was "Pay or we seize everything."

One day I disagreed with my manager on some action he was telling me to do to hurt some taxpayer. I refused to do it. Furthermore, I went into my manager's office and told him that he was an abusive jerk and that he should crawl back into whatever sewer he had come out of. I left the office and got drunk. The next day he called me into his office and I was afraid of the worst. He congratulated me and told me that he was proud of me for having the nerve to talk to him like that. Remember good is bad and bad is good in the IRS.

Closing a Case as in Business - Currently Not Collectible

I remember one older lady and her husband who had a construction company. He got sick and the housing collapse hit and they ran up taxes; after filing and paying for 65 years they now owed Uncle Sam. He was a twice decorated veteran with service in the South Pacific and elsewhere. They had nothing; he had a yard full of old construction equipment of little value. I advised them to shut down the business, sell the assets and walk away from it, and I would not pursue them personally for the employment taxes, due to the circumstances. At one point she had her son who helped in the business leave our meeting. She said "Mr. Schickel, I understand what you are saying. I could sell the assets of the business to our son and give the IRS the proceeds, but Junior is just not ready yet." She was 89 and Junior was 58. I closed that case as an in business 53 currrently not collectible account.

I have had many delinquent taxpayers who did business and did it well for years and then the market changed and they were left behind. In the case of construction companies, most buy heavy equipment under the old way of thinking - you would buy everything and just hope more and more jobs would come to you. Modern businesses tend to lease everything instead.

Sometimes a business cannot make any payments towards the delinquent taxes, but they can pay the current taxes. If it is a viable business, where they are paying current taxes, then the IRS can close the case as "in business currently not collectible (Status 53)." That means that the Government lets them stay in business as long as you can pay the current taxes. But they stay in business without having an IRS installment agreement. The reason for this is that then you and your employees are not unemployed and dragging on the system. But the IRS hates to close cases this way.

Exigent Circumstances Seizure

There is a special type of seizure that is used when the taxpayer is preparing to move or hide assets beyond the Governments reach. It is called a seizure due to exigent circumstances.

I heard of this only once in my career. A revenue officer had made a field call to a gift store on a Wednesday and talked to the owner and gotten some information and then they were supposed to meet the next week. On Saturday, the revenue officer was off work and pulled up to the bakery which was next to this store and saw a large moving truck and people loading up everything that was in the store. He had the case file and he wrote a Notice of Levy; normally his manager would have to sign off on it also. This was in the days before cell phones or email, but he was always well versed in the Internal Revenue Manual. When the truck was almost loaded, he called the local police and his favorite towing company and told them that he was going to seize the moving truck and everything in it. So just when they had finished, he pulled his car in front of the truck, blocking it in. Then he served the papers on the taxpayer who was screaming bloody murder. Then he had the truck towed away.

The taxpayer's intent was to place the assets beyond the reach of the Government. He caught a lot of heat from his manager, but the seizure was legal and the goods were sold at a public auction.

Tax Professionals Abused

One of the big gifts the IRS receives is the hundreds of thousands of tax preparers, enrolled agents, accountants, CPAs and tax attorneys and they are all doing the work of the IRS. It is like a secondary work force that directly benefits the IRS. They are highly educated, knowledgeable and professional and the IRS treats them like dirt. I have learned this in my own experience doing tax consulting and tax resolution privately. Compliance in a town or neighborhood always rises after the IRS takes an enforced collection action that becomes public. But the IRS does not treat tax professionals very well. They blanket them with deadlines and rules and regulations that make life difficult for everyone.

They have limited and poor electronic access to the IRS records for their clients and often have to wait on hold on the telephone for 1-2 hours to resolve a single case.

What Happens in the Field?

Revenue Officers and Revenue Agents want to come into taxpayers' homes and businesses without a court issued writ of entry. Never let them in. They are looking for ways to harm you and your business. I suggest that you speak to them at their office, preferably with a tax professional by your side. You would be amazed at how carefully the IRS agents speak when a lawyer, CPA or Enrolled Agent is in the room or if they know that they are being recorded. Versus how they speak to you in the office or in the field.

A Sound and Legal Way to Close Cases

Having a large inventory of cases caused me to be well versed with the laws. I will admit to being very creative in coming up with ways to close cases. One method that I used was what I called the "poor man's bankruptcy." Many businesses are organized as corporations, or limited liability companies (LLC). When they are in business, they can close, sell all the assets of that entity and then distribute the proceeds to their creditors, including the IRS. This has the same effect as going through bankruptcy. Some of the creditors may get judgments, but most won't. That is why having a corporate shield is such a great thing in the long run, if things go wrong with a business. The IRS will treat an out of business sole proprietorship or corporation more leniently than one that is still in business.

This does not make the IRS taxes go away. If the corporation owes $100,000 in employee withholding taxes, then by closing the corporation, the corporation still owes all the taxes. It is an entity by itself. But the corporation does not own anything. So it does not matter. The IRS will come after responsible officers for employment taxes - but when the business is closed they will only come after you for half the Social Security and Medicare and the income taxes withheld. So the Government will only come after you personally for 60-70% of the taxes owed. This is 7.65% for Medicare and Social Security and 20% income tax withholding. But it does bring you into a special class of taxpayers when businesses are closed. The IRS treats the matter differently and this opens up a number of payment and non-payment options.

The best part of this is that if you were a tradesman or salesman, you still are. You were a painter before and you closed your corporation. Now, you are still a painter. You can start a new business or work for yourself. I advocate that people who get into trouble with the IRS seek a tax professional who can guide them in this method. It does not work for businesses that have fixed assets required to produce income, like a concrete factory. This cannot be done for purposes of fraud. You cannot sell the assets to a friend or family member or for less than their full fair market value. You cannot spend the sales proceeds in an unreasonable manner. You have to deliver the proceeds to the IRS; then you will find the law gives you some breathing room. The IRS wants you back in compliance, so generally you can expect a hard time if you do this more than once.

Employment Tax Abuse

When deciding who I would personally assess for employment taxes (IRC6672) I was trained to assess everyone who was associated with the business. The philosophy was "shoot em' all and let God sort it out." I assessed everyone personally, even if I had no proof that they were responsible for the delinquent taxes. We all did that before 1998.

Collection Statute Waiver Abuse

Sometimes, I would also force taxpayers to sign waivers extending the amount of time the IRS had to collect, the taxes sometimes 25-50 years into the future. The law had changed in 1998, which ended that, but think how demoralizing and abusive this was to the taxpayer to know they were bound to the IRS for the rest of their lives.

Penalty Assessment and Abatement Abuse

Penalty assessment is big business at the IRS. The IRS even admits it. The IRS assesses penalties which are subjective and punitive as a deterrent to stop behaviors it does not like, like filing and paying taxes late. But there is also a penalty called failure to pay which is assessed even when a taxpayer is actually paying on an installment plan.

Two Secrets the IRS Does Not Advertise

Tens of billions of dollars are assessed in penalties every year. The IRS has the power to take away these penalties, based on two circumstances. "First Time Delinquent Penalty Waiver" where a taxpayer claims this was the first time they had had this problem and it was just one year. See Internal Revenue Manual (IRM) 20.1.1.3.6.1 at www.IRS.gov. Most penalties, and even interest can be abated.

A second way is to claim "reasonable cause" for penalty abatement. This can be found at www.IRS.gov in IRM 20.1.1.3.2A and explains how to establish that. Then you ask for the penalty to be abated based on your reasons such as your tax accountant told you bad information or you suffered from an embezzlement from your bookkeeper. Or you suffered from a theft or loss due to a hurricane or other disaster. Death, illness, being out of the country or in jail, fires, casualty, civil disturbance, tornados, hurricanes, floods and an inability to get records needed to file returns are all causes for penalty abatement. Many penalties can be abated when the IRS is in the mood to be reasonable.

Many taxpayers are told by IRS employees that penalties cannot and are never abated. Or that you have to pay the penalty first and then file an 843 Claim Form. The IRS information I have obtained shows that between 1989 to 1993 the IRS did abate about 40% of the penalties that it assessed. But you have to ask for it. In collection, they use a system called Reasonable Cause Assistant (RCA) - this is supposed to take the subjectivity out of penalty abatement. But it is not accurate, and punitive with its determinations and wrong at least 70% of the time, in my experience. No matter what the IRS employee tells you, the RCA can be overruled. (IRM 20.1.1.3.6.10.1) at www.IRS.gov. It is only as good as the instructions in its programming. For instance, the IRS will abate penalties in cases of embezzlement. But that RCA system states that embezzlements must have been discovered in 6 months for this to be allowed. It is unfair, arbitrary and capricious.

The bottom line is you have nothing to lose and the penalty amount to gain if you just file an appeal asking for penalty abatement due to your circumstances. Anything that affected your life may be used to help get the penalties abated. Your mental or physical health, your substance abuse - legal or illegal, etc.

The IRS is horribly negligent in not promoting this. It does not advertise it anywhere on their computer system, www.IRS.gov or any information about "First Time Penalty Abatement" and "Reasonable Cause for Penalty Abatement". Knowing this secret can save you big money.

There are 140 penalty provisions in the Internal Revenue Code. Accuracy related penalties are up 800% for the period 2005-2010.

Also in 2013, the IRS assessed individual and employment penalties for inaccuracy, bad checks, late filing, failure to make estimated tax payments, and failure to pay penalty and fraud. These penalties were assessed against 37.9 million taxpayers.

In 2013 the IRS assessed taxpayers almost $26 billion in penalties. But they ended up taking away 4.9 million penalties amounting to $11,458,194. This is important - when the taxpayers challenged the penalties - the IRS backed down 13-30% of the time. This is another IRS secret. Never automatically accept and pay a notice or adjustment from the IRS. Never! The IRS might be wrong or back down if you protest.

Jeopardy and Termination Assessments

One time I was called to a bank by the local police, because they had received a tip that a severed human head was in an oversized safe deposit box. After the bank and police opened the box, they found $3 million in brand new $100 bills. They relocked the box and called the IRS. I was the guy answering the phone that day.

When large amounts of cash are found and there is no explanation for where it came from or if tax has been paid on that money it causes the IRS to think that if you have $3 Million in cash sitting in a bank then you must have had at least $10 Million to start. So they do a Jeopardy and Termination Assessment to legally assess a tax against the money, not the person. The IRS assumes that it is illegal gain from a criminal enterprise. Actually the way the law works if you pay income taxes on your income legal or not, you are likely to avoid prison for tax evasion. The IRS said the tax on that money was $3 Million- unless the box holder could explain that the money had already been taxed.

On the day I made the cash seizure, the bank officer opened the box and I pulled the small backpack out stuffed with the money. All brand new $100 bills from the Federal Reserve Bank - still wrapped in the plastic. *Brand new bills*! It made me wonder what corrupt bank official was involved in this operation.

Part of me wanted to grab the backpack and run out the door. I can be *so human* sometimes. Thank God there were two armed guards blocking the exit. The box owner had sent a prominent criminal attorney to watch me count the money twice and then I handed him a receipt and papers explaining what would happen to the money. He said that was fine, his client had just wanted to make sure that the IRS got the full $3 Million. I have a feeling that this had serious consequences for someone somewhere.

IRS Seizure and Sale Abuse Cases

TIGTA issued a report stating that 30% of the seizures that the IRS conducted were illegal. Before the laws changed in 1998, I would issue a summons requiring a person to appear before me to give me tax information. At the same time I would have some of my fellow revenue officers in the parking lot towing away their car. I only did this in extreme circumstances. Some people would come back in screaming that their new car had been stolen. I remember one guy who was so sad that I gave him a dollar for bus fare just to make him leave my office. I remember other revenue officers would admire a ring or expensive bracelet, necklace or watch and then the taxpayer would take it off and hand it to them and then they would seize it.

I know one revenue officer who had a writ of entry to do a seizure signed by the judge. She got to the business and then the taxpayer who was a personal friend of the judge had the judge call them and rescind his order. The judge said if they did not leave right then they would be held in contempt of court and jailed. The revenue officers left.

Another time this same revenue officer was at an attorney's office and he went wild and pulled the phone cord out of the wall and locked the door and refused to let the revenue officer out for 6 hours.

Sometimes during a field call we would see things that were illegal: cocaine, marijuana, pills, porn, guns and sex toys littered around the house. Some houses had mold, excessive pets and vermin and looked like an episode of Hoarders. Very sad. We never knew what we were walking into. But we were prohibited from saying anything about this to other agencies after the law changed in 1998, and we had a gag order not to talk to other agencies. We were really always focused on closing the case. Doing the right thing was further down on the list.

Seizure Harassment

The IRS enforces the tax laws made by the United States Congress. The application of laws is variable and broadly applied to every situation. That is why those people, the IRS employees, charged with enforcing that law, measure the quality of the strength and mercy in a law. Most are professional, honest, fair and caring, and they seek to serve the Government as well as the taxpayers who pay their salaries. Some, though, are ignorant, uneducated, mean and aggressive.

IRS Abuse Nearly Destroyed This Woman's Life

There is a case of a woman who was a prominent and wealthy corporate attorney. She had no family and was very private, but she contacted me and consented to allow me to generally relate the circumstances of her story.

She was married to a man who was the greatest love of her life, she once told me. She had been making a lot of money from day trading, buying and selling stocks and making short-term profits. When he died, her world died along with him. She stopped working and was unable to cope with daily life. She could not even bring herself to open the mail or pay bills. She had a 200 acre ranch worth $1 million, a $200,000 house that was paid for, and a very large retirement account. She should have been set for life. Then the IRS got involved in her life.

I sent her letters and I tried to contact her. I went to her house several times, but she was not there. I left my calling card, but still no response. I did my research and knew something major must have happened in her life.

Since her husband died she failed to pay $60,000 in real estate taxes and lost the million dollar ranch. She owed $13,000 to her homeowners association and owed property taxes on her personal residence. The neighbors I spoke with knew that she was depressed and very private. No one knew how to get in touch with her.

One day I stopped by the house and found her chasing her dog down the street. We talked and she invited me into the house. I felt like I was entering a museum to her late husband. His Mercedes was in the garage and his golf clubs were in the corner with his golf hat on top of them. He had returned from golf one afternoon, sat down in his cattle longhorn chair and poured himself three fingers of Scotch. Then he died. Everything was exactly as it had been on that day. Except now a bust of him wearing his cowboy hat sat in the chair. It felt like he was still there in spirit.

There were piles of mail dumped on the floor by what year it was received. None of it had ever been opened. She allowed me to dig though the piles to show and explain the letters we had sent her. In one letter was a subpoena to appear in Federal court to force her to show where her assets were held. The IRS was going to seize her house, cars and retirement account. It was at that point, that I had received the case. I stood before the court and the woman brought in all the records I needed to get started. However, she still did not have the records needed to prepare corrected returns. I had her financial statements, but I did not want to take her house or anything else, until I was sure we had a correct tax assessment. I wanted to do the right thing even if it delayed the IRS case processing.

She was sobbing at the conference table as I went into the small courtroom. She gave me what was needed for that day and the judge released her back to IRS jurisdiction. I felt sorry for her being trampled by the big fear machine. My group manager had come that day and was upset that she did not go to jail for contempt of court. That always pleased him - to see people in jail for not cooperating with the IRS. He used to talk about how Collection needed to "draw a line in the sand" and "show people who was in charge".

She was so overwrought with anxiety and depression. It was hard for both of us. I said a quick prayer for the situation to remain calm and it did.

One day, when I had determined I was going to go out of my way and assist this poor helpless, depressed soul, I was called into my manager's office. The manager in charge of IRS Collection for Arizona and the Senior Manager of Collection for the fourteen Western States were both there to review this case. They told me to seize the IRA account and the house and the cars. I said No! I said that she had mental health issues and was under treatment with a psychiatrist. The big boss admonished me, "You are not a doctor! What do you care? She is an attorney and it will look good if we can jail her." I said I had seen a doctor's note reviewing her mental condition. Then the bosses all ganged up on me and told me again to do it. I did not want to be insubordinate, so I said, "If you order me in writing to do that and put it in the case history, I will do it. But I will continue to advocate for this woman through her Senators, her Congressman and the IRS Taxpayer Advocate." Management never did put that order in writing because then when it became a public relations nightmare-it would reflect back on them, not me. Doing the wrong thing does not let me sleep well at night so I do the right thing when I can.

I drove out to the woman's house again and handed her a summons to produce the missing records. At this point, the records were so old that the brokerage house did not even have them anymore and the IRS did not even have a copy of the original return. This should have been a problem if we had to go into a court of law and prove the IRS claim, but in Arizona it was not ruled significant. Southern Arizona did many strange things with the IRS laws.

I went to her house for two days and dug through piles of dirty, dusty records. I finally found enough financial information to figure out her taxes myself. I gave her a receipt and took them all back to the office to secure them. It took me two months to go through them and I discovered that the only person making money in that brokerage account was the broker. This is common for day traders I've worked with.

The most shocking part was that a few years before, the IRS had sent her a letter advising her that they were issuing a backup withholding order that required her stockbroker to do back up withholding, or 28% of the value of her account needed to be liquidated to pay to the IRS on her behalf, but she had never opened that letter. She should have been exempt, but she had not responded.

Her IRA account was $4 million at the beginning of the week. Which consisted of $2 million cash and $2 million on margin (borrowed from the brokerage house for investment purposes.) The IRS back up withholding order was issued which required the broker to pay in 28% of the value of the account to the IRS. The broker was afraid of the IRS but was legally required to do what was ordered.

The broker had to liquidate the stocks and send the IRS $1,120,000 within a two-day period. The broker issued a margin call which meant if she did not have more money to put into her account they would start selling stocks to protect their loan. She lost another $2.1 million due to those sales and commissions. (Because she was heavily invested in small startup companies' stocks.) The stock she sold made other investors sell their stock as well. The stock sales almost triggered a stock collapse of two small companies. Everyone thought that bad news about the companies must be circulating so a selling spree of their stocks was triggered as well. Then the remaining stocks lost an additional $780,000 in value over three days. The brokerage house sent her letters at the time, but again, since she did not open any letters, she did not respond. The woman lost $3,758,000 in a week. She suffered a second nervous breakdown after that.

All this happened without the IRS ever contacting her in person and offering due process rights or giving her any appeal rights and without the case ever having been seen by an IRS employee.

Then nothing happened because she did not yet have a tax assessment against her, but she was left with only $242,000 in her brokerage account. She had several hundred thousand dollars in other bank accounts. Due to her emotional instability, she was incapable of working.

The IRS stopped receiving tax returns from her so they made up bogus tax returns for her under the Substitute for Return Program (SFR). In two years, the IRS assessed her $4.5 million in taxes. They based this on all the stock sales that she made, but because the IRS did not know what was paid for the stocks, it was a very unjust calculation. The tax balances were legally assessed, and due and owing to the United States Government. That is when I entered the picture.

The SFR program produces huge tax assessments for people who have failed to file returns, but when this happens they do not get credit for any deductions or filing status. It is very harmful to anyone who is assessed under the program. The IRS does this right before a Notice of Federal Tax Lien is filed which destroys one's credit for ten years.

Although the Internal Revenue Code does have exceptions for financial hardship situations, if the person cannot advocate for himself or herself and cannot prepare forms and financial statements required by the IRS, there is no one who can help them. The IRS just plods along like a hungry bulldozer gobbling up assets without regard to ethical correctness.

Before I received the case, the IRS seized the money from the other bank accounts. I estimate she lost $400,000 there alone.

Eventually, I was able to gather the required records and the woman connected with a sympathetic CPA who prepared corrected tax returns. Instead of owing taxes she actually was due refunds for the years that the IRS had assessed. However, if you do not file a tax return within three years of its due date, you lose your refunds without recourse - forever. When all was said and done, she had over $800,000 in lost refunds.

She is not alone. I have worked many such cases of people who are afraid or unable to respond to the IRS requests and demands. They either cannot or will not. Some had physical or mental illness. It does not matter because the IRS will continue taking what they can find for at least the next ten years. This is just one case where fear of the IRS, or incompetence, lead to a person's ruin.

This woman's case was abuse but it is a story of healing. Because of the caring and compassion that resulted from my connection to her case, her earlier cases were resolved with her owing nothing and the $4.5 million tax assessment was mostly wiped away.

She only recently has come out of the depression and anxiety that was directly induced by the IRS. She credits me with helping relieve her fears with my belief that she could overcome her IRS nightmare and get back to some degree of functional life. She said that I was doing what God would do if he were in a body "loving my neighbor." She calls me every year or so and thanks me for the relief that she received through my service. Similar instances of gratitude and relief have happened many times during my casework. She told me last year that she is ready to work for other taxpayers to prevent this from happening in their lives also.

Then in 2015 she called me and told me that the Justice Department had come after her for $7,000 for court costs related to the summons enforcement action seven years ago. Because she was still unable to take care of simple business matters, the U.S. Attorney from the Justice Department got an order to have her arrested for contempt of court. So six Federal Marshals along with search dogs descended on her house and arrested her. They took her away in handcuffs and ankle cuffs and chained them together. She is 62 years old now and weighs about 100 pounds. Then she went before the Court and was jailed. The harassment never ends.

13

Audit Abuse

How the IRS Picks Who They Will Audit

The top secret computer program - Discriminant Index Function, (DIF) is used to compare all tax returns and then select those that are variations over the median for audit. Each return gets a DIF Score (Discriminate Index Function). This is a mathematical technique used to score returns for examination potential. The highest scored returns qualify for audit. That score will always be reviewed and if it is high enough you might get audited. The way this works is all the tax returns are processed and then categorized by the industry, type of business and similarities with other taxpayers in your same income level. Then the computer comes up with what it sees as similarities and difference. It comes up with a standard mean. They may look at returns that were filed by a certain tax preparer, or that were prepared by hand or those that rounded numbers up. Say from $24,999.57 to $25,000.

The program is very secretive and very subjective. Every year it focuses on a new group of taxpayers and businesses. The DIF system which chooses what returns are audited is top secret. DIF examiners do not know why a case has been pulled for review, so they use their experience and judgment to subjectively decide what issues will be covered in the audit and for how many years. Many of the leads prove to be unproductive.

I believe taxpayers have the right to know their DIF score in the same way they know their credit score. This would remove a lot of fear from the system.

The information is drawn from the DIF, National Research Project (NRP) and special return projects. The NRP uses a statistical draw of a number of returns. The draw is done using Social Security numbers and employer identification numbers.

This can involve cases that are partnerships, sole proprietorships, corporations and high income individuals. Or it can be to look at a certain item on the tax return - like interest, or employee expenses or home office deduction. The cases can also be selected by type of industry or type of business, like doctors, realtors, butchers, truckers or construction companies. These yield a higher rate of increased tax assessment than DIF cases alone. Usually in these cases 80% of the audits result in increased tax assessments.

Some of this comes from Market Segment Specialization Program (MSSP) and the Industry Specialization Program (ISP); this tracks all the statistics on a return divided up by the code listed on the form as to the type of business. Both programs accumulate statistics and come up with a mathematical equation of what is the standard deviation above or below the mean. Cases that do not fit this model will trigger an audit inquiry. Some can be easily explained with an audit letter and proof of the questioned expense. The National Research Program (NRP) is a comprehensive effort by the IRS to measure compliance for different types of taxes and various sets of taxpayers. It establishes a sample tax return for each type of tax that it claims is representative of the whole taxpayer population.

Two special programs called the High Income Fast Track Initiative (HIRTI) and another called the High Under Reported Income Program (which strangely does not have an acronym) both case certain cases to be put on the top of the pile of field cases to be worked. Both have a high potential for a lot of additional tax and for potential fraud case development.

There is also the secret Unreported Income Discriminant Function System, (UIDIF). This is a system that analyses tax returns in comparison with data from other returns and makes statistical comparisons as to the likelihood that there is unreported income. This could be more accurate if the IRS would share information with other agencies like county assessors and to compare the taxes paid and value of real estate, but they do not.

The National Research Project (NRP) also separates cases as "Abusive Tax Schemes and Transactions." This is for taxpayers or tax preparers who appear to be committing fraud. The NRP also segregates "High Income High Wealth" taxpayers, and "High Income Non-Filers." Some of these cases are worked by Special Enforcement Program (SEP) Agents. These employees are not to be taken lightly. They sometimes do not even make contact with the people they are investigating and just start issuing summons to collect date and issue levies to seize whatever they find.

Many new audits could be stopped and the cases closed using a method called "Survey without Taxpayer Contact." This can occur when a taxpayer is known to be in bankruptcy, when a taxpayer has suffered extreme hardship or illness or the taxpayer is deceased. The decision to survey a case is based on the professional judgment of the examiner. The IRS does not use normal industry standard practices for case building which allows it to waste Government resources auditing people and companies that should not be audited. That is why cases are closed as audited but "no change," (meaning that the return is accepted as filed by the taxpayer) or audited with an increased refund due to the taxpayer. Twenty percent of all cases are "no change" or give the taxpayer more money back. All cases can be surveyed (put on the shelf and never worked) based on the professional judgment of the Examiner. If they just had access to more information, it would make the system operate better.

The IRS can manage its inventory if they used this "survey a case" option. They currently use it to close cases without action because of resource limitations. (i.e. no money or employees to work the cases.)

Taxpayer Compliance Measurement Program Audits (TCMP) (now replaced by the NRP) and Return Preparer Audit Projects (RRAP) are audits that the IRS uses to determine how much of what is filed is accurate and is a statistical project that gives the IRS data as to who files and if what they file is accurate. It targets a certain group of taxpayers and businesses.

I have worked on one of these audit projects. We had sixteen employees who targeted an eight block area in Chicago. We went door to door and in every business and every house, we stopped everyone, and asked them their name, address and Social Security number or employer identification number. We wrote down their information. We wrote down license plate numbers of all the cars on the street and around the business. We were told by IRS Management, that if someone was not home or did not reply to us, we should return with a summons requiring them to come to our office and provide detailed information. We were looking for people who had never filed, who had underreported income, and people who were not in the system at all. We looked at their homes, apartments, circumstances to determine that they were appropriate for their reported income levels. These audits required that you prove everything on your tax return: birth certificate, Social Security card, marriage certificate, divorce decree, driver's license, and military discharge papers, rent receipts, mortgage papers, school records and immunizations shots for your children and proof for every expense. If you did not have it, the auditors raised your tax balances on the spot.

In those days it was still possible to not have a Social Security number and be self-employed. Today a Social Security number is required for infants before they even leave the hospital. In 1987, every person who was listed as a dependent age 5 and over on a tax return was required to post a Social Security number. In that year 7 million dependents disappeared. Many were believed to be household pets!

In 1990 every child over the age of 1 was required to have a Social Security number and then in 1997 even newborns were required to have one.

The IRS Can't Tell You How to Do Business

Many taxpayers think that the Internal Revenue Code says that you cannot deduct expenses from "hobbies." If you conduct your business like a real business, devote a certain amount of hours to it a week, and are "profit motivated," keep good records, then you will probably be able to defend the business expenses in an audit. One myth is that you need to make a profit in three out of five years in business. This is not true. The Government cannot tell you how to run your business. If you are formally conducting your business as advised by a tax professional, then maybe it will take you longer to make a profit. If you spend more money in the early years, you may be establishing yourself in your market. It is important to know that I have observed many tax professionals who are so conservative with their tax advice that they are doing a disservice to their clients. If you have a legitimate business expense put it on the tax return. The chance of you being questioned about are only 1% (chance of an audit) but now due to a declining work force the IRS will not even be able to keep up with that low number.

Big Corporations - Big Tax Assessments

The IRS prefers to use the resources of its accountants in the Large and Mid-Size Business Division in a program called the Coordinated Industry Case (CIC) program. This is where the IRS identifies 1600 of the largest businesses in the United States and assigns agents to do almost continuous audits on them. In fact, 800 large businesses in the United States have revenue agents who report to their corporate headquarters every day. I remember one huge international corporation provided beautiful office space and even a secretary to the revenue agents. One agent told me that for every revenue agent there were twenty-four high priced accountants that worked for the corporation that monitored what they were doing. We usually only saw those employees once a year at the Christmas party. But it was eerie, because the IRS was required to provide them with a desk in the IRS building so I knew of whole floors with empty cubicles, no employees, just managers and secretaries. This is a very successful program. It is said that it only takes up 20% of IRS examination resources but yields two-thirds of the proposed tax adjustments.

Knock, Knock – I'm from the IRS

One landmark study reported by U. S. News and World Reports stated that in 1953 of the 8,800 people surveyed in New England, 1,150 had failed to file a tax return for 1952. Agents collected $242,000 in payments, including $80,000 paid while agents were at the door. U.S. News and World Reports quoted one manager who said, "Even more striking, another $162,000 came from worried non-filers who rushed to pay before agents reached their door steps. One IRS office had 1,200 people lined up at its office before it opened the next morning. In the New England area, 13% of the taxpayers turned out to be delinquent. In Rhode Island, the delinquency rate was 34%."

IRS Commissioner T. Coleman Andrews was proud of the IRS agents' work. He said that the IRS had "collected $24 for every $1 it spent." In those days, before the Internal Revenue Code changed in 1954, the auditors and collectors did pretty much the same work. This caused an atmosphere that was ripe for fraud.

Years later Commissioner Andrews left for a job in the private sector. He told a reporter in April, 1956 "I don't believe in the Government reaching down into your pocket and taking money by force, by police state methods, which is what the IRS is doing everyday under our tax system."

Audit and RRA 98

RRA 98 was directed at Collection, but also impacted the audit staff. Not correctly reporting your income can result in additional taxes and not trying too hard to find a taxpayer who has moved is the frequent cause of large, mysterious and surprise tax assessments. Each auditor may have pet peeves that they will question on every case - meals and entertainment expense and travel mileage, gas receipts and mileage logs. The crazy part is on the tax return they will see income and then a line that says Cost of Goods Sold (that is almost never used correctly) but that is another long story. So say you have a million in income and $800,000 cost of goods sold. This large mysterious number is $800,000, but the IRS will only question what you did with the remaining $200,000. In that $800,000 number I have seen luxury items, vacation home expenses, rent and a car payments for the girlfriend of the corporate president. No one questions it as a matter of routine until you are audited.

We Liked Your Old Address Better

Worse are the audits that happen because the taxpayer never received notice and had no chance to appeal an audit. The auditor really has no incentive to actually find you and talk to you and get information. He sends notices to your old address and then of course you do not respond. Because you were never found and notified, he can close his case faster. This is an old auditor's trick. Say you were audited for 2008. In 2009 the IRS received 19.3 million pieces of mail that were undeliverable - many of them audit notices. You thought everything was fine for that year; you remember getting a refund. You have moved several times but always file a return. But the IRS sent the notice to your 2009 address and the mail was not forwarded. So they went ahead and assessed you $20,000 in new tax that year. You have moved and only were told by an IRS person to keep your records for 3 years. So you throw out those records in 2012. Now you find a Notice of Federal Tax Lien is showing up on your name filed in some far away county. You are so screwed, you just don't know it yet. Constructing those old records is next to impossible and this is the first you heard of it in 2014. This is a common nightmare I have seen many times.

The chief reason for this is when you move you can change your address over the phone with your creditors. The IRS does not allow this; you cannot change your address over the internet or on the phone. It must be in writing using Form 8822. Most people assume the IRS knows where they are because they still file every year. But that is not the fact.

Employee business expenses should be reasonable compared to occupation and income. The Internal Revenue Manual states that cases are to be reviewed with "heavy reliance on discretion, judgment and experience." But it is important to remember that the Government cannot actually tell you how to run your business. It cannot penalize you if you make bad business choices and end up losing money.

Many people in the IRS are new and lack the experience, judgment skills and are unable to comprehend the powers their positions hold. IRS employees do not have the time or motivation to use common sense to work out reasonable solutions to tax cases. In my work and with all the auditors that I have known, the most important characteristic is to be able to investigate, make a judgment and then move on. It is also important to be reasonable. That is what is lost in the IRS today. They are micromanaging their employees into a state of paralysis.

TIGTA reports that more than 62% of all audits selected from the Discriminate Index Function (DIF) were closed with no change. No increase in tax at all. This is a waste of Government resources. Clearly the IRS needs a better formula to determine where fraud and abuse is in the tax returns it audits.

Returns for regular income tax returns usually have no changes or an increased refund to the taxpayer in 20% of the cases.

In 1994, the IRS was conducting audits which were known as lifestyle/financial status audits and they matched up your living circumstances to what income you reported. For instance if you have three houses and cars and a wealthy lifestyle and report income of only $100,000 a year it raises serious questions about how you can afford to do that. I worked on projects where we pulled information on high dollar real estate transactions that were paid for in cash or with large cash down payments, we also summoned car dealerships to get records on individual who paid all cash for their cars. An offshoot of that was the car dealerships were not reporting this, and that led to charges against them as well. I personally loved these audits. When people are living beyond their visible means it can trigger an audit.

Sometimes their own jealous friends, family and neighbors will turn them in. I have witnessed many audits where a taxpayer will show business losses of $80,000 but show no income, and show mortgage interest paid on a million dollar house of $76,000 and car payments on luxury cars of $35,000 a year and then reported income of $40,000. The auditor would ask how they did that and they would be confused. Some would start talking and the story they told was always interesting. Some reported that they spent as much as they took in so they did not have to even file income tax returns. I always counsel anyone to report all of their income as required by law. But to be smart, at least report the amount of your expenses. If the IRS can track you spending $15,300 a month then you need to have income of $15,300 a month that is taxable. Be smart, not greedy.

These audits were very effective and large tax assessments were made. That is apparently why Congress killed the idea in its RRA 98 legislation. This helps the wealthy and those who derive their income from the underground economy.

14

IRS Service Center Abuse

IRS Correspondence

It is next to impossible to try to comprehend the letters that the IRS issues. They are dense, single spaced letters that you need someone to interpret for you. Even I have been confused in receiving IRS letters and refunds. I have filed taxes using Turbo Tax and then received mysterious refunds later from $200-$500 and asked my fellow tax professionals about the refund and we never could figure out why the refunds were issued. So I just cashed the check.

All IRS letters are confusing, lack details or useable information and violate English grammar and common sense. These letters cause taxpayers to call just to try to figure out what IRS is talking about in the letter. Again, the IRS uses in house employees with no knowledge of the English language to compose, design and edit these letters.

The CP2000 Program

The CP 2000 is a letter that matches what you have on your tax return with other information that the IRS has received from 1099's and W-2's and other sources. If there is a difference the IRS recalculates your tax and issues a letter that is a proposed adjustment but really looks like a bill. Most people pay it just because it does look like a bill and they are afraid if they do not, that the IRS will audit them.

This is the automated under reporter program - no employees review this information. There was a 9% inaccuracy rate in a study in 2007 by TIGTA - I have read other sources that claim a 20% error rate. Management blamed the IRS employees, not the IRS computer systems for the errors. But tens of millions of dollars were collected that were not legally correct. The IRS continues to over-charge taxpayers and is aware of it, according to TIGTA, but continues to churn out these letters.

The IRS said 98.4% of CP2000 letters are agreed to and paid. Some would argue that this is because of fear. People generally get a letter from the IRS and then try to call. TIGTA estimates that 32% of people who receive these letters try to call the IRS. Most just send a check. Out of 8.6 million letters, TIGTA found that 17,627 were not errors but those affected taxpayers never knew about and caused them to lose $29.2 million in lost refunds.

TIGTA estimated that over the next five years *243,345 taxpayers* will be over assessed because of the CP2000 program, resulting in millions more being collected illegally. IRS also sends 3.9 million correspondence audit letters similar in content to the CP2000. It also sends 3.2 million Math Error Letters and these are questions the figures on the returns, but look like bills so most people just pay them.

The Excess Collections Fund and Unidentified Remittance Fund

These funds are where money goes when a taxpayer sends in money and then never files a tax return. It is where money or credits are transferred when a taxpayer sends in money but the IRS claims they cannot identify who the money is from or to where it should be applied.

Sometimes this is for people who pay in taxes (to avoid criminal prosecution) and then do not file tax returns. Sometimes they file but have lost refunds. $1.4 billion of the excess collections fund consists payments of $50,000 or more and many were $100,000 or more.

According to one TIGTA study $4.7 billion was transferred into this account. In one study 224 taxpayers lost $116 million in refunds, because they were not notified by the IRS that they were entitled to a refund.

Where the IRS Gets Free Money

If a person does not file a return within three years of its April 15 due date, they lose their refund completely and forever. On April 16, 2014, the IRS took $760 million in potential refunds from hard-working taxpayers from the 2010 tax year which should have been filed by April 15, 2011. On April 15, 2015 another $1 billion was taken by the IRS from people who have not filed their 2011 income tax returns. All this money goes into the Treasury.

The secret to maybe getting a tax refund after the three years has passed is to not ask for a refund, but *ask to have the refund carried forward to the next tax year.* About half of the IRS computers will do this. You may also qualify for refunds to be transferred if you were physically or mentally unable to carry on your business affairs.

The Statute of Collections and Assessment

This is the greatest scandal of all. Congress wrote the law that only gives a taxpayer three years from the due date of the return to file and request a refund. But if they fail to file, they will ask for at least the last six years of tax returns. If there is a lot of unreported income, then IRS can look back 6 years in its audit. In no other case is this true - not in criminal or civil cases is the statute so short and arbitrary. This harms people by taking their hard earned refunds; many of whom have personal, mental or emotional or physical problems that prevent them from filing or having the returns prepared at all.

15

Criminal Investigation Abuse

IRS Criminal Investigation identified 5,314 cases in 2014 for investigation and forwarded 4,364 to the Department of Justice for prosecution. It claims a rate of prosecution 93%, and 80% of those convicted go to prison.

There is a lack of staff and resources that force criminal investigators to set high dollar amounts before they will even review a tax evasion case. The IRS does not prosecute its own cases. The IRS is required to go through and pay the Department of Justice attorneys to fly in from Washington D. C to prosecute their cases. This causes them to forego further investigation and to reach plea bargains in many cases. The IRS does have attorneys that are also Special Assistant U.S. Attorneys but they answer technical legal questions in local offices and appear in bankruptcy court proceedings where the taxpayer owes the IRS money. No one really seems to know who and why they are investigating someone so there is no oversight on systems outside of the IRS; no checks and balances. I have seen criminal agents spot a good looking woman on the street and then return to the office and run her license plate to find out who she is and where she lives - so they can arrange for some future connection.

Who is Criminal Investigation Interested In?

Usually Criminal Investigation is not interested in cases involving complex business fraud, items a jury cannot understand, old or sick people, no matter what they have done. This is because some defense attorneys have brought their clients to court in wheelchairs on oxygen and even with make up to make them look older and sicker than they actually are. A jury is unlikely to convict a person in that condition for tax crimes. They are interested in people that are highly educated, prominent, notorious, outspoken about the tax system or critical of the Government.

All CI agents are accountants or CPA's and my experience with them showed me that they don't really like tax cases as much as they like big flashy mob related cases, or money laundering cases, drug cases, human trafficking or sex/slave/prostitution cases the best.

In my career my natural intuition and gut feelings helped me to instigate 22 criminal referrals, but there are so many other suspicious cases that could be investigated and prosecuted if only the IRS had the resources. The IRS has dollar limits for criminal referrals and that limits the number of cases that can be referred to them. IRS Collection Management was very happy when I would make referrals. I was rewarded. I got credit for them and big awards and certificates and coffee mugs with the Criminal Agent logo and higher evaluations if I made at least 2 criminal referrals a year. I did not get any credit if the alleged tax criminal was prosecuted - I just got credit for referring them.

CI is very picky about which cases it chooses to investigate and prosecute. They love to pin perjury (lying) charges on people. These are people who sign tax documents that swear that nothing they signed is false. This is called the *jurat* statement written just above the signatures where you swear to the accuracy of your tax return. They strive for felony charges but also will charge some people with misdemeanors if they can be sure of a conviction. Some offices will try to pin both on you. But they get more credit for the felony convictions.

A friend, who was a criminal agent for many years, told me he knows within the first hour of questioning someone about alleged tax crimes if he can make a case or not - depending on how fast they crack and start spilling information without an attorney being present and before they offer Miranda rights protection. This method is used throughout IRS in Criminal, Audit, and Collection. It is known as the 80/20 Rule. You will get 80% of the most important facts in your case in the first 20 minutes of talking with the taxpayer. Then you can decide what to do with the case.

Criminal Agents usually only have one or two cases, so they have the time and resources to devote a lot of attention to you.

What Happens If CI Doesn't Get Who They Want

The IRS has models of who they would like to prosecute and my personal experience has shown if a potential criminal taxpayer is over the age of 65 - the taxpayer benefits from some age discrimination that occurs. He will be deemed unworthy of prosecution, no matter how glowing the case, even if it can proved that a taxpayer deliberately hid millions of dollars in income. But if you are one of those cases they identified but they were unable to find enough information to use to indict the person, watch out, because they will make sure that you are audited and the IRS takes the hardest line with your case. Criminal Agents came to my desk to tell me in these cases that they knew the taxpayer is dirty and I should make him suffer. This was not supposed to happen after RRA 98, but it still does.

Undercover Criminal Agents

Sometimes Criminal Special Agents like to play pretend. They go out and pretend they are businessmen involved in whatever business you are in. They drive up in a flashy car, previously seized, with a Rolex and other expensive jewelry on them that came from criminal forfeiture seizures from someone else. They will have government money to wine and dine you. Then they will ask to buy your business and then want to see your books, so then you will show them the books that you would show the IRS if you were audited. But then they ask for the "real books," to show how much you really make. Then they see those books and where you keep them, and the potential seller is told that they will pay huge amounts for their business. Actually in many cases the seller of the business is also lying and wants to inflate the potential sales price of his business. But this is what really happens: the IRS undercover agent goes back to his office with his notes and he usually also has been recording you and if he was able, had you in a location where you were being filmed or at least photographed.

This does not sound like fair play does it? It sounds like entrapment to me. But the courts have consistently upheld this sort of behavior. The undercover agent will go to all your customers and banks and creditors and issue summonses to collect data. By then it is too late to do anything but plan some time off in a federal prison.

Civil Forfeiture

In 2012, the IRS criminal agents did civil forfeiture seizures 639 times, with only 20% of the cases being prosecuted. CI keeps a portion of the money and goods seized. The person losing the money has the burden of proof on them to demonstrate the cash, cars and other assets were not tied to criminal activity. Most people don't have the money to fight the IRS in court so they just lose what was seized.

The IRS does not explain why they are doing it and in most cases does not accuse the taxpayer of money laundering, tax evasion or criminal activity. They just take the money, in fact, they get a portion of the money that comes back to their own budget. The original law was designed to catch terrorists, money launderers and drug lords who deposited less than $10,000 if it was done in an effort to evade the federal bank reporting requirement.

CI also enforces the Treasury forfeiture fund and does a lot of work not just enforcing the Internal Revenue Code, but also other financial crimes, and then come up with criminal charges and tax assessments over the next few years. CI can seize money or assets based on the belief that they have been illegally obtained or no income tax has been paid on them. They do their seizures (forfeitures) without any legal tax assessments being made. The greatest benefit to the Government is that the seizure is against the property not against a person. This clouds the rights that a person has in the case. How can a million dollars represent itself? These are also called jeopardy assessments when they are initiated on non-criminal cases.

One family run business had $447,000 seized from its accounts because of a pattern of cash deposits under $10,000 which were legitimate and based on the knowledge of the law that the family run business had. After holding the money for two years, where no federal criminal charges were filed, their lives and business were destroyed. Recently the Justice Department decided that the seizure was wrong and that the money should be returned. Too little, too late, in my opinion.

IRS only stopped this practice recently after the New York Times ran an article that pointed the spotlight on this dubiously legal practice.

Suspicious Activity Report

Criminal agents and the revenue agents have access to a secret list called the Suspicious Activity Report (SAR). This is where banks or individuals related to the financial industry make reports, some factual, some subjective and without substance and they are in effect snitching on other people. The SAR report is used by "anyone who knows, suspects or has reason to suspect that a transaction or pattern of transactions is suspicious and involves more than $2,000." IRS criminal agents and revenue agents have access to a secret report called the Suspicious Activity Report (SAR) which gives them ideas about where to poke around looking for criminals of financial/white collar crimes. This list is ripe, because it also includes all the people who have made cash transactions for more than $10,000. If you pay $20,000 cash for a car the dealer is required to report it. If you deposit more than $10,000 cash in a bank account the bank is required to report it. Big brother is watching everything you do. And you never hear about it. The bank and the Treasury Department/IRS can also track your currency from the serial numbers and the magnetic coding on each bill. I have read many creative reports on SAR documents - that are not true when I investigated them, but some people want to get other people in trouble with the IRS.

The IRS receives millions of these reports every year and it is impossible to investigate them all. Some are to report that a person may have come into a bank and put $6,000 cash into one account and $6000 into another account. The bank teller thinks they are doing it to avoid reporting a transaction over $10,000 so they file a report. It can be subjective, vengeful, discriminatory and racist. Banks reported many outlandish things in the reports I saw.

In 2013, IRS Criminal Investigation got convictions in 1,250 Identity Theft cases which resulted in convictions averaging 35 months in prison.

The IRS won criminal convictions in three employment tax cases (where the employer takes money from employee checks and does not pay it to the Government).

Two hundred and seven tax preparers who had prepared abusive and fraudulent tax returns were also convicted and sent to prison for an average of 27 months.

Criminal cases can come from many sources. I heard of one agent who used to watch HGTV, a network that specializes in real estate sales and renovations. It tells the names of the program participants and how much they have available to pay for new homes. That is easily searched to determine if they have reported that amount to the IRS. This information can also come from the acquisition of luxury cars, vacations homes or a high spending lifestyle without any apparent means to pay for it. At one time revenue officers and revenue agents could initiate their own case work and investigations, based on leads that they had developed.

After RRA 98, the IRS Agent had to write up an Information Item and that could lead to a case being opened.

Informants and Whistleblowers

Informants are people who turn in information to the IRS on spouses, jealous relatives, ex-employees, ex-employers, co-workers, neighbors, family, friends and small businesses that they believe violated the tax laws. Whistleblowers are people who are reporting on government agencies and on large businesses. In 2014, claimants received $53 million in rewards but the IRS collected $367 million more in taxes because of it. There is a formal network used to collect information from people who want to turn in their neighbor or boss. The IRS pays out great rewards for such information. An informant/whistleblower can get 15-30% of what taxes are collected, based on the information provided. A few years ago, the IRS paid one informant $104 million after he provided foreign banking secrets.

In the past, I have turned over information to the IRS that I learned while I was on my private time. People bragging about how they ripped off the IRS and telling all the details for anyone to hear at a party, bar or restaurant. I would watch for which car they left in and write down the license plate number. This was common in the IRS at that time.

Informants came from the IRS, local states attorneys, State Attorney Generals, Members of Congress and the White House. I have worked investigations on leads from all of these sources. It never occurred to me at the time that the IRS could be used as a political tool. I just did what the case required. But every case in the IRS is coded as to the source of information. As you can imagine if you got a code that said the case was from the White House or Congress that got top priority in my inventory.

It is amazing how people will turn in their neighbor.

The IRS is a great place to make both legal and illegal claims and get big money for Congress, with little effort.

16

Treasury Inspector General Abuse

As mentioned, the Treasury Department has a division known as the Treasury Inspector General for Tax Affairs (TIGTA) formerly known as the Inspection Division. They are known inside the IRS as the IRS Secret Police. They provided physical security if I needed an armed special agent to protect me from a violent or crazy taxpayer. They also helped catch people who attempted to bribe me. They would monitor telephone calls and film the bribe payments so the person could be prosecuted later. It was always very hush-hush when I worked with TIGTA. They did internal audit work and also monitored employees.

Being an IRS employee is hard enough, but when you add TIGTA in, it becomes a nightmare. They plant seeds of fear and discontent in the IRS. Most IRS employees fear them. TIGTA Special Agents can arrest you, have you fired or suspended, force you to resign, take your job, your pension, and your benefits and put you in jail. Fear of the Treasury Inspector General for Tax Administration (TIGTA) resonated in our lives every day. When we were in training a TIGTA agent told us that they were doing background checks and talking to people we knew 20 years ago, to make sure we were not communists or other people they did not like. They told me that if I had lied about anything on my job application I would be fired. They said that if I failed to put something on the application and they found out about it I would be fired. Most everyone fell for the fear and turned themselves in about DUI, traffic tickets, incidents that happened in college that involved the police. Most of them were never seen again. That is how it is when TIGTA is involved. People just disappear. The manager would tell us that they no longer work there and that we should not have any contact with that person in or out of the work building. Then all the locks were changed. All of them were banned from the building.

These same special agents have spied on me and tried to get me fired on at least three occasions that I know about, just because I was following the law and trying to do the right thing. I have also been under surveillance numerous times, and I am not alone in that. TIGTA Special Agents secretly talked to my friends, family, neighbors and the taxpaying public asking all sorts of personal and intrusive questions, and questioned my integrity and ethics. The Special Agents always made sure to warn/threaten the people being interviewed and told them not to say anything to me about their visits, warning the interviewee there could be serious consequences if anything was said. They monitored my personal mail, listened to my business and personal phone calls, and picked up my garbage after I put it on the curb looking for information that would incriminate me. I wondered why I lost friends for no apparent reason sometimes.

I have witnessed IRS management in strange and unprofessional relationships TIGTA. Very cozy. There is no separation of power.

TIGTA does encourage its agents to get friendly with the IRS employees to develop their "snitch network." So it is real hard to tell who is using who in the process. In fact they would like to have a cozy relationship with all IRS employees because they already maintain a network of informants and snitches and they want to add to their network.

They interviewed and intimidated me many times, questioning why I took certain case actions, or questioning my integrity and ethics. All of the cases resulted in proving my innocence.

TIGTA Special Agents have arbitrary but unchallengeable powers. They encourage employees to spy on each other and have informants throughout the IRS. As told earlier in my book, I worked on one large criminal case where hundreds of businesses and people were involved. I was called into to an office with two inspectors and they did the good cop-bad cop routine on me. They accused me of illegally accessing over 100 peoples' accounts on the IRS Master Computer. Just one illegal access violation can result in job loss, penalties, and prison. I was allowed to bring the NTEU union steward with me, and he was shaking in his boots.

I was not. I had accessed hundreds of Social Security numbers that all directly related to the tax evasion case that I was preparing. They were all legitimate. I had done nothing wrong.

The inspectors never told me directly what the result of that investigation was. For two years, I would wake up in the middle of the night sweating and full of fear. I was always careful about what I said on the phone or what I wrote. But I never caved in. Never! I knew that what I had done was not just legal, but correct and necessary.

After two years TIGTA came after me again, backed by a Collection Management member who was trying to force me out of my job. Again I had just been following the law and doing my job. The union, which was so full of fear of TIGTA they were afraid to ask about the prior case, finally demanded that TIGTA respond. TIGTA said that they had closed the old case two months after the interview as they found no evidence of wrong doing. A clearance letter had been issued to a second level boss of mine and she suppressed it. Intimidation and abuse can be found on many levels of the IRS.

I have worked with TIGTA seven times on bribery cases. I felt like I had a bull's-eye painted on my back and these TIGTA agents kept me in their sights, all the time. But they were always operating on incomplete facts, so they always lost.

I knew a man who worked at the IRS as a revenue agent and later a manager who worked on high profile strike force level cases.

Those investigations were designed to get people: politicians, hookers, drug dealers, mobsters, prominent figures, and assorted other criminals who had neglected to file and pay their taxes. Sometimes he was threatened with bodily harm by these people. Later in life someone made an accusation that he had threatened them with a full scale audit.

They can audit that person as far back as they find records. So the threat of an audit from an IRS manager carries a special hurt all its own. So TIGTA agents were notified by the person who was allegedly threatened and they started an investigation. Over a two year period, they listened to all of his telephone calls, reviewed his mail, went through his garbage, talked to his neighbors and friends looking for evidence that he had done things that were against the law. They harassed him, but never were able to prove this allegation. But they tried to destroy him. There was no consideration paid to the intrusion of his privacy and of the rest of his family. When IRS agents are on a mission to crucify one of their own they are like a bloodhound on the trail of a scent.

TIGTA agents are like Barney Fife/Keystone cops - they only can work 1-2 cases at a time, or they get overwhelmed.

17

Abuse from Taxpayers

The Social Security Loophole

Millions of people have discovered the secret that they never have to pay social security taxes and will still receive tens of thousands of dollars of Social Security benefits for the rest of their lives, based on their earnings reported.

A person can be self-employed for years and never file an income tax return. Never pay income tax or Social Security taxes. Then one day they can file ten years' worth of tax returns with the IRS and they will get 10 years of Social Security credit and will have not paid even one dime in to the government to get that credit. They avoid jail and plead poverty and they get away with it. I remember old farmers that had never filed tax returns were doing this in droves in the early 1980's in Illinois. Fraud is fraud.

Because of law changes, you do not need to ever file an income tax return and you will still receive full credit from the Social Security Administration for your Social Security and Medicare withholdings for disability and retirement if you have a job where you receive a W-2 form. Because a copy of your W-2 form is sent directly to the Social Security Administration.

Now this is another crack in the system: if you are self-employed, you have to file income tax returns with the IRS or you will not receive any credit for Social Security or Medicare.

I said you have to file, not pay. Yes, that is correct. Social Security will give you full credit for the amounts that you were supposed to pay in, even if you never have paid the taxes. Some people report all their income and some I think actually inflate their income to receive the maximum Social Security benefit. This is a broken system that needs to be fixed.

The IRS reports earnings to the Social Security Administration. It does not report whether the taxes have ever been paid. That is right. You can fly under the radar and receive a Social Security check without ever paying the Government for your Social Security. I saw this many times in my tax work. I was outraged, but unless Social Security audits individuals, this routinely happens. I knew about it, but was so busy producing for the IRS, I had no time to think about this - or even how and where to report it. I have verified this with other government officials.

One official was a 10 year veteran of the Social Security Administration as Claims Representative and had another 20 years as an IRS Revenue Agent and then another 5 years as an IRS Revenue Agent Group Manager. She gave me permission to quote her anonymously. She said *"Richard, you are very right about the 'loophole'. The right hand does not know what the left hand is doing. W-2's are filed with Social Security (not the IRS). Social Security posts the W-2 information and then provides that to the IRS for matching. That is why W-2 matching takes so long. The IRS, in turn, gives Form Schedule C (Profit or Loss from Business) data for self-employment earnings to Social Security. However, the IRS does not tell Social Security whether any or all of the Self Employment Tax (Social Security Tax) has been paid. A taxpayer can be delinquent in paying their taxes, have some of it written off as uncollectible, and Social Security will never know and has already posted their self-employment earnings for Social Security credit.*

Likewise, businesses that are delinquent in payroll taxes that have issued W-2's to employees but haven't paid in the payroll withholdings and the employee will still get full credit for both the payroll withholding and the Social Security taxes withheld. They will get withholding credit on their personal returns and get refunds of money that was never paid to the IRS, although the employer is delinquent and never pays the taxes. What an inefficient system we have."

I have seen some self-employed people just claim their whole gross income and then list no business deductions so that they get maximum credit under Social Security. This scam works best when the person is already over 62 or older and filing tax returns for the first time in years. The IRS is never going to audit a return and make you claim deductions, exemptions and expenses that you do not already claim.

This is a case of the right hand not knowing what the left hand is doing. But this is between two huge government agencies. There is no coordination between the IRS and Social Security Administration. But there are thousands of laws, rules and regulations and that is exactly what people are using to rip off the system.

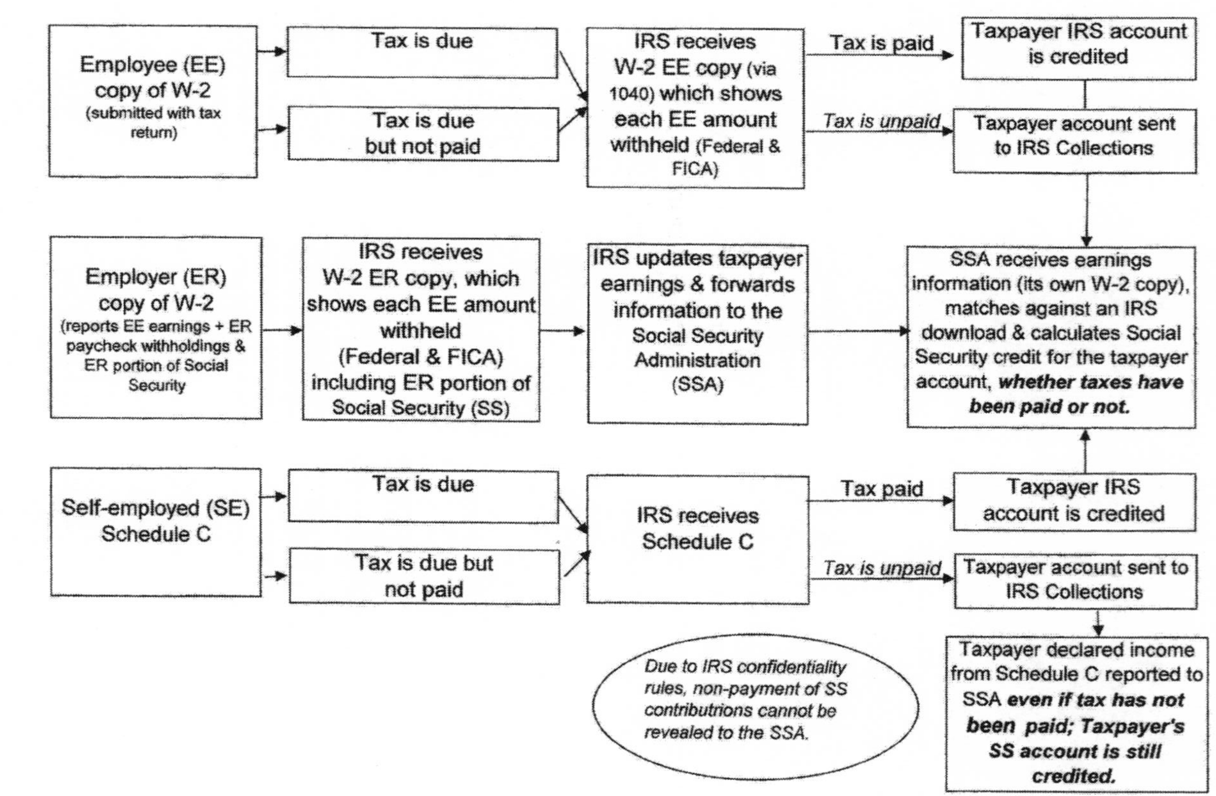
HOW TO CLAIM SOCIAL SECURITY BENEFITS WITHOUT PAYING A DIME INTO THE SYSTEM
Employee (EE) copy of W-2 (submitted with tax return)
Tax is due
Tax is due but not paid
IRS receives W-2 EE copy (via 1040) which shows each EE amount withheld (Federal & FICA)
Tax is paid
Tax is unpaid
Taxpayer IRS account is credited
Taxpayer account sent to IRS Collections
Employer (ER) copy of W-2 (reports EE earnings + ER paycheck withholdings & ER portion of Social Security
IRS receives W-2 ER copy, which shows each EE amount withheld (Federal & FICA) including ER portion of Social Security (SS)
IRS updates taxpayer earnings & forwards information to the Social Security Administration (SSA)
SSA receives earnings information (its own W-2 copy), matches against an IRS download & calculates Social Security credit for the taxpayer account, ***whether taxes have been paid or not.***
Self-employed (SE) Schedule C
Tax is due
Tax is due but not paid
IRS receives Schedule C
Tax paid
Tax is unpaid
Taxpayer IRS account is credited
Taxpayer account sent to IRS Collections
Taxpayer declared income from Schedule C reported to SSA ***even if tax has not been paid; Taxpayer's SS account is still credited.***
Due to IRS confidentiality rules, non-payment of SS contributrions cannot be revealed to the SSA.

Abuse in Action

Sometimes taxpayers had a personal vendetta against me for my actions. They sought to retaliate against me. I got awful, threatening letters accusing me of killing their dog or chasing their children around, and much worse. I was lucky because it was just verbal and written harassment. Some revenue officers have had their cars scratched or hit with gunfire. Or in rural areas, eggs, rocks and bags of dog feces have been thrown at their homes. Some have received threatening phone calls and false accusations. One friend of mine was under investigation for molesting the non-taxpayer's 16-year-old daughter. She had apparently answered the door and let him into the house because her father was on his way home. Her father arrived five minutes later. I heard there was a lot of shouting and then the revenue officer left. Then the father wrote letters to everyone and called the police saying his daughter had been molested. He also started a personal mission of retaliation against this revenue officer. He filed liens against the revenue officer personally and he filed suit against him in court. He was able to mess up the revenue officer's credit also. All because he did not agree with the taxes the IRS assessed against him. There was a big investigation and the revenue officer said that he had done no such thing and the daughter admitted that he had done nothing to her. But TIGTA, police and Children and Family Services were all involved. It was all supposed to be hush-hush but nothing in the IRS really ever is when there is a hint of scandal. We used to joke that the IRS runs on gossip. After he was cleared, it took the United States Attorney another two years to clear his credit, the bogus liens and lawsuits. This caused him great personal damage and he got nothing but grief from the IRS.

Man Arrested for Petty Theft

A friend of mine told me about a case he was involved with. He had worked a case where a man owed $6 Million. The IRS filed a lien against the man, who enjoyed dual citizenship of the United States and Israel, and he moved to Israel. He took all his assets with him. So my friend put out an alert that allowed for him to be detained when he tried to reenter the USA. So then he closed the case thinking the guy had won, he had beat the IRS.

Two years later, the man entered in Florida. They did not catch his entry at Customs so he went on about his business. His wife and kids had been visiting Disneyworld.

One day this man was at a convenience store and shoplifted a razor, toothbrush, toothpaste, shaving cream and deodorant; basic stuff under $20 in value. The owner of the store had him arrested. When he was being booked they found out that the IRS had put out an order to detain him until the IRS could question him. So they called Washington D.C. and then my friend was called as he was the original case agent. Washington told him to get on the next plane to Florida - the police were holding the man he wanted.

He arrived in Florida and the man was belligerent and arrogant and nasty. My friend asked for financial information and he refused - except to say he had nothing in the USA, it was all in Israel. The USA does not have a tax treaty with Israel – so the IRS was out of luck.

Then the US Attorney took him to Court to discover assets. The Judge set bail at $10 million. The next day the $1 million was wired in from Israel. (10% of the bond) He was released and told to appear at the next court date.

But he had enough of the USA at this point and drove straight to the hotel and got his wife and kids. He chartered a jet to Cuba and planned to return to Israel. This way he avoided going through Customs. A U.S. Marshall assigned to the case had a hunch that he might jump bail, so he kept an eye on this man. In many jobs - people develop a sixth sense.

When they were on the plane and cleared for takeoff, the FAA ordered the plane not to take off, to return to the terminal. There this man was arrested again and put back in jail. By now the Judge was very angry. So he ordered him held without bail; he was given the choice of paying the $6 Million that he owed to the Government.

Two days later the $6 million was wired in from Israel and the man was released. He had to pay the $6 million plus the $1 million in his bond, all because he stole $20 worth of toiletries! It was estimated that the man was worth about $50 Million.

This is Not a How to Cheat the IRS Book

I have no problem revealing these secrets. Some people have told me that this was like telling the bad guys how to cheat the government. Believe me, those who are motivated that way already know it. Criminals have all day to sit around thinking these things up. So I am not talking outside of school. I am just pointing out the gaps in the law and procedures that are costing the United States Government tens of billions of dollars a year.

File First and Claim the Kids

There are various widely known things taxpayers do to play the tax system. One of these, in the case of separated or divorced couples who have children, is to file their tax returns as quickly as they can to get the credit for all the children. There might be a state court order such as a custody agreement or divorce order saying who can get the credit for deduction of the child, but the IRS does not recognize state tax court decisions at all. Never has, never will. Many well-meaning people learn this the hard way. So the person doing wrong will win and the IRS will send an oversized refund check to them. If this is your situation file as soon as you can - the first to file gets credit for the children.

Your Kids are Worth Money to Other People

Another issue with children is when a poor family has children but has little or no taxable income, then they "sell" the income tax exemption to other people who are working. Each child/exemption is worth $3,950 so that means you can earn that much and pay no taxes at all on the money. Usually a person doing this will split the tax refund difference with the parent.

The IRS pays the refund out on the first return received, before it asks any questions. There are many tests for who can be claimed as dependent, but at return processing - it comes down to did they list it on the return or not.

Additional Child Tax Credit Fraud

There is a program called the Additional Child Tax Credit that allows foreign tax workers, some legal using Individual Taxpayer Identification Numbers (ITINS) and some using fake Social Security number and fake ITINs to claim credit for children in foreign countries. It is called the Additional Child Tax Credit. The IRS admits that last year this program paid out $7.1 billion to over 2 million workers who submitted fraudulent claims. One man was interviewed by the local news and he said "If the opportunity is there, why not take it?"

Alimony Fraud

Alimony Fraud is when a person claims to pay alimony which they can deduct off their income but do not in fact pay alimony. Or when the person receiving the alimony does not report it as taxable income. The IRS computer has no way of matching that, but a TIGTA study showed that the fraud of claiming alimony that was not paid costs the Government $2.3 billion a year.

Earned Income Tax Credit Fraud

Another abuse to the system is called Earned Income Tax Credit - this is a welfare program that Congress uses to encourage parents to work and benefits low to moderate income earners, who then get a big check at the end of the year. A family with 3 children, which earns $46,997, gets all income tax refunded to them plus they would get a check for $6,143. It is a law that had a good intent, but it is widely abused. In fact, the law was only supposed to be for one year, but it remained in the law because it was so popular and it encourages poor and working class people to work. This popular program paid out $63 billion in 2012. It is estimated that Earned Income Tax Credit has a fraud rate of 24% which costs the Government at least $15.6 billion a year, just given away to fraud.

Net Operating Loss Fraud

This is the Form 1045, Application for Tentative Refund where claims are made for business tax credits. It is rife with fraud because the IRS does not monitor what is being claimed on the tax Form 1045 returns. The website www.IRS.gov lists many abusive and fraudulent tax schemes.

Slavery Reparations Tax Credit Fraud

Another refund fraud is called the Slavery Reparation Tax Credit. This was in regards to an Order issued by Civil War General William Tecumseh Sherman which promised that each freed slave after the Civil War should receive 1 mule and 40 acres of land. They figured that the current value of that would be $40,000. So ministers and conmen would go around to African American Churches and sell this doctored up form for $250 and help people file for this false refund. The IRS did not disappoint them; it sent out tens of millions of dollars, before it figured out what was going on. The people who I met with who had gotten the money paid bills, helped out family, donated to their church and put on additions to their homes or paid off their mortgages. These were God-fearing Christians who believed their minister and the conman and really believed that the Government was finally making right on its promise. It was determined by IRS officials that it would not be politically correct to go after the people who had filed these claims, so we just let it go.

I could never collect a nickel on these refunds, because regular collection methods do not work on fraudulent refunds. I could not file a levy or a lien. The Government has the power to stop this by amending existing laws, but it does not. I would have had to file suit; regular collection methods never work in refund fraud cases. The U.S. Attorney said that it would not be politically correct to pursue the people who had received these refunds.

Federal Excise Tax Refund for Highway Use Tax Fraud

Another refund credit fraud is the Federal Excise Tax Refund for Highway Use Tax. This is where truckers or those who pretend to be truckers file for large refunds of credits never paid in on the Form 8821.

Illegal Immigrants and Un-Documented Workers

Despite what you may hear about immigrants "stealing" our resources and collecting food stamps, mostly the system abuses the people who it chooses to ignore. Illegal immigrants and undocumented workers are paying into Social Security, Medicare and for income taxes and will never receive a dime back in benefits. This is an abuse - but of the system. In fact, I remember hearing at an IRS meeting that 50-75% of these immigrants pay state, federal and local taxes and never get a dime back. It is estimated that they pay $7 billion a year just for Social Security alone. For all the complaining that we hear about how this group costs the Government money, many undocumented and illegal immigrants are employed in jobs where they have Social Security and income tax withheld, and they pay for Medicare and unemployment tax. This is a windfall to the Government, because these people cannot file and receive refunds and can never qualify for benefits under any of the systems.

I remember making a field call in a working class suburb and I knocked on the door and I said "IRS". Sixteen men who appeared to be Hispanic came running out the door and pushed me so I fell on the floor so that they could get away. They left the door to the apartment open. I saw no furniture just backpacks and blankets on the floor. I finally figured it out - they must have thought that I said INS (Immigration and Naturalization Service).

Receiving Form 1099 is Used to Hide Income

When an employee gets income, a form W-2 is issued to them. It is reported to the government and Social Security. But when a person is self-employed and bills his work under a corporation, the company paying the money is not required to report it on a Form 1099 as income to the other corporation. Unfortunately, some businesses think that this also includes Limited Liability Companies, partnerships and sole proprietorships; it does not. Actually the law says that corporation to corporation transactions are exempt, but many businesses ignore this and don't issue a Form 1099 at all. There are very confusing rules about this. This is an area where a lot of tax evasion can and does occur, because there is no connecting this business income to the actual persons receiving it. Then the receiver pays all business and personal expenses out of the corporate account and claims to have no taxable income. This maximizes their income short term, but they do not accumulate any Social Security or Medicare insurance benefits. Congress is aware of this, and has refused to change it, even in this day of electronic transactions when it would be effortless for companies to report this information. They already have it on their computers anyway.

Taxpayers Lying to Each Other

When a married couple owes taxes, sometimes one does not share this with their spouse. The longer this secret is out there the worse it becomes. I remember one story where the wife had taken over running the existing business and the much older husband was going to cash in his IRA for $300,000 to start a new business. She did not know what she was doing and ran up $400,000 in tax debt to the IRS. She prevented me from talking to him, with appeals and attorneys putting up interference. Last I heard, when he did find out, he beat her so severely she ended up in the hospital.

Underreporting Income Fraud

Many people who I have spoken with think they do not have to report cash income. That is not true - but it is widespread in some communities. I have seen cases where some cash can be spent and used to supplement a person's lifestyle. One of my taxpayers admitted to having about $600 a week that he did not report on his income taxes. I was able to find that after analyzing his bank statements and telephone records.

Cash leaves a trail. There are many clues that a person's income is more than they claim on their tax return. They have to have a bank account for at least the major expenses and usually you can locate credit cards from looking at their credit bureau report. They need a credit card to book airline tickets and rent cars and reserve hotel rooms. In the past it was different, where cash could be used to pay for more expenses. That seemed to change after 9/11. I would look at the house where a taxpayer lived and then their vehicles and then look to see if they had any adult toys like motorcycles, motor homes, dirt bikes, jet skis, antique vehicles, type of furnishings, antiques, collectibles, watches, jewelry, etc. I would get so much information just by observing lifestyle. Then I would ask them or their neighbor if they had a favorite place to vacation and if they also owned property there. Or did they have a favorite destination that they fly to and ask when and how often. All that fun that they are having costs money and that has to be coming from somewhere. Buildings and houses are registered in the county in the taxpayers name or in the names of people or businesses or trusts related to them.

The best source of information in any tax investigation is the HUD-1 statement. (The closing statement when the taxpayer buys a house or building.) The second most valuable statement is their mortgage application. That is where they will make sure to list all their assets and perhaps even inflate their values, in an effort to get bigger loans. It will list every asset they have. Even jewelry and stocks and bonds that may be stored in a home safe and previously unknown safe deposit boxes. The third most valuable form is the statement from their insurance company listing their assets and their insured values. I had to issue a summons for this information. When I was in such an investigation, I would also do a google search on the taxpayers and if I was very lucky, also find their Facebook account. That would have many photos and vacations and assets listed as they use such pages to flaunt their hidden wealth and lifestyle. It would be so funny later to see the taxpayers face when I would ask them a question that I knew the answer to before I asked and then they lied about it.

Cost of Goods Sold Fraud

Hiding income and expenses in the Cost of Goods Sold section of business tax returns is another common abuse. The IRS does not crosscheck this in collection efforts. This is an area where tax evasion and tax fraud occurs. I have seen some collection employees look at a Schedule C income from a service business form and it will show income (gross receipts) of $2 million and cost of goods sold as $1.6 million. On paper this leaves a profit of $400,000 and then other expenses like rent, utilities, supplies internet, etc. come out of this and then the net profit is maybe $50,000. Newer IRS employees only look at that number (the $400,000) and see if where it went is reasonable. That is a flaw in collection, a lack of training in accounting methods that would disclose this return was fraudulent.

Retirement Contributions Fraud

There is no automatic computer program that monitors and matches retirement account contributions and withdrawal transactions. Like a Simplified Employee Plan account, this is costing the Government untold tens of millions of dollars a year in fraudulent claims.

Made-to-Fail Businesses

Another abuse to the system is when a taxpayer sets up their business operation to fail. They structure everything to make money and hide assets. I have seen several cases like this. I knew one woman who opened an antiques business and bought $100,000 in antiques and then two years later closed the business and kept all the antiques. She had used the $100,000 to lose money and this made her other employment income tax free because she lost money from her business. Nothing I could do except write this up as an "Information Item" and send it over to Audit who would probably do nothing about it, because they are so short staffed. Also audits goals are not the same as collections goals, so my referral would never be acted on.

Businesses that Hide Behind the Shield of the Law

I love to garden, but weeds love to grow and have more time in my garden than I do. This is the same as with criminals. They devote all of their time, money and attention to analyzing the tax system and then figure out how to exploit it.

A business will hide behind a legitimate business front and know they are protected from the IRS/Treasury Department scrutiny. Take for instance businesses that deal with large volumes of cash. They register as money services businesses. These are places where you pay a fee and they will cash your check or convert your cash to a check or money order. Since they charge a hefty commission, they are sometimes not enforcing the law. The law states that all cash transactions over $10,000 must be reported to the IRS/Treasury Department. This is under the Bank Secrecy Act, which was supposed to combat money laundering. (i.e. cleaning up money gained from drugs, prostitution or illegal activity.)

I have worked businesses that have hidden behind the shield of this law. They form a business that cashes checks; they were then called a money services business and now are legally exempt from reporting large cash transactions. The businesses were pulling cash out of a bank once or twice a week for almost a million dollars, and it all disappeared. All cash. I tried to get Criminal Investigation interested but they said this was exempt under the Bank Secrecy Act so they were not interested in it. The way an operation like this works is that it is set up to receive and launder money, avoid taxes on that money, and then produce large amounts of cash. In order to have this much cash flow through a local national bank, you also have to have the bank manager and at least some of the tellers in on it. And also probably some connection with the Federal Reserve Bank to not make this look unusual. When this much cash is floating around, it really will provide a temptation to pay off and bribe many people.

Most of the deposits to the bank account come from a foreign country and are wire transferred in.

Money Laundering

Working so close to the border with Mexico, I have witnessed money laundering. Large Mexican corporations buy large commercial retail projects and apartment complexes for tens of millions of dollars and the money is wired in from some foreign corporation's bank account and an American Corporation is set up to manage the property.

One of the favorite ways to hide money today is by buying prepaid credit or debit cards. Another place to launder money is at a casino or race track or through a business that may have some legitimate purpose, but it is flooded with lots of cash. Cash is hard to move and hard to hide. So they don't mind paying taxes on it, because this not only cleans the source of the cash but makes it legitimate money that can be used for anything.

Catch Me if You Can

Some people survive their encounters with the IRS and instead of being angry or vengeful, they just get smart and read the tax laws and the IRS procedures and figure out how to "play the system." Some try never to have anything to do with the IRS. They are motivated by greed and are drawn to what they see as "free money."

In my work, I met many people who thought they were smarter than me and the government. Many suspected sociopaths and psychopaths sat before me in my office and outlined their plans for getting away with tax evasion. They delighted in it, because I just sat there and acted stupid, like I did not understand what they were talking about. Then I acted naïve and even dumb as I asked what appeared to be innocent questions about the tax matter or the business and holding companies they had set up. In one case, I had a business that was very successful and was being sold to a Mexican firm, but the sale was required to go through a United States Corporation.

I listened and listened to this one man and he told me how he was going to file bankruptcy the next day. It would be a fraudulent bankruptcy. I acted very pleased because that would allow me to close his case. He was filing bankruptcy, not his corporations. He was trying to hide the sales from me and the bankruptcy court. I monitored the sale progress and the day that the sale closed. I contacted the parent company in Mexico and issued a levy that requested they pay all the proceeds from one of the sales to the IRS. My powers as an IRS officer did not extend to foreign countries, but because they were going to close through an American subsidiary, my levy attached. Eventually, I collected $347,000 plus there was a three year contract for the rest of the sales price, $3,157 a month. That is how much this man was going to get. He thought he was so smart he claimed to be bankrupt. I went after him for tax fraud and the case would not go anywhere - the Criminal Special Agent told me that the structure of the business made the case "too hard for a jury to understand." I tried to get him for bankruptcy fraud - but the U.S. Trustee said it was too complex and he was not interested. But I did get considerable pleasure every month when I posted that check for $3,157. I collected $113,652. It made me smile.

Nuns, Priests, Rabbis and Ministers Abusing the System

I have worked with at least a half dozen Catholic priests and nuns who were in positions of power and authority, who have abused the employment tax trust fund. They took the money out of the employee's paycheck as withholdings and then used it for whatever charitable purposes that they wanted.

I have also had ministers and rabbis who disagreed with the tax laws and did not pay what was required. Their protests did nothing to stop my collection efforts or the federal money spent on abortion, nuclear weapons, the military and war. I have worked on cases where organizations were run by ministers, priests and nuns that did really amazing social and charitable work and stole monies from the government.

Some have tried to use the Bible to get out of paying taxes and I always quote the Bible right back *"Render unto Caesar what is Caesar's and render unto God what is God's."* It is short and simple. Many just try to protest taxes or disagree with how the money is to be spent.

When I first started I had a crusty old manager who I talked to a case about where a priest stole employees' tax withholdings. I asked if I should abate the penalties because he was a priest after all. We had both been raised as Catholics and he looked at me and said. "Get over that crap! He is a priest, but he is also a thief." So I assessed the penalty that I could against him, but he and his corporation which had closed still walked off without paying $70,000.

I have had many religious people pump up their egos by taking money that did not belong to them and giving it away to the poor. But stealing is stealing. Strangely enough I had to explain this to them.

All people who conduct religious events stand to receive cash income, from giving their blessings, their time, for conducting weddings, funerals, baptisms, communions, confirmations and bar mitzvahs and bat mitzvahs. Cash income is worth more than what you make. If a priest does a wedding it is common for them to receive $200-$300 dollars. If this were taxed, it would probably come down to $130-$195. If you receive wages - you know what I am talking about. It is just unfair for people who have cash income not to report all of it, all the time. Moral and ethical issues come into question here - to me it is just a question of fairness.

I am not saying that all religious people are like this, I am only talking about those specific cases that I have seen. Sometimes, I would have a priest or a minister making a confession to me about all their vices, lusts, desires and anything else that they think will divert me from collecting money that they owe. I always had power in these situations, because if I did not get cooperation from them, I could go to their Bishop or Cardinal or Board of Directors. This actually worked with members of the military also - if I did not get cooperation I would find the Commanding Officer and get my case quickly resolved.

I did not get a response from one free spending nun and she was into the IRS for nearly $1 million. I found out what order she was in and then called the Superior of that Order. The way it works with anyone who has taken a vow of poverty, is they can earn whatever they can, but then they turn it in to the Order and then ask for sufficient money to pay their living expenses. They do not keep cash on the side. Unfortunately some people, religious or not, will just not learn these valuable lessons in this life. I remember that I told this nun that she was not Mother Teresa and to stop spending other people's money because it was against the law. She said she knew how to spend the money better than Congress, and she told me to "fuck off."

First Time Homebuyers Credit Fraud

This is a credit worth up to $8,000 which was used to encourage taxpayers to buy homes from 2008 to 2010. It was a response to the collapse of the real estate market. In late 2009, TIGTA reported that at least 19,000 filers hadn't purchased a home when they claimed the credit. Another 74,000 people claimed the credit of $8,000, but they already owned homes. The credit was claimed by 500 people under the age of 18 including a four-year old. Many criminal prosecutions came from this mess. In fact, it was so attractive and so much money that 53 IRS employees filed for this credit illegally or inappropriately.

Like-Kind Exchanges Fraud

Fraudulent or incorrect Like-Kind Exchanges under Internal Revenue Code 1031are a tax tool to delay capital gains taxes. The IRS does not have the computer technology to accurately track when wealthy people or individuals buy and sell property and then defer the gain so that no tax is paid. Many people have been known to use this for vacation homes or other properties used for personal use; the IRS has no way to monitor this systemically without an audit.

The IRS has no systemic way to monitor the sale prices of residential homes or rental homes either. It does no research on free internet sites such as Zillow.com that could verify any of the numbers on the form without an audit.

Similarly, stock purchase prices and sales prices are not monitored either. The sales price is matched to the sale price reported by the brokerage house, but again what your basis is in any of these assets is a mystery to the IRS - they just believe whatever a person puts on the tax return, trusting that they will tell the truth. Without an audit, no one is looking over your shoulder. Since January 1, 2011 the brokerage houses are required to report the complete transaction, both buying and selling.

Brokerage houses were able to keep track of new stock purchase prices and they did but for years were not required to report them to the IRS. Now they have to, if they know it.

Higher Education Tax Credit Fraud

Congress wants people going to higher education to have a tax break, so it is written into the law. In 2010 the IRS paid 2.1 million people $3.2 billion, even though they did not qualify for the education tax credit or related credits. It is suspicious that half of those returns were prepared by tax professionals.

Unethical Tax Professionals

I have known tax professionals that owe large income tax or employment tax balances and use it as advertising. I knew one who was convicted on non-tax related felony charges. One tax attorney would show his own personal Notice of Federal Tax Lien for over $1,000,000 as proof of how he got away without paying taxes. He advertised that "If I can beat the IRS – you can too!" He was very successful and attracted many clients that way. But strangely this income did not show up on his tax return when I was reviewing it. Tax attorneys and businesses that advertise on the radio and television making false claims as to what they can do for you with the IRS are also unethical. They violate the Circular 230 which governs how tax professionals are supposed to conduct themselves and their tax affairs.

Chronic Delinquent Taxpayers and Serial Non-Payers

Many business people apparently go into business with the intention of never paying the taxes incurred by the business. These can be corporate income taxes or excise taxes or employment (payroll) taxes. They do this because they can operate their businesses for 30-40% less than a business that complies with the tax laws. Not paying corporate income tax, or the income tax withholding of 20%, the Social Security taxes/Medicare taxes of 15.3%, or the unemployment insurance tax which is 1-6%, allows them to underbid jobs. Since they never pay the taxes or not even file the returns, they can run this scam for years without being detected by the IRS computers.

These are either service businesses or they lease most of their equipment. When the IRS comes in and tries to collect from the company, it finds no assets or equity in anything. So it turns to the responsible officers of the corporation or LLC. The officer/member has already set his/her lifestyle up where they also lease everything. So the IRS or the responsible officer closes the corporation/LLC that has the balance due.

Then, the responsible person opens another corporation/LLC and runs up tax liabilities. I have seen some people do this four, five, even six times. Each time, they are hiding money and staying one step in front of the IRS. In fact, some of these delinquent taxpayers are more familiar with IRS Collection Procedures than new Revenue Officers.

The IRS can transfer the taxes over to the person who is really behind these tax delinquencies, but it is an administrative and judicial nightmare and rarely done. Congress has the power to simplify this process.

Loans to Shareholder

This is a deduction that is used to hide cash income. When a business closes, the IRS has no systemic follow up to monitor this. The money that was a loan should be reported as income if the loan is never repaid. But many times, it is not and many people get away with this tax dodge. This also applies to businesses that start up and then buy assets and inventory which are deducted as an expense against other income. Then they fold those companies after one or two years. The IRS does nothing about this scenario, either. The law says that those assets should revert to becoming income to the person receiving them.

Lost Treasures Found

Some people delight in confusing the tax collector. In my early days, I would collect tax returns that showed income because taxpayers filed but did not pay to avoid criminal prosecution. But then they would write in the payment section that the money had been deposited in a National Bank in the United States in the name of the IRS and for the benefit of the taxpayer.

I would go around to local banks and never found the money. I had about a dozen of these and I never found the money of these wise guys. In those days it was easy to open a bank account without showing any identification or proof of Social Security number. I had to wait years until the banks would turn the money over to the State Treasurer's Office of Unclaimed Monies and then I would levy on it.

When I worked in Chicago, the Chicago Tribune would print a huge special section on unclaimed money in the State. There were hundreds of IRS employees, but I was the only one who read the article and acted on it. It was a Sunday and I went into my bosses' office on Monday and explained and then contacted the State and then issued levies and in those accounts I found $2.1 million. It doesn't take much to be a shining star at the IRS. Just a little initiative goes a long way. Eventually the IRS National Office was informed and this became a standard practice throughout the United States. As I write this, I checked the State of Illinois and State of Arizona and again see dozens of accounts in the name of the Internal Revenue Service. I wonder if anyone is following up on this since I retired.

Prisoners Winning the IRS Lottery

Refund Fraud due to prisoners filing tax returns is a big money business. From 2004 to 2009, prisoners illegally claimed $800 million in refunds. The IRS proudly talks about how it prevented $677.2 million in false refunds. That is fine. The problem with this is the IRS admits that it issued $122.8 million to prisoners in that time. In 2012 alone, 138,000 inmates filed for $1 billion in fraudulent refunds, most got caught, but $70 million was paid out to inmates.

This happens because the IRS does not buy information that is used by private business that tells whether the addresses are jails, prisons, hospitals, post office boxes, mail box stores, rooming houses and other places that may seek to hide the origin of the money.

Tax Exempt Organizations Fraud

Tax exempt (charities) organizations are often the targets of fraud by unscrupulous individuals. Many of the people attracted to the cause of the organization are not business people. So they help the fund raising efforts and then embezzlement often occurs. TIGTA reports that 1,200 tax exempt organizations owe IRS tax balances of over $100,000 *each*. According to TIGTA, 64,200 tax exempt organizations (3.8%) owed nearly $875 million in Federal tax debt as of June 16, 2012. There is so much fraud in the application and approval of tax exempt status by the IRS. I have seen a case where a wealthy lady was a hoarder and liked poodles. She had 23 poodles. She created a not for profit whose goal was to take in poodles and arrange for their viewing and adoption. She then took most of the expenses of running her house as business expenses and soon she had 45 poodles. She put them up for adoption on her website, but after people visited her dirty house, they rarely adopted the dogs.

Another man I knew was very concerned about the issue of preserving and protecting rare and antique books. He loved books. In fact he bought the house next to his to store the collection. It is only about 40 feet away from his house. He has it open to the public the first Saturday of each month, by appointment only. The 2000 square foot house is packed full of rare books and the Government, in effect, subsidizes the purchase and running of his "private museum."

Yet another man was passionate about giving money to a charity that helped children. So he raised tens of thousands of dollars in his high society fund raising parties. In effect his social life was financed by his tax exempt organization. At the end of the first year he had donations of $100,000 and he did donate $10,000 to a charity, but the other $90,000 was gobbled up in administrative expenses.

Some very wealthy people also wish to further their own political interests by forming a Super-Pac (a 501(c) 4 not for profit organization) and fund it so that they can influence elections.

There are many cases where the IRS is granting tax exempt status to people who do not have charity as their goal at all. Since the Tea Party Scandal, the IRS has made it extra easy to apply for a not for profit organization status. This is just another IRS created crisis in the making.

Government Contractors as Delinquent Taxpayers

It is not just the IRS employees and other Federal employees who owe taxes, it is also Federal contractors - private companies that work to do government tasks from running prisons to building bombs. This is nothing compared to the rest of the Federal government. There are 27,000 defense contractors, 3,300 civilian agency contractors and 3,800 general services administration contractors that owe the United States Government $7.6 billion in delinquent taxes. This is outrageous. **"You are only as good as the company you keep."**

Outside contractors who provide goods and services to the IRS collectively owe $589 million in unpaid federal taxes.

But it is not just outside contractors who do not pay their taxes. It is also other federal government agencies. As of December 31, 2011, there were 39 agencies delinquent in filing tax returns and another 70 agencies who owed at least $14 million in unpaid taxes.

18

IRS Seizures and Sales

I remember one man who was interested in Lincoln Continentals. He had not paid taxes in years and maxed out his credit cards to purchase them. He had used the tax money to buy 27 Lincolns and he knew they would appreciate in value. He said he just had a sense they would be worth a lot of money one day. They were all stored in an old barn. If his investment had played out one day he would have been a rich man. But, he seemed to forget that he had taken all the money from the Government and private creditors. But really the money is from the people - you and me who actually pay taxes. A week before I was going to seize them he convinced someone else to buy the collection. He paid his taxes and all his bills and had $25,000 left over. He actually thanked me - he said he thought that he had gone a little crazy over the old Lincoln Continentals.

He Could Have Been Really Rich

I remember one IRS seizure in Phoenix that featured a rare car. It was a 1967 Ferrari 330 P4. The man who it had been seized from owed a lot of taxes. According to news reports, he had been disputing income taxes since the 1970's. He had served time in prison for drug charges, performing illegal abortions, and for concealing three of his Ferraris from an IRS investigation. In anticipation of hiding his assets from the IRS, he had invested his money in high end autos. He put them in a building in Florida and thought he had outsmarted the IRS. He had 18 Ferraris, an old Indy race car and an Avanti. According to news reports; the collection in the building was worth $60 million. I heard he felt so positive about this that he did not feel he needed any insurance on the cars as they were all in his building according to news reports. Then Hurricane Charley hit and he lost all but one car. The one that the IRS was able to seize from the collection was away for repair in Arizona. That same month the IRS filed a Federal Tax Lien against him for $2,921,293. So then the IRS seized the 1967 Ferrari 330 P4, one of only three made, with an estimated value of $20 million. The IRS minimum auction bid was $2 million. The taxpayer was able to pay $600,000 to the IRS just before the sale and made other arrangements to get the IRS off his back.

Recent stories found on the internet show that this same man sold a landfill for $7.5 million in a recent year and claimed that year to have no income. The IRS saw it differently and assessed him more than $1 million. He is facing up to 5 years in prison for this.

They Hide - I Seek

I have met many very successful businessmen who are able to attract lots of money and make a game out of hiding it from the IRS. All of them have accrued assets but lived very simply in huge houses.

When I went on a tour of Frank Lloyd Wright's Taliesin Complex in Arizona, the tour guide told us that Frank Lloyd Wright did not agree with taxation and was always in trouble with the IRS. He said the famous architect would buy rare cars and store them all over the country in a game where the IRS agent could seize them if he could find them.

Anything to Save a Few Bucks

In another case, a man hid his properties under secret trusts and other people's names to avoid paying income taxes. A bank held title to the properties and would receive the real estate tax bills and for a small charge forward them to the owner. So in this case the person had 112 houses and large apartment buildings and because of the small fees charged by the banks, he was paying out $10,000 a year just to get the property tax bills. But this was the price for secrecy. Other investors understood this. But this guy was greedy.

At first, while researching this man I could only find that he owned his house and had an income from his small business. But my sixth sense told me that there was more. I already had checks that he had written for the prior 3 years and then finally I found a $20 check on his personal account, dated 3 years back to a small bank in a faraway town. So I issued a summons to that bank to see what it was for.

A week later, I was sitting in the bank's board room surrounded by 30 boxes of records outlining the details of the 112 properties he owned. He owned - in whole or in part - a 160 unit apartment complex, smaller apartment complexes, condos, and homes. I also learned of other properties he owned in Europe. A rough estimate of his wealth was about $67 million. To save the $10,000 fee, he had listed his name on every title that the bank held, where it said send tax bills to his name. At that time there was no way of crosschecking this on computers. Computers were not widely used then. All the records were on paper in huge dusty old books in the County Recorder's office.

This led to a criminal investigation and a huge tax audit that eventually resulted in the Government collecting millions of dollars in unpaid taxes. If you had looked at his business or tax returns - no way could he have purchased this much property. I tried to talk to him, but he returned to the European country where he held dual citizenship. This saved him from the criminal charges so we just got the tax money from his properties instead.

When he had been in business, I remember his customers telling how he used to say the IRS is so stupid that you can get away with anything - because the IRS will never figure it out. So this small act of greed - trying to avoid $10,000 in bank fees - ended up costing him millions of dollars.

Tax Protester Advice

Another case that I remember is when I went to a large 100-year-old house that was falling down. I knocked on the door looking for a man who owed $693,000, a man from a pioneer family who should have been labeled as potentially dangerous and a tax protester - terms the IRS used to use to identify some taxpayers. But nothing was on the case file telling me who he was or that he might be a problem. I talked to his wife and found out that he had just gotten out of federal prison for tax evasion after a 40-month sentence. He had been a successful inventor who one day had just had enough with the tax system and everything else. He had planned his revenge for years; he had divested himself of his assets before he did anything illegal. Friends and family owned all the stuff that he used or needed in his life. He even had a patent on some tool but he sold that for a lot of money before he owed any taxes, and it disappeared into the stream of cash. When I finally did meet him, he just laughed at me and said that I was a pawn of the rich people who run this country. Then since he had no income or assets, I closed the case as currently not collectible due to financial hardship. I guess he won in the end.

The Mills of God Grind Slowly But they Grind Exceedingly Fine

Sometimes, I am not the only force working on a case. I remember one man who through a string of corporations owed $2 million. His was a service business and he had not paid any employment taxes. He had disguised where the income from the business had come from through fake names and employer identification numbers.

This was another case I sent to Criminal Investigation, but they were not interested because the money was already gone. There was nothing for them to seize. I was trying to figure out what part of this huge international corporation was paying him $500,000 a month. When I finally found out, I issued a levy and then I heard from him. He was begging, pleading and crying and then cursing, screaming and threatening. This was the third corporation he had done this with and he took his ill-gotten proceeds to Mexico and bought beach front houses. My simple levy brought down his whole house of cards. He did not want to discuss, negotiate or compromise on his position. Add on to that his cocaine addiction and he said that he had really high overhead every month. The first month I levied I got $247,000 - a drop in the bucket. The corporation dropped him and he was out of business. There was a second check under levy for $147,000. He was on his way to my office one day and got hit by two other cars and his neck was broken. He cannot walk or feel anything below his neck. I released enough to cover his medical insurance and the family living expenses and collected another $47,000. I felt like some power higher than me had helped me to resolve that case.

19

Physical and Verbal Threats to IRS Employees

IRS EMPLOYEES ARE PHYSICALLY ASSAULTED and threatened at least 50 times a month, I learned in one training class I attended. I read a report that claimed that IRS employees are subject to more assaults than the FBI, the U.S. Marshall or the Drug Enforcement Agency combined. That would make sense since all three of those agencies require their employees to have guns. Being a revenue officer was not only hazardous to my physical health but also my emotional health. It was depressing to be hated just because of who I worked for.

When you think about the IRS, maybe you have never thought of the risk to employees from threats and assaults. Many jobs in the IRS involve making contacts with taxpayers at their homes and businesses, and there is a high risk of assault. They have to drive into sections of cities that are dangerous or hostile to government agents. They are verbally assaulted and sometimes physically assaulted – some have even been killed in the line of duty. Most of the time, the IRS does not know exactly where these employees are. There is no systematic or electronic tracking of their whereabouts. The IRS does not have any accurate system for tracking the movements of its own employees like the U.S. Postal Service or Fed Ex or UPS. An employee can go missing for days without a question being asked.

Even dogs and errant children can be tracked with technology today. Not IRS agents in the field!

The IRS was really good at getting me into potentially dangerous and completely unsupervised situations often in places that were far from the middle of nowhere. I have been pushed, backed up to the wall by a man grabbing my necktie, I have had a table flipped over on my legs, had people pull guns on me, and been threatened by a mobster who wanted to kill me and blow up my family. I have had things thrown at me, been spat upon and verbally threatened on dozens of occasions. I have been physically assaulted 5 times in 33 years. One of my fellow revenue officers was threatened seriously enough for his house to be kept under watch. He said his kids got rides to and from school from an armed Government agent.

Many jobs in the IRS involve making contacts and cold field calls to taxpayer's homes and businesses, and there is a high risk of assault. They drive in parts of cities and the country that are dangerous. Some cities have areas delineated by the IRS as High Risk Assault Areas (HRAA). If I had field calls in those areas, I would just drive by but was instructed not to get out of the car.

Occasionally IRS employees are threatened from within. One IRS employee worked in an administrative position in the IRS and had access to Human Resources Records. She stole the identities of at least 160 current and former IRS employees. She applied for charge cards with retailers and banks to get cash from ATM's, and goods and services illegally. The key to this is she changed their addresses without their knowledge so it took a long time to discover the fraud. The conspiracy resulted in over $1 million in goods and services stolen. She is awaiting sentencing.

It is dangerous being in an IRS office especially between April 14 and April 20. This is because some people start protesting taxes on the 14th. I like legitimate freedom of expression in the form of protest - but some people have serious delusional beliefs. Then on the 15th the protests continue. Once a man left his two children with me at my office one April 15th for a whole day because he said he was not able to feed them because I had taken his bank account and paycheck. I held off calling the police as we stuffed them with candy and ice cream. Then a sympathetic police officer found their mother and turned them over to her - she was separated from the husband.

April 19 is the anniversary of the Waco, Texas massacre of 78 men, women and children by the FBI and what used to be a sister agency of the IRS - the Bureau of Alcohol, Tobacco and Firearms. Then also on April 19, 1995 was the Oklahoma City explosion of the Federal Building which killed 168 people and injured 680, many of them federal employees. This is a fringe part of society that I tried to avoid. I recommend not being on federal land during this time. April 20 is Adolph Hitler's birthday and that day brings out a whole different group of strange anti-government protesters.

Security in the Field and the Office

On February 18, 2010, IRS Revenue Officer Group Manager Vernon Hunter was in the Austin, Texas IRS office when a non-taxpayer flew his airplane into the IRS office that had 190 employees. He killed Revenue Officer Hunter and seriously wounded 15 other people. Checking people at the door cannot help that. In early 2000, one office I was in was chosen because it was in a private building and 400 IRS employees were to be working on 3 floors - in the mid-section of the building. A security expert who came to talk to us said that it made it a less likely target for a crazy taxpayer or terrorist attack. That is clearly not what happened in that privately owned ten story building in Austin. The delinquent taxpayer who hated the IRS just flew his airplane loaded with extra gasoline into the side of the building. This resulted in a large explosion and fireball according to news reports.

Being in the field making cold calls is also a very dangerous time. One ex-IRS auditor named James Bradley age 63 had retired and been audited and he owed $2,500. The IRS sent out an old revenue officer who knew him. His name was Michael Dillon age 61. Mr. Bradley had paid $2,000 but still owed $500. It was most unusual for the IRS to spend the expense of a grade 12 high ranking revenue officer for a $500 balance due. But they did it because they always harass current and ex-IRS and other federal employees if they owe tax money. When Revenue Officer Dillon asked for the money, Mr. Bradley shot him three times with an M-1 rifle at point blank range according to news accounts. So the IRS named a federal building and a National Award after Mr. Dillon. Poor guy, all those years in the IRS and he could have already retired. But he had devoted his life to his job and lost his life.

Please Don't Shoot

When I was a new revenue officer, I was making a field call in the dead of winter in rural farmland 60 miles from the next big town. They used sand on the roads to protect the crop land from salt and I was in training with my coach. We went to a large ranch house. I had everything pretty much under control during the interview. The IRS demanded that I be "Firm but Fair" in my contacts with my taxpayers. I was being caring and sympathetic and was getting the financial information I needed to close the case. Then my coach started telling the guy what a lowlife he was and then the guy exploded. He threw all the papers off the table and kicked his chair over backwards. I stepped between him and my coach. I got them all settled down and we sat down again. Then I was almost done; the man had lost his marriage and his farm and soon his house to a bad economy and a big drinking problem. He had no work and was at the end of his rope.

In those days I could not close a case without getting the taxpayer to sign the form. I know, another dumb IRS rule - the IRS felt that it was important for the taxpayer to sign under the penalties of perjury statement although they rarely, if ever, prosecute anyone for lying on the financial statement or the tax returns.

So I had two more lines to go on the form and then the coach said another antagonistic remark and the man exploded. He picked up a captain's chair from the dinette set and smashed three shelves on the wall knocking all the plates and cups on the floor; broken dishes littered the floor. I decided that we should leave right then. But my coach kept saying things and then the taxpayer went to get his shotgun. I was literally backing out pulling my coach behind me. He kept saying stuff that could get us killed. I had a tiny Nissan Sentra and I slipped and slid out of the driveway.

When I got to the road, I turned the wrong way. Just before I hit the gas we saw him come out with the shotgun. This scared the hell out of me and still in the car the coach kept bad mouthing this guy. I drove to the end of the road. There was deep snow on both sides and a chain at the end of the road. I saw a farmhouse at the end of this long road so I got out of the car and walked over in my dress shoes and knocked on the door, and the farmer told me he thought I was lucky that the guy had not shot me - everyone around there knew he was a crazy drunk. How could I get out? So this wonderful, amazing farmer took me out to the barn and put a plow on the end of his tractor and plowed his road so that I could get to the state route and get the hell out of there. I could have been killed. But I was happy to know that at least the buckshot would have to go through my coach first.

Making field calls was dangerous because I wouldn't know who would open the door. The IRS does not purchase or share any information that would help to identify taxpayers or people they are in contact with (family, friends, business associates who may be afflicted with mental health issues, or who have been accused or convicted of crimes.) Sometimes I would knock on a door and find people who had been found guilty of assaulting a police officer, murder, rape, bank robbery, battery, serial drunk driving, unlawful restraint, or abduction. You name it, I have met them all. Once an off duty stripper au natural answered the door and I interviewed her for ten minutes. Some people who get out of jail still are not in a good place and believe me - you don't want to be the one knocking on their door. The IRS really does not care that much about employee safety and security - in the building or out of the street.

For instance, in Chicago, it was not unusual to receive bomb threats over the phone. We had a Federal Protective Service Officer come and tell us that most of them were false and we should not get too worried about it. They did not want us to have to disrupt our work day thinking we might get blown up. Originally when a bomb threat came in the people on that floor and the floor above and below it would be ordered out of the building. Then a search with dogs etc. would take place. The IRS is very vulnerable when it is located in public or private buildings. A person with an issue against the IRS just needs to get in the building and if they are in the elevator they can leave a package or explosive etc. It is right next to the wall where the IRS people already are. So this security expert told us from then on they would only evacuate people within 25 feet of the bomb threat area. You are probably thinking this is funny and crazy at the same time. Then this security expert said that with every bomb there is an acceptable kill rate - so many people per square feet. He was serious; there are security people in the IRS who actually determine how many employees it is OK to lose.

In 2014, at the Tucson IRS office, a suspected bomb was blown up less than 25 feet away from IRS employees and taxpayers who were doing business as usual. No notification, no evacuation. We always knew there was a threat by the increased line of Federal Protective Service Cars (Federal Police) parked around the perimeter of the building. This was supposed to scare people off who wished us harm.

After the Oklahoma City Federal Building was blown up, we got increased security but like I said a well-placed car or truck bomb could change all that in an instant.

I worked for the IRS National Office for 6 months and they have some great security. But the local offices never had any security until 9/11, when security greatly increased in all offices. Buildings were reconfigured to prevent vehicles from getting too close. Now taxpayers have to take off their jewelry, belt, and shoes as well as have their purse, backpack or briefcase hand searched and x-rayed just to get in the building.

National Office was different because in many conference rooms they have floor to ceiling draperies - like from the 1960's and they cover one wall of the room. Behind the curtains are these huge vault doors 6' across at least. The secrets of the IRS are contained within.

In all the times when I was assaulted or threatened, nothing ever happened to those hurting me, except the IRS sent out a couple of agents with guns to scare the hell out of the big mouth crazy person who had assaulted or threatened me.

Tax protestor is a term that the IRS used in the past to describe a person or organization that advocates non-filing and non-payment of Federal Tax Returns and balances due.

In the early 1980's there was a lot of this activity in rural communities in Illinois. One time I had to seize the home of a prominent tax evader in a small town in a rural area. He was a big shot with the group called the Posse Comitatus. They not only do not pay taxes, they also advocate that others do not pay taxes either. So I did all my seizure paperwork and planning and requested two armed criminal agents to protect me. Remember, I only had my cardboard credentials to protect me.

I learned that this tax protester owned several weapons. The law required that I go to the door and hand the papers to the owner of the house. I planned all the details of the seizure. So did the Criminal Agents - but each from our own perspective – as it turned out.

It was a glorious fall day - and agents reached in the trunk and pulled out two bullet proof vests. I asked where mine was. They said "You don't get one." I said "But I am the one going to the door. You will be behind me." They very seriously said "Don't worry - if they shoot you fall to the left and we will take him out." If I was nervous and stressed before, now I was downright afraid. Especially since I have never heard in 33 years of an IRS Criminal Agent ever firing his gun in the line of duty. They have some reputation for being like Barney Fife from Mayberry. So I walked up and knocked on the door and the man's wife and a group of people answered the door and I served the papers on her. Without incident. We got out of there quickly.

Then a month later, I held the sale in a room in a rural post office. 100 people were marching around the building with posters expressing anti-tax and anti-government sentiments. I went in with the two criminal agents who again were looking bulky due to wearing their bullet proof vests under their coats. Potential buyers were afraid to come in at first. So I waited and waited. Finally a man came in with $22,000 in cash and I held the sale and sold the house to that man. I was so relieved. It is very embarrassing to the collection effort to seize something and then have to release it back to the person I seized it from.

I found out later he was an undercover government agent from the Treasury Department. He used funds from a special fund to purchase the house. The Government would have been embarrassed in its tax compliance efforts if the house was seized and we could not sell it. In that case, it would have been handed back to the tax protester and this would have looked bad.

When the sale was over and we wanted to leave, we heard and saw the crowd. They were getting wild and started throwing eggs and tomatoes at the Post Office building. The Postmaster was losing his cool and told us we could not get back to our car - it was surrounded.

Some people had tire irons and baseball bats and this was not turning out very well. So the Postmaster made me promise never to use his Post Office for anything ever again. Then he loaded us into the back of a Post Office Delivery Truck and had us delivered to another post office in the next town. We waited for some other criminal agents to pick us up there. Two days later they returned to pick up the Government car and it had a smashed windshield and dents.

Dangerous Tax Professionals

The IRS has a separate problem with tax professionals that it seems to have no control over.

There are 84 tax professionals who are CPA's, tax attorneys and enrolled agents who the IRS identifies with warning codes as Potentially Dangerous Taxpayer (PDT) or Caution on Contact (CAU). This means they have said or threatened to do things that were violent to IRS employees. In fact there were four physical assaults to employees by tax professionals over a two year period. But they are still tax professionals licensed to practice before the IRS. Go figure.

Although this number is a small percentage of the 2.3 million tax representatives, the IRS employees have no access to this information when they make contact with these representatives. This is in part because the IDRS system is unable to mark every case in a way that would warn the employees that the representative is dangerous. This is just another sign that the IRS does not take care of their employees.

Dangerous Taxpayers

You Do Not Want to Be a Member of this Club!

As mentioned, there are people who do not want to pay taxes at all. One such group of people advocates bringing down the government through passive and violent methods. This group was classified by the IRS as Illegal Tax Protesters. Tax protestor is a term that the IRS used in the past to describe a person or organization that advocated non-filing and none payment of Federal Tax Returns and balances due. Technically the IRS was required to stop using that term after 1998, but you can believe that it still vigorously tracks such illegal activity. The former IRS Historian Shelly L. Davis stated that the IRS kept lists of citizens "for no other reason than their political activities might have offended someone at the IRS." She charged that "anyone who offers even legitimate criticism of the tax collector is labeled as a tax protester."

These are people who are either protesting the use of the tax money, saying they do not wish to pay for war or atomic weapons, or they are people who are challenging the legality of the tax laws. Protesting is not against the law. But regardless of why they are protesting, these people are still being tracked by the IRS. You can protest but still pay, or can stop filing and paying. This is against the law and will get you into trouble eventually. Now the IRS may classify these people as PDT - Potentially Dangerous Taxpayers - or as Frivolous Return Filers, or Non-Filers. This is kind of like being found guilty of something but without any legal hearing. No 1st Amendment rights or due process rights are in force here.

I also met several well-known people who organized thousands of people by telling them they did not need to file or pay taxes.

The IRS called them "Tax Protestors Promoters." They officially advertised they had never filed or paid Federal income taxes. People believed them. The ones who did not file or pay went to jail. Really now, don't you think the other tax avoidance promoters really did file and pay their taxes? It always made me wonder. The IRS could never say yes or no publicly without the alleged tax protester's consent. And since your tax records are always confidential, that would never happen. Those people make a lot of money traveling around fleecing people who get into trouble with the IRS years later.

In the past, there were illegal tax protestor designations, high profile cases, sensitive cases, highly sensitive cases, or project cases, all giving the IRS employees special directions on how to deal with that case. Then there were the residents of High Risk Assault Areas, which were urban areas the government officially recognized as too dangerous to send unarmed tax collectors and auditors into. All of these make for special classes of taxpayers, who may have done nothing to warrant this designation.

Being an IRS employee is not an easy job on the best of days. Think about it. It seems the whole U.S. population hates you. People are verbally abusive and it can get physical quickly. I am talking about being hit, threatened, and thrown against the wall. One day I was supposed to be at work to open a call site at 6am but for some reason I was late. Thank God, because when I got there, a pipe bomb had gone off five minutes before. It shattered windows and had started a fire. I would have been walking through that door if I had been on time that day. Being a revenue officer was a job I was good at, but it was never easy.

Due to the abuse, some employees suffer more than others and resort to self-medication to survive. I heard a group of employees talking once about how hard it was to sleep or relax. One said the real problem is the alcohol (consumed the night before) starts to wear off at about 4am. Another employee shared a solution that worked for him; he said he keeps Nyquil PM next to the bed and takes a shot of it and gets another two hours of sleep. This is tragic.

Other IRS employees use religion to cope; it is not uncommon to find employees at their desks reading their prayer books and Bibles. Other agents use prescription drugs, anti-depressants mostly; some also had blood pressure pills and Valium. One of the common threads at the IRS is food. We loved food, especially coffee and chocolate. It helped to deal with the stress. Some employees have calendars that count off the exact number of days until they can retire, even if that is years in the future. They have trouble facing each day.

Many groups have employees who are so burned out from just trying to figure out the job that they barely have time or energy to relate to each other. In fact in one office I was assigned to, the Group Manager canceled the Christmas parties because he felt we were too busy with work and he also said he had forgotten about Christmas.

IRS Employees in Danger

The IRS has 25,000 employees who make physical contact with taxpayers. Taxpayer cases can be coded PDT and CAU as previously explained also. Sometimes rightly and sometimes based on vindictive testimony by an IRS employee. Taxpayers with this code include those that advocate violence against the Government or the IRS or the employee or his family, or that have filed liens or erroneous law suits against the IRS employees to damage their personal credit, those with a propensity towards violence, and those who have made suicide threats. In the past, I could call other government agencies - federal or state or local - and report I had a suicide threat from a taxpayer who is in need of help - but that RRA changed that to "protect" the confidential nature of the tax problems. That leads to the tax issue that I wrote about previously, regarding the lady who was the tax lawyer who was not capable of handling her own affairs and has no family backup. Now this problem is reported to TIGTA, which has a lengthy review process to determine if they should make contact or not with suicidal taxpayers. The process is so cumbersome that I have heard that by the time TIGTA made contact some taxpayers had already killed themselves.

20

Identity Theft

THE IRS IS SUPPOSED TO provide an Identity Protection Personal Identification Number to each victim of refund/identity fraud. This would help them to get their refund faster in the future. The law requires it, but TIGTA found that 11% of taxpayers did not get this number and suffered because of it. Although they did issue 13,220 PIN's to deceased taxpayers. TIGTA also points out in a report that 759,446 taxpayers got a PIN - but no instructions on what to do with it and how important it was to keep confidential - it was like a second Social Security number.

During January to May most IRS resources are devoted to the filing and processing of the tax returns and getting the tax refunds out within 45 days. This is very important to know. If the IRS does not issue a refund within 45 days, they have to pay interest on it. In 1985 the rate was 13%, it had been as high as 16% in 1983 and stayed over 10% for most of the 1980's. Today the interest rate is 3%.

Plus the Revenue Reconciliation Act of 1998 (RRA) mandated that returns would be issued more quickly. This ties in with a family needing their refund to pay off their Christmas bills or take vacations. It is good public relations to get the refunds out quickly. This is key to understanding the current refund/identity fraud problem. Some IRS manager must have really screamed and in those days it was not uncommon to hear managers yelling at employees. Somebody was going to save the Government so much money if they could just get the refunds out faster. Now the IRS has electronic filing and that made the demand increase for faster return processing and faster refunds, on average in 9.6 days. The computer does not ask questions or do a background search or match any of the information you put on the tax return. For instance - you have never filed before but now are claiming $10,000 in income and a refund of $5,000. The IRS will pay. (Or if you have not filed for the last two years and file for a refund of $314,000 and want it sent to an address in Hungary, you are likely to get your check. One address in Hong Kong received 555 refunds. Another in Hungary received 603 refunds at the same address.)

The IRS does not cross check when a person files for a refund to see if they have any income or tax withholdings. It trusts that the taxpayer must be telling the truth. This is a strategy that does not work in today's business world. When was the last time you bought a car just on your good word and a handshake? It is as simple as looking at past income history and 1099's and W-2's that would be required to be filed electronically which would provide instant access. The IRS does not do this and that is the crime here. The IRS issues checks that no one in the business world would ever issue. Based on "trust". The IRS issues refund checks to people who make false claims on tax returns.

This is because of another old IRS idea that every case can be worked in the "bulk pipeline." That means that the cases are not worked by people, but mostly by the computer. The antique computer decides to send the checks out. That is what it was programmed to do 54 years ago. It only takes a new computer or extensive reprogramming to make this change. A clerk could look at tax refund claims that look suspicious. If you owe the IRS, you automatically lose your refund. But the computer screws that up also sometimes. The IRS is consistent at being inconsistent and chaotic and is most effective at striking fear in the hearts of taxpayers.

Identity Theft and Refund Fraud

The only reason that there is refund/identity fraud is that the IRS allows and encourages it. It is hard to say they are being robbed when the IRS willingly and knowingly continue to issue checks. It is irresponsible.

There are many kinds of refund fraud. It basically means that a person files a fake tax return claiming a refund is due, and the IRS pays it. The IRS does not check and compare the information claimed on the return for at least six months to a year later. The IRS just assumes that the return is legitimate, so they pay the refund.

I believe that the greatest leaks of confidential tax information is occurring right in the unsecured data transmission or leaks by employees in the IRS and Social Security Administration. There is too much identity fraud of old and disabled people to suggest otherwise. These people do not have active credit purchases, new mortgage loans or other financial transactions that would put their name, address and Social Security numbers out into the business world. Many of these people are not required to file tax returns because their income is too low.

Sometimes the IRS is afraid to be in charge. It holds the money, it has the power to require businesses to file all W-2 forms electronically, and it can program the computer to figure out when suspicious activity is happening. They do not have to wait until after it has happened and then try to correct it. The IRS is putting out small brush fires and failing to see that the whole forest is on fire.

The Internal Revenue Service has great discretionary authority to issue procedures to do a better job at assessing and collecting taxes than it does. The IRS used to do that. They made plans and announcements that worked to make the system better. They did not worry about what Congress and everyone else had to say about it.

What is the Source of the Social Security Number Leaks?

Where does the information come from? There are many companies, and payroll processing firms that have access to a great deal of information: names, Social Security numbers, addresses and dates of birth. There is a growing black market for this information. But I suggest that the market is small. It is too labor intense. I had unlimited access to millions of taxpayer accounts on the computer. I did not even need to go into each account. There are lists on the IDRS computer that will show me all that information for 10 taxpayers at one time.

Large amounts of data have already escaped IRS attention. Unlimited access to the Master File and opportunity exist for an employee to quickly download millions of taxpayer accounts. These have a double value. They can be sold on the black market, or that individual can file for refunds directly. The IRS has put at least 3,000 employees into the Identity Fraud program and I was trained also in it. The IRS and its computers cannot question whether the refund you claim is good or not, because they always pay even though they have not received or processed the W-2 forms. The W-2 is due from small employers who still file paper W-2's by March 31 and if the W-2's are electronically filed they are also due by March 31. This reminds me of the old Chicago elections - where they said vote early and vote often. So in this case file early and file often. Then the IRS does not match the W-2 data to what people claimed on their tax returns until July and August.

In order to electronically file the W-2s you have to submit 250 or more. This is like a science calculated to make some people very rich and few are caught, let alone convicted. It is white collar crime taken to the next level. The refunds - sometimes hundreds - go to a single address if they request a paper check, but more often than not, they go to pre-paid debit cards which are untraceable and a good source of cash and items. They also favor using direct deposit bank accounts. You can retire and have your Social Security check sent to most countries except North Korea and Cuba and the same goes for your fraudulent income tax refund. Tens of thousands of refunds are wired into either a foreign bank account or into domestic accounts and then transferred online to foreign banks. The IRS does not have any access or control over this once the refund is issued.

Many people think white collar crime is one without a victim, likes it's no big deal. Like taking the tax money you hold in trust for your employees. My view is there are victims all over the place. Our middle class, working class, veterans and children all suffer, in part from Congress and in part from lack of funds designated to their causes.

Then there is the fact that the IRS regularly shares confidential tax data with 300 state and federal agencies. Who knows who has access to the information at that point. Do those people that have access have the same level or integrity and background checks as IRS employees have, I wonder.

The IRS system of trusting what a taxpayer puts on their return without any verification is a system that does not work anymore. It is like a person going to the bank and withdrawing money even though they don't have an account at that bank.

The IRS response after you have experienced Identity Fraud is almost as bad as the fraud itself - they often delay your refund up to 6 months. The person whose identity is stolen is usually the last person who learns about it, because so many people have no regular need to file tax returns because their income is too low.

The name of the game with filing tax returns to file first, because the IRS will give you credit for whatever you claim on your return, it will credit you income, withholdings, dependents and filing status, all without crosschecking or verifying anything. As mentioned earlier, this is a contentious issue with couples who have separated or divorced and a state court may award the dependents to one or the other parent. The IRS will pay the money to whoever files first.

The IRS does not abide by anything that a state court says; as a federal agency - it does not recognize state court actions at all. If you sue the IRS in state court, they will notice it and then have it transferred to a federal court and then they can decide, under the right of sovereign immunity, if they will let you sue them or not. Then you are bound by Federal Court rulings.

The IRS stated that its refund fraud program caught $24.2 billion in false refund claims, but admitted $5.2 billion was actually paid out in 2011. In 2012 $3.6 billion was paid out. In 2013, 3 million fraudulent refunds were filed and it is estimated that the number is even higher. The Treasury Inspector General projected that refund/identity fraud could cost $21 billion a year by the year 2016, despite the IRS efforts. This takes away taxpayer's confidence in the tax system. Most of the refunds are paid as direct deposits into bank accounts.

I do not like to propose conspiracy theories; but with this much "free money" it does make me wonder if some group is orchestrating this fraud.

Refund Fraud

There are many kinds of refund fraud. It basically means a person files a fake tax return claiming a refund is due, and the IRS pays it. The IRS does not check and compare the information claimed on the tax returns for at least six months to a year later. They just assume that the return is legitimate, so they pay the refund.

As a trained investigator with experience in forensic accounting, I wonder how so many cases of identify fraud involve people who are deceased or have little income and do not need to file tax returns. From what I have seen in my work and from what I have read, identity fraud is usually committed against people who have little or no income. The IRS and its employees have access to all this information.

As reported above, IRS employees already have unrestricted access to the entire name, address, Social Security number, income information and credit information; some have been convicted for abusing that. The IRS does have a system for detecting that. But even a first line employee could access hundreds of thousands of accounts before it would even be detected. That could take anywhere from a month to several years. There simply are no online audit controls to stop this.

The movies *Oceans 11, 12, and 13* were all exciting stories about high-profile robberies. The robberies required huge amounts of planning and strategy in order to gain large amounts of money. But cash and gold all takes a lot of room to pick up and move and then clean up through elaborate money laundering schemes. Direct deposit straight from the U.S. Treasury into your foreign bank account is so much quicker and cleaner.

Business Identity Fraud

An emerging problem is with business identity fraud. This can occur because each 1099 or W-2 form contains a business's Employer Identification Number and address. This can be used to file for large tax refunds on business returns. This is especially hard to find out about within the IRS system. Defunct businesses also have these EIN's and they can be used and no one knows. In the past, every single county recorder's office in the United States had copies of the Notice of Federal Tax liens that contained names, addresses and Social Security numbers and employer identification numbers. About 12 years ago they reimaged the copies to block out the numbers. But originals of these documents still exist in most counties either on paper, computer images, microfiche or microfilm. These are all sources for Social Security numbers and Employer Identification numbers.

Individual Identity Fraud

The strange circumstances of each case are not considered. Like you have filed for years and make $24,000 a year. Then suddenly you file and show income of $250,000 and request a $45,000 refund. Bam - you get the check. Estimates differ; I have heard that as few as 40% of these refunds are issued up to a higher percentage for lower dollar refunds. The IRS taught me in training that 80% of the tax-related identity theft occurs through electronically filed tax returns. Two years ago, I was told in my identity fraud class at the IRS that at least 450,000 identity theft cases were being worked. Some in just a few days. In 2014, the IRS processed 199 million individual income tax returns and 80% of them received refunds that averaged $3,000. Some received refunds in as little as 7 days. Let's think about that for a second. So 159 million taxpayers in effect loaned the United States Government $374 billion interest free for up to a year. That is what happens. It is a huge scandal taxpayers have grown comfortable with this system. Some use it as an automatic savings account - they are so happy to have the return of their own money - like it is an inheritance from some long lost uncle.

Identity Fraud/Ghosting

This is when you or someone else uses your identity for fraudulent purposes. There are many cases like this before the IRS. Criminals steal the identities of people who are dead, and mentally or physically disabled. In the past they could get information from Notice of Federal Tax. They would take advantage of the known lack of coordination between the IRS, Social Security and other federal agencies. Some people bribe employees who do payrolls for this information. They would manipulate the credit and banking systems to produce false entities that would then file for the IRS funds. That is why it is called ghosting.

When these people gain control of your financial/credit identity then they are able to easily manipulate the system and gain access to your personal affairs. Some just do it at the Federal Level so the fraud does not affect your credit, so you may not know your privacy has been violated for a year or more after the fraudulent refund has occurred. Each state or county maintains their own birth and death records and it is easy to put together another person - at least - on paper and use their name, Social Security number etc. Birth certificates have no pictures or finger prints. The County Clerk, the County Recorder, the Bureau of Vital Statistics are all rich information sources that can be used for tax fraud and ghosting.

What is the Underground Economy?

The most organized crime in America is the underground economy. These are people with jobs that work for cash or have businesses that are cash based. This is not reported to the IRS or taxed. These can be service businesses such as, carpet layer, carpenter, electrician, plumber, car sales and personal care. This might include your gardener, babysitter, nanny, cleaning lady, home health care aid, housekeeper, your hair stylist, your waiter or waitress or a person selling items at a flea market or on Amazon or EBay. People selling used cars, trimming trees, or anyone who has access to a cash business may not be reporting all or any of it.

A person who has a job may earn $60,000 but a person who is an under grounder can earn only $40,000 and have the same lifestyle - because they do not pay any taxes.

Sometimes a person in this economy will be receiving welfare, Earned Income Tax Credit, and unemployment compensation, disability or Social Security. All of these have income level restrictions. Benefits could be cut if income exceeds established levels.

Some businesses have cash and credit sales. The cash sales are never reported or only reported for part of the day. You can usually figure out which businesses these are. Any business that offers a cash discount may not be reporting the cash. At some retail stores or restaurants - cash sales are not counted. I remember one restaurant where it was standard policy to not ring cash sales after 5pm on the cash register. A few years ago credit processors were required to report to the IRS the amount of credit that they had processed. This caused a great deal of previously unreported income to suddenly be accounted for.

There are many estimates of how large the underground economy is. The government knows (I have heard estimates) of how large it is from IRS Economists. Many believe that the numbers that the IRS acknowledges are low - they have estimated that the underground economy is at least $2 trillion. The amount of taxes that could be collected from that amount would be $600-700 billion (tax gap) a year in lost tax revenue as of 2010. Over ten years that would be $6-7 trillion dollars that could pay all of the deficit and all other expenses. This occurs because of tax evasion, tax fraud and unintentional taxpayer errors - due to the complexity of the tax code and under reporting of income.

Most tax professionals that I know think that this number is much higher.

The United States is one of the only countries in the world that taxes all income earned by their citizens anywhere in the world, even if it has already been taxed in the place where they live. Currently the IRS is trying to collect taxes from the Lord Mayor of London who has United Kingdom and U.S. passports but has not lived in the United States since he was 5 years old (44 years ago)! The IRS often gets involved in ridiculous cases like this. It is embarrassing. They get these big ideas like let's tax all income of American citizens and corporations earned anywhere in the whole world, but they don't even have 100% compliance in the United States.

The international tax gap is estimated to be $40-133 billion a year. This is when an American citizen or corporation earns money outside the United States and does not report it as income. I have read reports that claim $21 to $32 trillion is being hidden from tax collectors around the world in countries that hide income.

Another report I read said U.S. corporations are currently holding $2 trillion dollars offshore to escape U.S. taxes. If this were taxed it would produce another $700 billion in tax revenue.

I was so busy collecting from and punishing those taxpayers who filed returns and did not pay, that I could do little or nothing to those who did not bother to file at all. It was unfair to me as a wage earner and to all those who were in the United States. I could always tell when I was around people who had extra cash. Many were from foreign countries where they were not used to paying taxes. They could be found around the high end shopping centers driving the Bentleys, Rolls Royce's, BMW's and Mercedes. But like I said, in the old days I could spot someone like that and then turn it into a criminal fraud case. Maybe I heard them brag about how they screwed the IRS in a restaurant and I happened to be sitting at the next table. It did not take much to make me interested in what I viewed as "the enemy" then.

The good part is this underground economy produces jobs and cash income. Many of the people I have worked with did not save this money, but used it to pay bills, buy homes and commercial real estate, and buy things. Sometimes I wonder if a national sales tax would make sense. This underground economy is good for the economy - but not for Uncle Sam.

While I was busy working my inventory of 50 cases, I was aware of this underground economy and saw it in action. My taxpayers would sometimes admit to not reporting cash transactions, when I asked how they were paying the bills with the income listed.

The IRS admits that the actual voluntary compliance rate is only 84% and I think that that is probably overstated. But think of it this way, in a crowd of 100 people 16 are probably not filing or paying any taxes. It kind of makes you feel stupid to be in that group that is paying.

All income is taxable. This income can be from legal or illegal sources such as prostitution and gambling (yes your football pool is all taxable). So are drug sales, bribes, crime. The Internal Revenue Code does not care if your income is legal or illegal. If you rob a bank, then the amount you took was income. The General Accounting Office claims that at least 40% of the underreporting comes from sole proprietors underreporting receipts or over-reporting expenses. This could be resolved if businesses were made to report payments to other businesses.

Currently if a corporation pays money to another corporation, it does not have to report it to the IRS with a Form 1099. This provides a clear path to a person whose intent is to not pay taxes. They file for corporate status at the state level and then never file tax returns at the federal level. It works. Many taxpayers have all their income go into a corporation and then the corporation pays all of their living expenses - so they claim that they have little or no taxable income. You would not believe how many times I saw that.

Congress has had opportunities to stop this, but, this might affect some of their friends - so do not expect this to occur in the near future.

Where Did the Money Go?

In my tax collector work, I spent most of the time trying to figure out where the tax money had gone and tried to see if I could get it back. Employment/payroll taxes are where I concentrated my efforts. These are the income tax, Social Security, Medicare taxes and the unemployment taxes. This is the money that your employer takes out of your check. In the case of Social Security, in 2015 you pay 6.2 % and your employer pays 6.2%. For Medicare, you pay

1.45% and your employer pays 1.45%. This all adds up to 15.3%, plus whatever else you have withheld to cover your income tax, usually 10 to 20%. Most of the time, this system works well. The government gives the employees credit for the amount of withholdings claimed, even though the money may never have been collected by the Treasury. So this is an area where some business owners commit the perfect white collar crime. They take the money out of your paycheck and then they keep it. This would not work, if the government did not give you credit for your withholdings. If people applied for Social Security or unemployment or a tax refund and the government told them that their old boss had kept the money, I believe that there would be lynch mobs of angry employees. Many employers who took tax money could be hanging from trees in their front yards.

When the IRS gets around to sending someone out in the field to figure out what is going on in a situation, it will be at least 6 months to two years after the fact. If a business has tax liabilities of $50,000 a quarter, this could mean that $100,000 to $400,000 is gone - probably lost forever. If the IRS just had adequate staffing, it could make contact early on while it may still be resolvable. When you have a business that owes taxes for over two years, it is probably going to end up being forced out of business or in bankruptcy.

I was not able to find more recent statistics, but TIGTA reported in November, 2004 there were 128,000 people who owed $12 billion in employment taxes. There was an additional $58 billion in unpaid payroll taxes that had not been worked yet. In addition to that, an additional 318,882 individuals had already been assessed the Trust Fund Recovery Penalty (TFRP).

To give you an example of this, a business might owe $100,000 plus penalties and interest. Of this, the IRS will look to responsible officers of the business to assess the TFRP for about $70,000, and assess it against them personally. The other $30,000, plus penalties and interest, will be written off if the business closes. Usually there is a lot of IRS paperwork needed to establish the penalty, but mostly the tax balances are never collected. The people who took the money have spent it or hidden it. So they have figured out how to commit a white collar crime and will never have to spend a day in jail.

Over a three-year period, only 112 people were charged with criminal activities for failing to pay the payroll taxes. Eighty-six percent of them were convicted and served an average of seventeen months in jail. Only 112 people charged out of 318,882 cases, proving incredible odds in favor of walking away from the situation a rich person. In 2012 alone, the IRS wrote off $5 billion of employment tax delinquencies as uncollectible.

The IRS never uses words such as "theft", "thief" or "stealing" when describing employers who have taken this money for their own purposes. Yet I was a witness once to an African American man who stole two cases of beer and four cartons of cigarettes from a convenience store. He was sentenced to county jail for three months. Justice is hard to find on a consistent basis in the United States.

21

Who Manages Your Money?

Darryl Strawberry was a great baseball player, but a poor steward of his own money. He trusted others to take care of his finances and owed income taxes for 1989, 1990, 2003 and 2004. He pled guilty to tax evasion and was sentenced to six months home confinement and 100 hours of community service and ordered to repay $350,000 in tax, penalty and interest. When a person owes a tax balance it doubles roughly every 6 years. He had a provision in his major league contract with the Mets to receive $8,891.82 a month up to $1.28 million in retirement, according to news reports. The IRS is scheduled to hold an auction of that right and it will seek a minimum bid of $550,000 for the right to receive the remaining payment up to 1.28 million dollars.

Joe Louis was one of the greatest heavyweight boxers in the United States. He earned a lot of money and then gave it away in support of the war effort. He was reported to have earned $371,000 in his first two years as a professional boxer (1937-1939). He is said to have helped out his friends and family. He also paid back the Government for the relief (welfare) payments that his stepfather had received during the Great Depression.

In 1942 he gave $65,200 to the Naval War Relief Fund. Later that year he won $45,882 from another match and gave that to the Army Relief Fund. He then enrolled in the army.

Because of the high tax rates, Joe Louis had to pay 79% tax rate on those earnings. By the late 1940s the tax rate had risen to 90% and Joe Louis was audited and found to owe $500,000 to the IRS. He was not allowed to deduct his donations to the Navy and Army funds. With interest and penalties his balance grew and grew. He died owing the IRS. He not only had poor management and tax advisors but he also lacked education and business knowledge. He was good at what he did, but despite his good works, he lost almost everything he had.

Many actors and entertainers have had tax problems. They relied on managers, finance people, bankers, accountants, accounting firms and lawyers, who failed to protect them. Buster Keeton, Bud Abbott and Lou Costello (Abbott & Costello) lost everything to the tax man due to having poor or dishonest money managers.

The actor Wesley Snipes went to jail for tax evasion and owed $17,000,000. Boxer Mike Tyson owed $18 million, and singer Lauren Hill owed $18 million. The most troubling case was of Willie Nelson who owed $16,700,000. He filed for an offer in compromise to settle his tax debt. The IRS was going to accept $6 million, but he did not pay that. He later filed another offer with the IRS and settled his debt for about $12 million. It was his legal right to do so, but it really hurt the compliance effort for many years after as people said they wanted a deal like Willie Nelson got. So it was not in the best interests of the IRS.

Some people are caught for tax evasion, because they are greedy or arrogant. One example is the real estate and hotel mogul Leona Helmsley. She made the comment "Only the little people pay taxes."

But years after he served, Joseph Nunen, a former IRS Commissioner also was convicted of tax evasion and jailed. So no one is safe when the IRS wields it hefty sword.

Movie Producer Joe Francis, known for his *Girl's Gone Wild* Movie series, was worth tens of millions of dollars, but was convicted of tax evasion and owed the IRS $33,800,000. Actually he owed that amount for a while, until a court found a technicality and relieved him of the tax burden.

The Trusted Rip-off Artists

The Internal Revenue Code is complex and can be incomprehensible to the average person.

The policies, procedures, rulings, tax court cases and the fact that much of what the IRS does, does not make logical sense, and quickly confuses even an educated person. The tax law creates a world unto itself filled with methods that do not help the average man to pay the minimal amount of tax.

Many people turn to a tax professional to get tax preparation done or get tax advice. Some of it is right and some of it is wrong. But what we are really talking about here is what the IRS is all about: fear, worry, uncertainty and confusion. This allows tax professionals great power to advise their clients about delicate financial matters.

Many people rely on and trust their tax professionals, managers and advisors to help them out with their finances. Many wealthy and prominent people have run up huge tax bills because they did not receive honest, competent assistance from these tax professionals.

It's a Ponzi Scheme

Many people are able to generate vast amounts of cash in their businesses. They become attractive targets for people who want to separate them from that cash. Actors, entertainers, sports figures, doctors, lawyers, wealthy people and even accountants are a big market for embezzlers. The money comes pouring in and managers, investment managers, accountants, tax attorneys and other friends and family all want a piece of the action. Most are given absolute control over the investment and spending of the money. Some people, like the Bernie Madoff victims were seeking an unrealistic gain in their accounts. Greed and ignorance frequently let people be fooled into thinking that the investment that they have will double or triple their money in 90 days or less. They allow themselves to be deceived. Many Ponzi schemes happen all the time but the Bernie Madoff scandal affected 4,800 victims and stole $65 billion.

I had one taxpayer in his eighties who was a victim of Bernie Madoff. He was worth $20 million but he lost $6 million in the scam. He felt old, embarrassed, used and foolish. He had made his money in manufacturing. He said that he made a nickel on every product sold and he saved it to make his fortune. As a Revenue Officer, I was only talking to him because he had cash flow problems in one of his businesses and while he paid his taxes, he was requesting that penalties be abated. I decided to abate the penalties and it was approved by the IRS.

He told me how he could not believe that Madoff had screwed him financially as they were both Jewish. I said that I had seen these types of cases before and the one running the scam never seemed to care about the outcome and who got hurt. He continued and told me that he had been a child in a concentration camp in World War II and he was standing in a line next to grown men waiting to be shot by the Nazis. The shooting started and the man next to him fell on him and saved his life. Jewish prisoners came to remove the bodies and they sheltered the boy. He gave me this advice "The lesson in life is to not worry about death. Death is going to happen no matter what you do. You have no choice in when or how. So why worry about it?" He said that he "found joy in life from a cup of coffee, a good meal, a beautiful woman and a fat baby. " He told me to "stay busy and help others and I would be happy." He said that the best advice he could give me was "to help myself first." He thanked me for helping him by abating the penalties. He said I was a good man. He said that Madoff had tried to break his spirit but he was surprised and glad to find a good man in the IRS.

Conmen I Have Known

I have seen many Ponzi cases in my career. The person running the scam was usually a charismatic guy who appeals to people who are greedy. They claim to raise money for businesses or projects or investments from people that they meet at the country club, golf course or at an expensive restaurant. They offer people investment returns of 20-60% a year. The potential investors look at the car the promoter is driving and the house where he is living and maybe get invited up to the promoter's vacation house to be wined and dined and impressed. They believe that the promoter is doing so much better than they are. They want to invest - they want the great rewards - so they write the promoter a check for $50,000 or $100,000 or $250,000. These are usual sums - and the investors do no research, they just trust the promoter. Doctors seem to be especially susceptible to this.

In fact, people who market these schemes do have amazing lifestyles, and boats and cars and houses. One man even had a Lear jet. But the fact is that they don't own any of it. Those are all props - like in a movie.

In a Ponzi scheme the later investors are paying for that lifestyle and the disbursements of the earlier investors. This is because people look at the conman's stuff and are envious of his success. They don't know that this is all just to impress the investor. Whether it is family or friends, everything they create is to impress the investor. It is all a false front. As I learned in my life - all the false riches on Earth do not buy you piece of mind or real satisfaction.

So eventually the schemes collapse and people lose their money. But the charismatic guy who sold them the investment always seems to have a Teflon shield that allows him to blame the Government or the economy or someone other than himself. So he moves on to the next scam.

In fact that movie with Leonardo DiCaprio called *Catch Me If You Can*, about a conman, is very real and I have seen it played out at least a dozen times in my career.

Embezzlement

I became obsessed with embezzlement cases, fraud cases and forensic accounting methods to discern where the money went and how much their income really was.

I can't remember how many times I would make a cold field call to a business that had taken taxes out of an employee's paycheck and just kept the money. But sometimes it was not the business owner but a bookkeeper who had embezzled the money.

I remember one case of a medical doctor who was making a good living and wanted to sell his practice so accountants came in and did a due diligence audit and found that over the prior four years, his bookkeeper had stolen 1.4 million dollars. The doctor was taking home $600,000 a year so he thought everything was fine. He had no idea. This is a practice that happens frequently to doctors, lawyers, accounting firms, banks, and small businesses all because they put their trust in a person or system that did not reveal that money was being stolen. Businesses would benefit from an outside auditor coming in at least every two years and looking at office procedure and the books and records. Most embezzlement cases are routine and there are many signs to look for to discover embezzlement.

In the case of penalties being assessed for not paying the taxes, a reasonable cause argument that would relieve the penalties is to file a police report against the embezzler (whether they actually go to trial or not) and ask the IRS to abate the penalties. In over three quarters of the cases, the person or business who suffered the loss refused to go to the police, because they are embarrassed. They do not want the public to know what happened.

In the case of the doctor, he did have her arrested for embezzlement and theft and I was able to take away $241,000 in penalties.

In many cases I have found that old friends of the taxpayer sometimes going back 30 years are the ones who get jealous of their success and start stealing small at first and then greater and greater amounts, until they are finally caught. If they have a chance and suspect that they are going to be fired or arrested usually they will burn the records and the computer data is erased and destroyed.

The thief usually has some story about why they needed the money-to help family or friends, or some sick or dying person, or for drugs, prostitutes, alcohol, or gambling. It does not matter where it went, it is rarely recoverable. They might go to jail or have a judgment against them that will affect their futures, but it seems too many like the "*wild ride*" and think all that free money was worth it. Sometimes, when victims did not want to file a police report, I would advise them to issue a Form 1099 reporting the verifiable stolen amount as income to the thief. This causes the person to be assessed and taxed by the IRS and it is a satisfying method for some people to resolve the nightmare situation.

22

IRS Survival Strategies

THE FOLLOWING IS A LIST of the most often asked IRS questions and answers to guide you in your contacts with the IRS.

Question: I don't know how to respond to the IRS. What do I do?
Answer: Read what they have sent you. There is important information regarding your rights buried in that pile of papers that you received in the mail. Study the system and figure out what you have to do first. Then give them exactly what information they request. Determine what they are trying to use that information for and then learn your rights, be prepared to file an appeal at every opportunity. If you are talking to an employee, then write down their employee number and also request their eFax phone number or you may never be able to locate them again.

Question: I have been calling the IRS for days and they never pick up, or leave me on hold for over 2 hours before they answer. What should I do?
Answer: The IRS is so short staffed that it admits that at least 60% of all calls will not be answered during peak periods. A written letter of inquiry or response should be sent certified mail to the address found on the last letter that you received.

Question: I am poor with keeping receipts and records. Now I got a notice that the IRS is going to audit me. What do I do?
Answer: Do not despair! There is a rule named the Cohan Rule, after the composer of the song "I'm a Yankee Doodle Dandy," George M. Cohan. It is a ruling by Judge Learned Hand that establishes that if you are busy earning a living and not keeping track of your expenses you can still be entitled to estimate your expenses and receive credit for them on your tax return, as long as they can establish some basis for the deduction. In Mr. Cohan's case he was also an entertainer who traveled and did shows all across the United States. So he could backtrack and explain that he had train fare and food while on the road and hotel room expenses.

The IRS would prefer to use Section 274 of the Internal Revenue Code, but with a good CPA or Tax Attorney, you might find relief using, at least in part, the Cohan Rule.

Question: Can I go to jail for not paying my taxes?
Answer: Yes, but the odds are against it. Eighty-two percent of all people convicted go to prison. But that number is less than 4,000 a year on average. If you are being audited or owe the IRS, your life will seem like a living hell for a while, but no jail. But if you have income and do not file tax returns, then yes you can be investigated by the Criminal Investigation Special Agents and their goal is for you to be found guilty in court and go to jail. Fraud or misrepresentations made to the Government will also get IRS attention.

Question: I have an approved installment agreement to pay my back taxes, but they still keep charging me a failure to pay penalty. Why?
Answer: Because that is what Congress put in the law. You pay this penalty even when you are making payments. The failure to pay penalty is applied even when a person is in an installment agreement. It can be applied at the rate of 5% per month up to a maximum of 25%. Congress can change this but has not. Also a

delinquent taxpayer faces penalties for failure to file in an amount as high as 25%, penalties for failure to pay in an amount as much as 25%, plus an estimated tax payment penalty of approximately 1%, with the potential for other penalties for accuracy errors, or fraud and interest. Penalties can be as much as 150% of the original tax balance.

Question: I have an installment agreement and I had extra money so I sent three months payments all at the same time. Now I got a letter that they are defaulting my agreement. Why?
Answer: You can send three separate checks towards your installment agreement and hope they post them correctly, but mostly they won't. Just send one check every month. There is a built in skip on every installment agreement. If you miss one payment it will not automatically default the agreement. The IRS does not advertise this. So many people miss a payment and then worry and start calling or writing the IRS, who is not prepared to respond.

Question: I am a small businessman, I report my credit card sales, but not my cash income. The IRS can never catch me - right?
Answer: The IRS identifies all businesses that have assets less than $10 million as small businesses. It does not depend on the amount; you are structuring your business to evade taxes. That is illegal. They can catch you in a dozen ways. I heard of one case where prostitutes were targeted for nonpayment. It was a massage parlor. So the IRS went to the laundry that supplied its sheets and towels and used that number to back into the number of clients that they provided with services and the average that they would have paid. Or there was the case of the blacksmith/metal fabrication workshop. He had never filed tax returns and claimed to have no income. The IRS went to his steel supplier and reconstructed his income that way. It may have been too high - but he was forced to either accept that the IRS prepared number or file his own returns with the proof of what

he put on the returns. So yes you can get caught. When the IRS has the will there is always a way.

The informal motto of The IRS Criminal Investigation is "Greed follows prosperity and we follow greed." They will look for the most egregious cases of non-tax compliance and prosecute them. In 2013 they worked 5,557 cases and referred 3,865 for prosecution. Of this, 3,311 were convicted of tax and financial crimes related to tax evasion, money laundering, and narcotics. The IRS claims a 92% conviction rate. In 2014, CI opened 17% fewer criminal cases due to short staffing. Tax criminals usually receive 18-25 month sentences in a Federal Prison. The chances of you getting caught are about the same as you winning the lottery. It's extremely rare, given that there were 130 million tax returns filed in 2013. If you are unlucky or extremely greedy and this happens to you, the mental, emotional, and health-related costs of a criminal investigation will depress, deplete and destroy you.

Question: My tax return is going to be different from other people, I donate a lot of money to charity. What should I do?
Answer: When you file your return, make sure you keep all of your donation records and the copy of the receiver's letter proving it and the check you used to make the donation. I advise that you attach photocopies of all your proof to the return and that will prevent an audit. There are many audit triggers and this includes high donations to charity - especially if they exceed 50% of Adjusted Gross Income.

Question: I want to avoid an audit. What will trigger an audit?
Answer: There are many things that will trigger an audit. But most of them are only known by a few in the IRS. This is determined by what areas the IRS wants to investigate in that tax year. Sometimes it will go after certain types of business, like realtors or beauty shops/

barbers. Or it will question certain types of expenses like losses or business expenses.

The Nation Research Project (RCP) audit is an audit on everything in your life. They will want to see your marriage certificate, Social Security cards, spouse and children's cards and birth certificates, etc. Some audits are based on your lifestyle. You must be able to show that you make enough money and that you report it to show how you pay for your lifestyle.

Question: I have a corporation and corporations hardly ever get audited. My CPA told me the odds are good it will not get audited. Is this true?
Answer: Every year about 33,000 corporate income tax returns are audited by Revenue Agents who come to your business and sit there looking at your records for days or weeks. They always are there to come up with a tax balance. Don't put anything on the return that you cannot prove or does not have some basis in the law. Large businesses get even closer attention, because anything that corporation does will have a major and far reaching impact that could have large and immediate tax consequences.

Question: I heard that all my income is taxable. I sold my comic book collection, my car and had a garage sale. Is this all taxable income? How would the IRS ever find out?
Answer: The Internal Revenue Code states that all "gross income from whatever sources legal or illegal is taxable." But you have some basis in the collections and the car that you can subtract from the sales prices (what you paid for the comic books or car and the contents of the garage). The IRS can find out if you make a lot of money because most people are afraid to keep cash and put money in the bank or buy something for cash - beyond their known income level. Cash leaves an audit trail. This can occur with sales on Amazon

and EBay or selling antiques, or expensive automobiles that have increased in value. People watching shows like CSI, think that the IRS and the Treasury Department already know everything about everyone, and if they don't, they can easily find it out. It is true that with a summons, the IRS can get all of your information; it is not instant and it is not easy. They have access to every detail about your life. The IRS will request every transaction, every financial document, phone records, credit card records, passport records, once an audit is started or when there is a tax balance due.

Question: I have a $6.5 million estate and am trying to avoid the estate tax by using "pay on death" and joint tenant's accounts at the bank and on my properties.
Answer: Good idea, but it is illegal. You are trying to evade taxation. If the IRS finds out, they will construct an Estate Tax Return for you and assess taxes and go to all those people you left your estate to and collect from them directly. There are many legal ways to reduce estate taxes. Consult a tax attorney.

Question: Can I get an installment agreement if I owe the IRS?
Answer: Yes, if you owe under $10,000 or can pay it down to that amount, you qualify for an automatic agreement. You easily also qualify for an installment agreement if you owe $50,000 or less. Under this agreement it can be without a Notice of Federal Tax Lien being filed.

Question: I like to receive my refund every year. It is usually about $3,000. It is like a forced savings account. Is this a good idea?
Answer: Let's see: you are making an interest free loan to the Government every year and you are happy? The Government holds your money for 12-16 months and you are paying interest on any credit card balances that you have. Think about it, this forced IRS savings plan is probably costing you 10-25% in credit card interest

every year. You should adjust your withholding and then pay off any credit cards balances, then set up an automatic savings plan.

Question: I was told the IRS tracks when people buy vacation homes, expensive cars, homes, artwork and other collectibles. Is that true?
Answer: No myth, that is correct. Cash leaves a trail for the IRS to follow. But they do not systematically track this. But it will come up if you are under audit or your tax preparer is under audit.

Question: I heard that you can get cash awards from turning in your neighbors, friends, family and employer for tax crimes. Is that true?
Answer: Yes, it is true that you can collect 15-30% of the amount the government eventually collects because of the information that you provided. The largest payout was to a man who also spent 2 ½ years in jail. He received $104 million, which worked out to be $4,600 for every hour he spent in prison. The IRS hotline number is 1-800-829-0433 for information. You will need to file Form 211 to actually report the alleged tax violation. They no longer accept information over the telephone. All reports can be done anonymously, but then you will not be able to claim the informant's award.

Question: I filed my return and forgot to include income. But I am afraid to amend the return because someone told me that would trigger an audit. Is this correct?
Answer: Wrong. Amended returns are routinely processed. It is rare for them to be assigned to a field auditor.

Question: I was really scared by the IRS Agent when he was at my door; he said horrible things. Is this what will happen when I try to deal with them in the future or should I hire a tax professional?
Answer: Each IRS employee is different. You will find many of the stories and orders that you were told to do by the Agent or Officer were not actually what they were supposed to legally say to you. You

will notice how differently they speak if you hire a tax professional. If you feel that you have been harassed you can contact TIGTA and report that employee: 1-800-366-4484.

Question: Someone told me that he has a business and writes off all of his expenses so ends up with no taxable income. Is that possible?
Answer: It is for a while. The IRS expects that you will should make a profit in 3 out of the first 5 years of a business, or it may disallow all expenses and reclassify your business as your hobby. There are exceptions to every type of business. In fact the Internal Revenue Code does not use the term "hobby." The business may have a loss that can be supported beyond the first three years. The IRS looks at a person's total income and lifestyle to determine if it is a business that is motivated to make a profit.

Question: When I was finally able to pay my many years old IRS tax balance, I was given a payoff amount by the government agent and then 4 months later the IRS came back and said I owe something called accrued failure to pay penalty and interest for another $12,154. How can this be - what can I do about it?
Answer: Nothing can be done, unless you can convince that agent and his manager that the government made false representations and made an error that damaged you. That is rare. The reason that this happened is because the old IRS computer can only assess failure to pay penalty if there is a credit balance on the account. So when you made a large payment then a credit was on the account and that triggered the computer to calculate the failure to pay penalty, which can grow to 25% of what your tax was to be calculated. The worst part of this is that it may have been years since this penalty was last calculated. You can ask for the penalty to be abated but this is rare and the IRS will not abate interest in a case like this either. In the meantime that old computer cannot charge interest on the

penalty that is accruing but has not been assessed. This hurts both the taxpayer and the Government and costs millions of dollars every year. This is not fair or equitable to those taxpayers who pay earlier. The Treasury Inspector General estimates that this costs the Government $171 million a year in lost interest.

Question: My friend said she had identity fraud happen to her where someone used her name and address and Social Security number to get a large refund. She said it took over a year for her to get her actual refund and for the IRS to resolve it and she felt like the IRS was treating her like a criminal. She is a retired old lady - she only gets Social Security - how can this happen?
Answer: It happens because the IRS is overwhelmed and unprepared to identify and battle identity fraud. TIGTA has issued its own reports that find that customers with identity and refund fraud do not receive quality customer service.

Question: The IRS sent a letter telling me they were holding my current years' refund (which I need to pay medical expenses) because I have not filed in the last five years. I was taking care of my dying mother and had no income. What should I do?
Answer: Continue to wait and write to them to explain. After six months they have to issue the return with 3% interest. Request a copy from the IRS of any income reported under your name and Social Security number for the past five years. Or file a Form 911 telling that this is causing you hardship. You will talk to the Taxpayer Advocate which is a watchdog agency outside of the IRS. The Taxpayer Advocate will only accept your case if you have made numerous contacts with the IRS and have been unable to resolve your case. They can be very effective when they help a taxpayer. Or you can seek help from the manager of the person that you speak to on your phone call. Or you can write to your Senator, Member of Congress or the President seeking help.

Question: I am afraid the IRS will come and seize my house or car or business. What can I do?
Answer: The IRS can seize your house, but probably won't. Happily, the number of seizures is down from 12,000 a year to an average of 764 a year, in the last 5 years. The IRS did 25% less seizures in 2013 than in 2012 and I project this number will continue to decline due to loss of experienced employees who know how to use the seizure tool effectively. I made over 100 property seizures in my early career.

Question: What triggers an audit?
Answer: Just filing a tax return enters you in the "IRS Tax Lottery". Every single item on a return can be questioned. But using the DIF and other scores certain items will be reviewed for an audit. The IRS will scrutinize large, unusual or questionable items. (LUQ) They will compare your return to millions of other people or businesses like you. They will make sure that your income is sufficient to support your exemptions claimed and your lifestyle.

Question: If I sell my house, can I keep all the profits and pay no income tax?
Answer: Yes and no. Consult a tax professional. You will have to live in your house for a certain amount of time and only a certain amount of money is exempt. The IRS does not have an effective online computer follow-up that allows them to monitor when and how much you sold your last home for and how much you made or lost on the sale. This is what you must provide in an audit. If you have a cash sale, there is usually no record monitored by the IRS to track that.

Question: I received an IRS letter that said I should have tip income. Why?
Answer: What did you write on your tax return under occupation? Waiter? Bartender? Taxi driver? Beautician? Barber? Hair designer?

Porter? Doorman? The IRS keeps it pretty simple. They respond to what you tell them. If you are in a job where tips are the norm, they will ask why you do not have any tips. If you receive a W-2 it will indicate if you should be reporting tips. That is how the IRS knows to look for tip income.

Question: How do I get out of the tax system once and for all?
Answer: You can die and in most cases that will get your Social Security number permanently closed on both the IRS and the Social Security computers. That computer program is known as the "Death Master File." Some people have tried to bribe employees to do that. Some IRS and Social Security employees have been arrested for taking money for doing just that.

Otherwise, you can try to live with the IRS after you. No Social Security, no disability, no unemployment, and no benefits of our society, like food stamps, welfare or medical assistance. Today you need a Social Security number for almost everything, even to open a bank account or to have credit. So it is almost impossible to disappear these days. That is why many people have figured out how to use corporations and LLCs and holding companies to water down income and pay no income taxes.

Question: A friend told me that tax avoidance is illegal. Is that true?
Answer: Tax avoidance is both legal and encouraged by the IRS. Tax evasion is illegal.

Question: I am old and disabled. I want to file my taxes but am unable to pay for it. I just want to walk in to the IRS and have them answer my questions and help me do my returns. How do I do this?
Answer: As of January, 2014, IRS walk-in offices/taxpayer assistance sites stopped providing answers to tax law questions, and no longer gives tax law advice, and they will not help old, sick or handicapped people file their tax returns. There are programs outside the IRS

such as Tax Counseling for the Elderly administered by AARP. If you try to call them, good luck! Due to budget cuts they only expect to be able to answer 40% of incoming calls in 2015. Sometimes I have been on hold for 2 hours and that is on the special hotline for tax professionals. One time I was on hold for an hour and it was towards the end of the day and the employee picked up the phone and said her shift ended in ten minutes and that she could not help me, so she hung up!

If you write them a letter you may just receive a letter telling you that they are behind and need 45 days to respond to you and then you may not ever hear from them again. There are some free software programs where you can prepare your own tax return. Unfortunately many people do not own or have access to a computer or even know how to use a computer.

Question: I want to do one of those Offer in Compromises that they talk about so much on the radio and television. What are the odds of me getting such a deal?
Answer: There were 11.5 million delinquent taxpayers in 2013; of these only 74,000 offers were filed and only 31,000 (42%) offers in compromises were accepted. That is only .002% of all delinquent tax cases. The IRS does accept some offers because the taxpayer is old, sick or has access to money that the Government would not be able to reach. You have a better chance at getting an installment agreement, or having your collection or audit account deferred for a few years. If you have a financial hardship ask that your case be declared currently not collectible. Your odds might be better if you buy a lottery ticket and then win enough money to just pay the IRS and be done with it. The ads on TV show that everyone is settling their tax debts with the IRS for pennies on the dollar are wrong. But do not think that you can negotiate with the IRS by threatening bankruptcy or because you want a better deal. Offers are determined by your numbers not your speech.

Question: I don't make enough to get audited. True?
Answer: If your income is less than $25,000, there is a less than 1% chance that you will be audited. But if your income is under $25,000 you probably have more important things to worry about like paying your rent, car payment and buying food.

If your income is under $200,000, there is only a 1 % chance that you will be audited. Incomes above $200,000 have an audit chance of 3%. This has made some people reckless with the information that they put on tax returns. In 2013, the IRS did the fewest audits since the 1980s. In part this is because additional information filing requirements allow the IRS to match more data reported to them with the data you put on your tax return. Audits are a way to bring fear into the equation. The audit is where you have to bring in your actual books and receipts and prove what you claimed on the tax return. Unlike the IRS of the old days, when the auditors had more discretionary power, now there is very little reasonableness during an audit. You either have the records or you lose that deduction. During an audit, you will be asked dozens of questions that are designed to make you disclose income or gifts that you may have forgotten to list on the tax return. In that forum, you are presumed guilty until you can prove yourself innocent.

There were 100,000 fewer audits in 2014. There will be no collection on 190,000 cases in collection in 2015, due to a reduced number of employees. This means 3 billion dollars will not even attempt to be collected. In fact, three Automated Collection Sites were closed and the employees were reassigned to work on identity fraud cases instead. These do not yield any tax money to the government.

The odds are against being selected for an audit, if the taxpayer puts down reasonable expenses in relation to their income. The IRS tracks this and builds accounting models via the NRP program. So they know the percentage that people would normally have for housing/mortgage interest, real estate taxes, medical expenses and charitable contributions.

The IRS has business models by industry and by market. The IRS knows that a dentist, for instance, would have certain expenses in a statistical range. They look for deviations from the norm. It works pretty well at locating audit targets

Question: I move often, and I file every year, so the IRS always knows where I am. So I don't think I need to file a change of address (Form 8822) - Is that correct?
Answer: Wrong. Part of the IRS may know where you are. But the auditor or tax collector may not. He may send letters raising your taxes to the address you listed on the return. Your mail forwarding order will have expired and they will audit you, make big tax assessments and then start collection against you. This includes the Notice of Federal Tax Lien, one of the greatest tools of IRS Collection all without your knowledge. In our credit based society, this can destroy your financial life for the next ten years. All because the auditor does not try to find out your new address - which might already be somewhere else on the IRS computer. You must file Form 8822 the IRS Change of Address Form.

Question: If I just ignore these letters from the IRS will they stop some day?
Answer: Sorry! The IRS never forgets you. One day they will come to your door. Seize the day and if you can't handle talking to the IRS, hire a tax professional to help you out.

Question: If I have an installment agreement, then will the IRS stop charging me the Failure to Pay Penalty?
Answer: No! You pay this penalty up to 25% for as long as you have a tax balance due, installment agreement or not.

Question: My friend told me I don't have to file or pay taxes because the 16th Amendment, which created the Income Tax laws, was not

properly ratified. Plus I heard that the Supreme Court overruled the income tax and said it was unconstitutional. Is this true?
Answer: This is misinformation. All Federal Courts have upheld the Income Tax Law that was passed in 1916. It is correct that the Supreme Court said that an older, different Income Tax passed in 1894 was unconstitutional and it was struck down in 1895. Following this advice will get you in big trouble and the IRS will assess huge penalties against you.

Question: The Internal Revenue Service advertises that the tax system is based on voluntary compliance. Can I refuse to "volunteer?"
Answer: Bad Choice! The IRS likes you to think that you have some choice about whether you should file and pay taxes. When you don't, watch how fast they force you into compliance.

Question: Cash income like gambling winnings, tips, and other cash income is non-taxable. The IRS can't prove it anyway. Am I right?
Answer: Wrong! The IRS can look at your lifestyle and see what you have paid for rent, mortgage, car payments, education costs, insurance utilities, etc. and add it all up and then make up tax returns for you where you will owe money.

Question: Will I will get a bigger refund if I go to a CPA or tax preparer?
Answer: If you have a complex return you can go to ten tax professionals and get 10 different tax returns results. Some unscrupulous preparers will prepare fraudulent returns that will guarantee you large refunds. Later they get caught and you get audited. If something sounds too good to be true, it usually is. I use Turbo tax - but there are many programs that are pretty easy to use if you choose to do the returns yourself.

Question: Can the IRS Revenue Officers, Revenue Agents or Tax Auditors arrest me and put me in jail?
Answer: No! They do not have that power. They can make your life a living hell and you may wish you were in a quiet jail cell. IRS Criminal Special Agents can make arrests and so can TIGTA Special Agents. But Revenue Officers, Revenue Agents and Tax Auditors can refer you to IRS Criminal Investigation for investigation for tax evasion, tax fraud or perjury. This can then lead to your arrest for tax crimes.

Question: If I wait to file until October 15 (on extension) is it true that I will not get audited? Because the IRS runs the lists comparing income reported with income reporting systems in June.
Answer: Wrong! All returns get a DIF Score (Discriminate Index Function) and that score will always be reviewed and if it is high enough you will get audited (if the IRS has enough people to work the audit).

Question: What does the DIF score look for when it is comparing my numbers to other taxpayers?
Answer: In my experience, I have seen home office, travel and entertainment, casualty losses and charitable contributions deductions most often. I have also seen Foreign Bank and Financial Account Form (FBAR) as a cause for an audit. But the funny part of this is that each return is reviewed by a DIF examiner who may have their own standards - so it is a very subjective process.

Question: A friend told me that the IRS also uses Special Projects to audit groups of people. They choose different businesses and individuals each year. Is that true?
Answer: Very true. In a recent year, the IRS went after S-corporations, real estate partnerships, construction companies and individuals

earning over $1 million. They also like to audit people who list numbers in their tax returns that do not match up to other data that has been reported to the IRS.

Question: If I don't have any assets in my name, the IRS cannot do anything to me, right?
Answer: Partially correct, you can live a life where you work for cash and are paid every day and own nothing, have no bank account, car or ownership in anything. But the IRS can come after your friends, family and significant others and for example ask why they have assets when they do not have any means of support - no way to pay the mortgages or other expenses. I knew an attorney who was a big gambler and playboy. He had a huge house and put it in his girlfriend's name and went out drinking, gambling and carousing every night. I knocked on the door, the girlfriend answered. She talked at length, I listened. I shared some information about how she owned the house according to public records and that she could do whatever she wanted with it. One day a month later, I was pleased to learn that she had kicked him out of the $600,000 house that was in her name and paid for in cash and taken back his expensive BMW also paid for in cash.

She had filed all the income she received from him, so she was in the clear. It was cheaper than trying to pursue the case in Court.

Question: If I am fair and honest with the IRS, will the IRS be fair and honest and reasonable with me?
Answer: Keep dreaming! Many people have wished for this to happen, failed to get representation on complex tax matters (because they thought they could do it themselves and save money) and have lost millions of dollars, experienced hardships, lost valuable rights that they did not even know they had. Protect yourself first, get the best advice you can afford about your tax situation.

Question: Can I ever get the IRS off my back? I filed on time and owe back taxes from 5 years ago. They keep sending me threatening letters.
Answer: Taxes that were filed on time and are more than three years since the due date and filing of the return may be dischargeable in bankruptcy court. See a bankruptcy lawyer.

Question: Will the Taxpayer Bill of Rights make the IRS protect me?
Answer: No! The IRS is run by people and some people are nice and some are not. Wake up! You may get some protections from it, but you have to exercise all your rights. Most IRS rights expire in time.

Question: The IRS can't take my wages or bank account or my retirement account or my house without going into court and allowing me to have my day in court, right?
Answer: Very wrong! The IRS can take most everything you own, just based on the testimony of the IRS Revenue Officer or Criminal Agent in a secret session they hold with a Federal Judge. You have some rights after the seizure. But if you don't have a good tax professional even those rights will evaporate with time.

Question: If I disagree with the IRS - can I fight them in court?
Answer: Yes and no. To even get into U. S. Tax Court will cost you $20,000 for the attorney and filing fees. Many people would be helped if they used the IRS Appeals system first if they have a disagreement. It is very rare for an individual to be able to go to tax court and win against the IRS.

Question: I always thought the IRS was there to help me.
Answer: Wrong! The IRS is here to audit tax returns, look for tax cheats and unreported income and collect money and close cases! It is designed to assess and collect new tax balances. It talks about

doing the right thing, but its first mission is to audit and collect money.

Question: I heard I don't need to keep my receipts or tax records because of the tax law changing. Is that true?
Answer: Wrong! That is very limited and applies to tax court. If you are audited or suspected of tax fraud you will need your records. The IRS can assess new taxes against you generally for 3 years, but if you have omitted over 25% of your income it can assess up to 6 years. There is no statute of limitations on fraud. I have seen cases going back 25 years. So in a criminal case it is common for the last ten years to be looked at. If record storage is a problem, you should scan them into your computer and then also save them on a cloud. Be aware that many cash register receipts have ink that fades and will disappear in a year or so. Tax records are more than just you receiving bills and having those. You must also prove that you paid the expenses in order to qualify for the deduction from your income.

Question: I don't want to file tax returns or pay taxes because I don't like big government; I don't want to pay for armies and wars; I don't want to pay for nuclear weapons, and I don't want to pay for food stamps and welfare. Can't the Government just leave me alone?
Answer: Remember high school civics class. You vote and elect people to represent you and they determine how much to tax you and how the money will be spent. If the IRS knows you have income and you do not file taxes it will make up perfectly legal returns allowing you no deductions under the Substitute for Return (SFR) program. No one in the IRS cares what you think about the tax system or public affairs.

Question: I have a business and don't want to file the employment tax returns. What can happen?
Answer: The IRS will estimate how much they think you owe- add 20% and then file returns for you. The good part of both of this is if

you pay the tax balances plus penalty and interest, you are accepting the tax returns as filed and so is the IRS. So they can't come after you later to make changes. But this will hurt your employees if they need Social Security disability or unemployment checks when they file their tax returns.

Question: Do I have rights before the IRS?
Answer: You only have rights if you know about them and use them. Read Publication 1 - Your Taxpayer Rights. Most people don't. Either they don't read all the letters explaining the rights or they don't understand them or they don't file timely responses and appeals.

Question: It is time to file my tax return and I am short $10,000. I am just going to wait until I get the money and then I will file and send the money I owe. Will this work?
Answer: No. File on time or the IRS will assess a Failure to File Penalty of 5% a month for 5 months up to 25%. If you file five months late you will owe another 5 % per month up to 25%.

Question: If I have an installment agreement with the IRS - I don't have to pay any penalties. Right?
Answer: Wrong. You will be charged either 5% a month for failure to pay penalty - even while you are making payments or if they choose .5% a month for up to 50 months, the IRS will decide.

Question: I heard that if I structure my business with many partners in a large partnership, that that makes it too hard for the IRS to audit the business. Is this true?
Answer: Yes, an effective Audit Avoidance Plan is to form a Large Partnership. In fact, when the person does not want the IRS to monitor their tax affairs then, it is good to be organized as a partnership.

Large partnerships (assets over $100 million) have an audit rate of only .008% according to the Government Accountability Office. Because a partnership does not pay any tax itself, it passes whatever loss or profit down to its partners. So the IRS has to audit not just the partnership, but also the individual partners at least on that issue. This results in huge audit cases and most of the time the IRS is not prepared for that. Audit rate for corporations with assets over $10 million fell by 20% between 2013 and 2014. There will be 300,000 less of these audits in 2015.

Question: Is it true that the IRS can't make me do anything -even respond to their summons and subpoenas?
Answer: You are correct and wrong. The IRS will document that you are ignoring your tax obligations and you will be in contempt of the Internal Revenue Service and they will refer you to the Department of Justice which will bring you before a Federal Judge who will give you a chance to testify or produce records and then if you refuse - the Judge will throw you in jail for being in contempt of court. Usually the U.S. Marshall will actually arrest you. Many people are in jail for this as I write this.

Question: If I get audited will I owe more in taxes?
Answer: Not always. In fact about almost 2 in 10 people who get audited get refunds or no change is made to their taxes.

Question: My friend told me that if I get my refund check, then the IRS believes what I put on my return and then they forget about me.
Answer: The IRS is under great pressure to pay out tax refunds within 45 days of filing or within 45 days of the due date of the return, whichever is later. So the IRS usually pays your refund first and asks questions later. Sometimes three years later.

Question: Aren't you afraid to write a book about the IRS? Don't you think they will come after you and make all sorts of trouble and accusations in your life?
Answer: I am tired of being afraid of the IRS. They will do what they always have done; try to suppress the message and discredit the messenger. But the truth needs to be told here and now and my intention is to help the IRS succeed in its mission for the next 50 years.

23

Solutions to the IRS Situation

Goals:

- Restore full faith and confidence in the IRS. Private collection is not the answer. This has been tried and failed many times.
- The philosophy of the Internal Revenue Service should change to finding out what they can get right here, right now in making case settlement determinations. This includes the automatic use of installment agreements and currently not collectible determinations, and also the use of offers in compromise. This precludes the need for a tax amnesty.
- Have a clearly defined Mission Statement that encourages voluntary compliance, broadening the tax base and is focused on verifiable business results, like dollars collected and audits that result in increased tax assessments.
- Hire a company that is expert at designing huge computer systems and give them a contract that will update the IRS computers for the next 20 years.
- The IRS should stop trying to draw a line in the sand and prove a point with people who refuse to pay their taxes due to moral, constitutional, anti-war or other reasons to protest. So much money is being spent there that could be going to other places where their efforts would result in increased filing and paying compliance.

Employees:

- Do psychological and personality tests of employees before they are hired. Test existing employees; if they clearly are not suited for their jobs they should be offered other positions or given early retirement incentives.
- The attitude of some IRS employees is judgmental and vindictive, as if they are on some higher moral ground. I think they need to get over themselves and their limited attitudes and focus on true customer service. And make sound financial judgements and tax evaluations based on the financial circumstances of each taxpayer. Let God judge people not the IRS employees.
- As a result of my own experiences within the IRS, I think that revenue officers of the future should be trained in strategies to control their egos and adrenaline levels.
- The policies, procedures and protocols that govern employee actions should be streamlined and simplified.
- IRS employees should be encouraged to be reasonable and use their judgment to "do the right thing" and care about the taxpayers whose cases they are assigned to work on; this is not a combat field.
- Each Social Security number should be assigned a PIN number to prevent identity fraud. In the future, a system should be implemented where a taxpayer uses a thumbprint to sign their tax documents.
- Reasonable deadlines and expectations should be stressed in all communications with taxpayers. Right now, the IRS tells you to hurry up and give them money or information and then you spend months or years waiting for a response.
- If the IRS had a website where taxpayers could report changes in their circumstance this would save a lot of time in collection and audit and even criminal cases later. For instance if a

person was dead, relatives could report that. If a person had gone through bankruptcy this would be reported. If they suffered any financial hardship or mental or physical breakdowns these could all be reported. Then an indicator on the system would classify them and decide if that could affect the case status in the future.

- The IRS needs to be able to serve taxpayers 24 hours a day and 7 days a week. An interactive website and the use of email would allow this to happen.
- Each IRS employee should provide their eFax phone number to reduce the burden taxpayers have in trying to reach IRS employees working on their cases.
- The failure to pay penalty is applied even when a person is in an installment agreement. It can be applied at the rate of 5% per month up to a maximum of 25%. Congress can change this but has not. So a delinquent taxpayer faces penalties for failure to **file** in an amount as high as 25%, and penalties for failure to **pay** in an amount as much as 25%, plus an estimated tax payment penalty of approximately 1%, with the potential for other penalties for accuracy errors, or fraud and interest.
- People who are appearing before the IRS because they have been summoned should be given their rights, before testimony begins.
- The Taxpayer Assistance Program should be given free rein to encourage the IRS to do the right thing in cases where they have not done so.
- The IRS has the ability to access high tech tools and information to monitor tax transactions and that should be encouraged.
- Computer matching should be done on all documents that are required to be filed, before tax refunds over $5,000 are issued. This is not possible now, because the law does not require the 1099 and K-1 forms to be filed before the returns are due.

Reviews should be done by a human being. Suspicious cases will be referred higher up the line.

Collection

- Loosen up the requirements for installment agreements and offers in compromise. Give everyone who owes $50,000 or less an automatic 6 years to pay their taxes with direct debit payments. Just like a car loan. File a notice of federal tax lien only in cases where the delinquent taxpayer owns property that has equity greater than $50,000 at the time of the installment agreement. A Notice of Federal Tax Lien can get you fired from your job and ruin your credit for 10 years. How can the IRS expect people to recover and pay off their tax debt with the lien crippling them? The goal of the IRS has always been to encourage people to file and pay voluntarily for their entire working lives, 30-40 years. This ensures a consistent income stream to the Government.
- A report issued on March 15, 2015 gives excellent analysis of the installment agreement and offer in compromise programs and how they do not benefit either the IRS or the taxpayers. It speaks of IRS employees who are not adequately trained in the law and in judgement and do not feel empowered to apply the financial standards to make case resolutions. It also talks about employees who do not have flexibility to make decisions to resolve cases.
  See http://www.IRS.gov/Tax-Professionals/SMALL-BUSINESS-SELF-EMPLOYED-SUBGROUP-REPORT
- Another way to resolve cases is to encourage that delinquent businesses liquidate and reform new businesses and those are closely monitored to ensure that they stay in compliance. (Poor man's bankruptcy)

- Another case closing is called: "In-Business 53." This means that you stay in business and may or may not have an installment agreement, as long as you file and pay current taxes. In effect the IRS is formally leaving you alone. These are rarely given.
- Collection cases should be assigned within six months of the liabilities being accrued - the longer the IRS waits the less chance that they will ever see full payment on the delinquent accounts.
- Revenue Officers are not given time and support to apply their technical skills. Many more cases could be closed if all revenue officers would be allowed to analyze the Queue inventory and suggest by their own years of experience which cases could easily be resolved and collected and closed.
- The reason most employment taxes accrue is that the IRS allows it. If the taxes are not paid for 2 or more quarters, the balances can grow quickly. Usually the IRS takes 12-24 months to make a personal contact. By that time the $50,000 that might have been owed for the first and second quarter have now grown to a balance of $100,000 to $200,000. What would have been a case that could have been fully paid is now a monster uncollectible case. In 2012 alone, the IRS wrote off $5 billion of employment tax delinquencies as uncollectible.
- Raise the tolerance levels when small balances are owed. For example if a person owes $2,500 or less, the IRS should send one letter and then shelve the case.

Offer in Compromise

- Use the offer in compromise program to settle accounts that are currently not collectible. Follow the lead of credit card companies where they send out letters saying that they will settle credit accounts for some percentage less than face value. The older the account the greater the discount. This gives people the good feeling of having settled their debt with the IRS and allows them to receive money from outside sources like friends and family that the IRS would have no access to or standing with. This would be in lieu of a tax amnesty program, but just as big a revenue raiser. The greatest feature to the offer in compromise program is that if the taxpayer does not continue to file and pay their taxes for the next five years, all the original tax, penalty and interest comes back to them. No second chances, no matter what.

- Another way to resolve cases is through the promoting of the offer in compromise system. Only 60,000 offer in compromises are filed each year and only about 30,000 are accepted. Less than .002% of all cases are closed that way. It should not be so expensive, exhausting and non-productive to file an offer in compromise.

Audit

- Audits in the same or following year should be the goal, not three years after the tax return is filed.
- If audits will yield less than $5,000 the IRS should bypass the case. If the IRS has information that indicates that any proposed adjustment will not be collectible, it should not propose any tax increase. I advocate taxpayer education over taxpayer punishment.
- The IRS also needs to look at what they audited in the past and determine why they have such a high percentage of audits that result in increased refund or audits that result in no change in the tax due. It is ridiculous to continue to use outdated and outmoded audit selection methods.

- Audit cases should be reviewed for collectability - if there is not going to be a chance of ever collecting the money that will be assessed, then the case should be closed.
- Taxpayer education is no longer emphasized. All business taxpayers should be required to watch an IRS video outlining their duties and responsibilities as a business owner and an employer. They should be required to watch a follow up video every year as part of their continuing business education. This will help many business owners in their dealings with the IRS and when they are making tough business decisions regarding letting employees go or restructuring their business to make them more profitable. Profitable businesses that are in tax compliance are good for the Government and the people of the United States.

Tax Professionals

- There is no current effective way to determine if your tax preparer or tax professional is trustworthy or competent. The IRS could publish statistics that it controls over these tax professionals regarding their error rate and any disciplinary action or complaints recorded by professional organizations, bar associations or licensing authorities or the IRS.

24

A New Direction For The IRS

THE CONGRESS OF THE UNITED States chooses through its actions to continually attack the IRS in public forums and in budgets that fail to provide for the Mission of the IRS. The Constitution grants the Congress the right to tax. Congress uses issues like Obama Care to stir up negative publicity for the IRS, to protect their friends and business interests, the wealthy and corporations. Whatever the cause, no government agency can be sustainable, let alone efficient, if it is faced with yearly budget cuts, arcane methods of budget keeping, an antique computer, and increasingly complex tax laws.

All 535 Members of Congress are responsible for the Tax Code, not the IRS. All the Members of Congress going back 70 years are personally responsible for the inequities in the tax code. Many of these members have inserted thousands of special provisions to the tax code that benefit small groups of taxpayers who have lobbied the Congress for special tax treatment.

In order for conditions to change at the IRS, the Congress must make changes first. Congress must acknowledge that we have an unfair, unbalanced tax system that is a burden to all citizens because it does not seek to fairly and equally apply the tax laws to all of the people. (Remember the 14-20% of the people who never file or pay taxes?)

The more I write about this, the angrier I get. How is it that we have three tax systems? One for the W-2 wage earner employees who are trapped in a box and subject to the IRS sticking a hot poker in from time to time. Then a second system that benefits wealthy individuals. Then a third system that corporations and other businesses benefit from by having no income tax due - despite huge receipts and profits and allows them to benefit from thousands of tax breaks.

My life has been about building bridges between the Internal Revenue and the taxpaying public. I try to build bridges of education of the tax law and the tax system as administered by the IRS. I treat everyone I meet like a human being and try to be fair and equitable.

This is the reason that the tax system needs to be reformed. The IRS leans on the little people, making quasi legal interpretations and applications of the tax laws which harm them. The perception that wealthy individuals and corporations enjoy a different standard of tax compliance undermines the whole system and makes future compliance on all levels less likely.

The complex and confusing Internal Revenue Code is a problem created by Congress, not the majority of the people who voted them into office. Recent polls show that 78% of people disapprove of Congress. So when will the people who pay for this country rise up and start to demand a fair and balanced tax system?

A broken tax system corrupted by greed - hurts all of us. For far too long the IRS has used internal management that has come up through the ranks and lacked the education, experience, knowledge and credentials to effectively administer the tax system. IRS management is myopic, fearful and paranoid of outside assistance. The best person to be in control of the IRS would not be a political appointee with no tax background, but a tax lawyer, Certified Public Accountant or an academic with a doctorate in taxation. The IRS is not just a latchkey operation where a takeover specialist can just come in and make changes.

Owing delinquent taxes places a very high emotional burden on many taxpayers who are just trying to do the "right thing" and contribute to our society. If the IRS is given a regular budget outside of the main budget, with scheduled increases, the resulting increased number of audits and collections could result in more revenue being assessed and collected, which could be used to pay off the deficit and pay down the national debt.

The IRS is capable of doing excellent tax administration if it is allowed to do what it is supposed to do. The IRS deserves credit for being able to operate at all, given its antiquated computer system, its aging employee population, the increasingly complex tax laws and the budget cuts it has suffered for the last four years. Looking at how the IRS is still operating is remarkable – it is like watching a tired, old three-legged dog go for a run.

Let's start with the tax professionals that abuse the taxpaying public with false and unethical ads promising that they will get offers in compromise and tax settlements for pennies on the dollar. What they promise is illegal. When determining what to charge in my tax consulting business, I called several of the big tax processing mills. I said that I owed $10,000. The IRS grants an automatic installment agreement for that amount due. Three of the largest firms told me they could "help" me out for $3,000. Like I said, part of my personal mission statement is to "do what you can, with what you have, where you are."

That is why I decided to become an Enrolled Agent in the first place, because I had a delinquent taxpayer who owed $17,000 and had paid $7,000 to a firm that later went out of business. I showed up at the man's door and he got physically sick from the fear of dealing with the IRS. He also qualified for an immediate installment agreement. The whole process took about 20 minutes. I was outraged at what that company had done to him, and wondered how many tens of thousands of other people had been treated like that.

The IRS is afraid to control or regulate or censure these practitioners, even though many in the IRS are strongly in favor of it. The IRS is afraid that it would give the appearance that they were trying to deny taxpayers their rights to representation.

The reason that these firms do so well and are able to generate so much income to buy television and radio ads, is because they are selling hope. A glimmer of hope. That by hiring them, you will be able to get the IRS off your back for good. That you will be able to settle your tax debt with the IRS for pennies on the dollar. It is a nice dream, but in most cases they are unable to deliver on their promises.

I am grateful for the many experiences that I had working at the IRS. One of the best was that I was able to trust my gut feelings and determine which taxpayers were being honest and which were not.

For me, it just got so that working at the IRS was not fun or satisfying anymore. I did not feel that working there any longer was taking care of myself, first, best and always. So I retired on December 31, 2013 after 33 years. Now I am free to share my story. The names and circumstances of the cases I talk about have been changed to protect the confidential nature of the taxpayers. Some stories are a compilation of incidents. Most of the cases are just distant memories.

My hope is that by reading this book, you can become your own, successful, knowledgeable advocate in your case before the Internal Revenue Service. My editor suggests that if there is so much that needs to be fixed within the IRS, what about other federal agencies? It all comes down to funding and support from the Congress. Things need to change, and they need to change now. If you agree, talk to your family, friends and co-workers, people at church or at leisure talk about what you think about Congress and the IRS and paying taxes.

Endnotes and Sources

Monty Python
CNN Money 11-7-2013
Joint Committee on Internal Revenue Taxation 6-5-1975
Senate Finance Committee 9-23-1997 David Burnham
Wikipedia- IRS Commissioner Stories
U. S. vs. Nunan 236 F 2d 576 (1056)
Unbridled Power Inside the Secret Culture of the IRS, Shelly L. Davis
Schoenemnad Hofstra Law Review Vol. 16.291
U.S. News and World Report 5-26-1956
Heritage Foundation
Tax History.org
Edgar R Feige "The Underground Economy and the Tax Gap"
Congressional Budget Office
Senate Finance Committee

The best source for all this information is: The Treasury Inspector General for Tax Administration (TIGTA) Semi-Annual Reports to Congress. This data is from the report for the period October 1, 2013 to March 31, 2014 and prior. TIGTA is very effective as an external auditor of the IRS processes. It shows through its reports where the IRS is most vulnerable and then people reading those reports can determine how best to play the system and steal money from it.

Source: Journal of Accountancy, Nov, 2004: Avoid the Payroll Tax Trap.

Source: The IRS Chief Financial Officer's Office if Unpaid Assessment Analysis

Postscript:
I am writing a book called *What To Do If The IRS Is After You*, written from interviews of retired IRS employees. This book will take you through the whole IRS. It will offer advice and IRS secrets unknown outside of the IRS. It will tell you what you would learn if you had received a letter from the IRS and brought it over to your brother-in-law, the former IRS Officer, and asked his advice as to what you should do. That is the kind of advice that the book will share and along with that, it will offer business and tax plans to keep you from getting in trouble again. That book will be available in Spring, 2016.

Made in the USA
Lexington, KY
11 March 2018